Screening for Perinatal Depression

*Edited by Carol Henshaw
and Sandra Elliott*

Foreword by John Cox

Jessica Kingsley Publishers
London and Philadelphia

Figure 6.1 (pp.73–76) 'Integrated Perinatal and Infant Care (IPC) model and suggested clinical pathway' reproduced with permission from South Western Sydney Area Health Services. Box 9.1 (p.101) from Day, A (2001) 'The challenges of detecting and managing postnatal depression in a multicultural society.' In *Postnatal Depression and Maternal Mental Health: A Public Health Priority*. London: Community and Health Visitors' Association. Reproduced with permission. Figure 9.1 (p.103) reproduced with permission of the Community Practitioners' and Health Visitor's Association (2003). Figures 9.2 (p.105) and 9.3 (p.105) from *How are you feeling?* booklets, Community Practitioners' and Health Visitors' Association (2003). Reproduced with permission. Figure 11.1 (p.130) and 11.2. (p.131) from MAPPIM Team 2003 (unpublished). Reproduced with permission. Figure 13.1 (p.145) from Green, J.M. (1998) 'Postnatal depression or perinatal dysphoria? Findings from a longitudinal community-based study using the Edinburgh Postnatal Depression Scale.' *Journal of Reproductive and Infant Psychology* 16, 143–155. Reproduced with permission of Taylor and Francis (UK) www.tandf.co.uk. The Edinburgh Postnatal Depression Scale on pp.200–201 from Cox, J., Holden, J.M. and Sagovsky, R. (1987) 'Detection of postnatal depression. Development of the 10-item Edinburgh Postnatal Depression Scale.' *British Journal of Psychiatry 150*, 782–786. Reprinted with permission from the Royal College of Psychiatrists. The Edinburgh Postnatal Depression Scale on pp.202–203 from Cox, J. and Holden, J. (1994) *Perinatal Psychiatry: Use and Misuse of the Edinburgh Postnatal Depression Scale*. London: Gaskell (Royal College of Psychiatrists). Reprinted with permission of the Royal College of Psychiatrists.

The right of the contributors to be identified as authors of this work has been asserted by them in accordance with the Copyright, Designs and Patents Act 1988.

First published in 2005
by Jessica Kingsley Publishers
116 Pentonville Road
London N1 9JB, UK
and
400 Market Street, Suite 400
Philadelphia, PA 19106, USA

www.jkp.com

Copyright © Jessica Kingsley Publishers 2005
Foreword copyright © John Cox 2005

Library of Congress Cataloging in Publication Data
Screening for perinatal depression / edited by Carol Henshaw and Sandra Elliott.
p. ; cm.
Includes bibliographical references and index.
ISBN-13: 978-1-84310-219-9 (pbk.)
ISBN-10: 1-84310-219-6 (pbk.)

1. Postpartum depression—Diagnosis—Great Britain. 2. Medical screening—Great Britain. 3. Pregnant women—Mental health services—Great Britain.
[DNLM: 1. Depression, Postpartum—diagnosis. 2. Mass Screening. 3. Perinatal Care. WQ 500 S433 2005] I. Henshaw, Carol, 1961- II. Elliott, Sandra.
RG852.S37 2005
617.7'6075—dc22

2004024489

British Library Cataloguing in Publication Data
A CIP catalogue record for this book is available from the British Library

ISBN-13: 978 1 84310 219 9
ISBN-10: 1 84310 219 6

Printed and Bound in Great Britain by
Athenaeum Press, Gateshead, Tyne and Wear

Screening for Perinatal Depression

of related interest

Surviving Post-Natal Depression
At Home, No One Hears You Scream
Cara Aiken
ISBN 1 85302 861 4

Good Practice in Adult Mental Health
Edited by Tony Ryan and Jacki Pritchard
ISBN 1 84310 217 X
Good Practice in Social Work 10

Mental Illness
A Handbook for Carers
Edited by Rosalind Ramsay, Claire Gerada, Sarah Mars
and George Szmukler
ISBN 1 85302 934 3

New Approaches to Preventing Suicide
A Manual for Practitioners
Edited by David Duffy & Tony Ryan
ISBN 1 84310 221 8

Supporting Parents
Messages from Research
David Quinton
1 84310 210 2

Understanding Your Baby
Sophie Boswell
ISBN 1 84310 242 0

For our husbands, James and Mike, and our children, Richard, Lee, Paul and Michaella

Acknowledgements

We are grateful to Guy's and St Thomas' Charitable Foundation who funded Sandra Elliott's salary during the time she worked on this book, our partners and families who have had to put up with long hours of absence and the women whose needs inspire us to continue with this work.

Contents

Acronyms and Abbreviations

ADDS	Atypical Depression Diagnostic Scale
BDI	Beck Depression Inventory
CES-D	Center for Epidemiologic Studies Scale (Depression)
CEMD	Confidential Enquiry into Maternal Deaths
CPHVA	Community Practitioners' and Health Visitors' Association
EPDS	Edinburgh Postnatal Depression Scale
GHQ	General Health Questionnaire
HADS	Hospital Anxiety and Depression Scale
HRS-D	Hamilton Rating Scale for Depression
IPC	Integrated Perinatal Care
MAPPIM	Maternity and Perinatal Partnership in Mental Health
MCH	Mother and Child Health
NSC	National Screening Committee
PDPI	Postpartum Depression Predictors Inventory
PDSS	Postpartum Depression Screening Scale
PND	Postnatal depression
POMS	Profile of Mood States
RCT	randomized controlled trial
RDC	Research Diagnostic Criteria
SCID	Structured Clinical Interview for DSM-IV
SCL-90-R	Symptom Checklist 90 Revised
SDS	Self-Rating Depression Scale

Foreword

The last four decades have seen a burgeoning of research and clinical services across the world within the field of perinatal mental health that was surely unexpected over 40 years ago when Brice Pitt published his seminal paper, and in the late 1970s when the Marcé Society was founded. It was not entirely foreseen either when the Edinburgh studies were underway at that time and the Edinburgh Postnatal Depression Scale (EPDS) was on the drawing board. So what is happening to global society that continues to drive the subject of perinatal mental health closer to the top of the public health agenda? Is this linked to changing patterns of family life, greater awareness that the parent–infant relationship may be affected by mental disorder or to more vociferous women's voices? Whatever the explanation, this book is both a symptom and sign of the present-day public health prominence of perinatal mental disorder.

Carol Henshaw and Sandra Elliott, two of the most prominent pioneers at the present time, have used their scholarly reputation and differing clinical perspectives to edit this formative book. They have brought together in constructive dialogue those most concerned with prevention and, above all perhaps, included a cogent user perspective. The call to complete existing research projects and to validate the EPDS as a screening tool in the sense understood by the National Screening Committee, is a timely challenge to the next generation of Marcé followers. Bon voyage to screening. Bon voyage to the EPDS – it is in good hands.

John Cox
Emeritus Professor, Keele University, Staffordshire UK

Introduction

Carol Henshaw

This book arose out of two workshops and one conference on screening for perinatal depression that were held at the Marcé Society Biennial International Meetings in Manchester, UK in 2000 and Sydney, Australia in 2002, and a conference organized by the Keele Perinatal Mental Health Education Unit at Keele in 2003. Sixty people from 12 countries actively involved in screening in clinical and/or research settings attended the first workshop and debated best practice in screening. Our thoughts developed following the second workshop, the conference and the debate following the publication of the National Screening Committee report.

The burden of affective disorder related to childbearing has been clearly delineated. Ten to fifteen per cent of women experience a depressive episode after delivery (O'Hara and Swain 1996) and a similar number of women are depressed during pregnancy (Bennett *et al.* 2004; Kumar and Robson 1984). The strongest predictors of postnatal depression are a past history of psychopathology, dysphoric mood during pregnancy, a poor marital relationship, low levels of social support and the occurrence of stressful life events. There are weaker associations with neuroticism and a negative cognitive attributional style (O'Hara and Swain 1996). Two per thousand recently delivered women will suffer from puerperal psychosis (Kendell, Chalmers and Platz 1987) and those with a past history of serious mood disorder in the postpartum period or at other times are at very high risk of recurrence after delivery (one in two or three). Unipolar postnatal depression is clearly distressing for the woman and burdensome for her partner who may be juggling caring for her, a new baby, other children and a job and who may also be suffering from a mental health problem. There is a substantial literature outlining the impact of maternal depression in the first year of the infant's life on his or her cognitive and emotional development, with effects persisting beyond school entry (Murray 1992; Murray *et al.* 1999; Sharp *et al.* 1995). More recent work has shown higher and more variable salivary cortisol levels in the adolescent offspring of postnatally depressed women (Halligan *et al.* 2004). The implications of this are not fully understood but clearly the impact of postnatal depression extends far beyond infancy. Hence, identifying and treating perinatal depression must be a priority.

There are a growing number of treatment studies but the evidence base is still very limited when compared to that for depression unrelated to childbirth (Boath and Henshaw 2001). Preventing postnatal depression has so far proved largely unfruitful (Bradley, Boath and Henshaw 2004; Dennis 2004b, 2004c), and so improving the detection of women who are depressed and engaging them in treatment is essential.

Definitions of screening

Screening has been defined in a variety of ways. One of these is:

> the systematic application of a test or inquiry to identify individuals at risk of a specific disorder to benefit from further investigation or direct preventive action amongst persons who have not sought medical attention on account of symptoms of that disorder. (Peckham and Dezateux 1998, p.767)

Although the focus of screening was initially on conditions such as cervical cancer, breast cancer, deafness in infants etc., more recently attention has turned to psychological problems, particularly depression.

In 2002 the United States Preventive Services Task Force recommended that clinical practices that have 'systems in place to ensure accurate diagnosis, effective treatment, and follow-up' should screen adults for depression (US Preventive Services Task Force 2002, p.761) and there is a debate about which tool should be used or whether two simple questions are sufficiently accurate in, for example, general practice consulters (Arroll, Khin and Kerse 2003). Several North American medical academies and colleges now advocate routinely asking patients about depression during history taking. In our context this definition fits well with the identification of women who, while well during pregnancy, are at risk of postpartum onset of serious mental illness (Chapter 10).

Case finding is defined by epidemiologists as the search for additional illness in those with medical problems, yet this definition accords more closely with the use of a screening instrument in a pregnant or postpartum population (who are not considered medically ill) in order to identify those who are suffering from a current depressive disorder. Confusion is not confined to these settings and screening has been described as 'a double-edged sword, sometimes wielded clumsily by the well-intended' (Grimes and Schulz 2002, p.881).

This book is aimed at two audiences: maternity service professionals (i.e. obstetricians, health visitors, midwives and early childhood nurses or health visitors who encounter women with mental health problems during pregnancy or after delivery) and those working in mental health services whose clients become pregnant. This presented us with a challenge in writing the book, which we hope is part of the process of encouraging joint working and moving towards a shared literature. For the last 20 years or so organizations devoted to childbearing mental disorder have remained largely discipline-specific. The Marcé Society was founded in 1980 by psychiatrists and the vast majority of presidents have been psychiatrists until more recently, although the membership is becoming more mixed. Members of the Society for Reproductive and Infant Psychology are in the main psychologists and the International Society for Psychosomatic Obstetrics and Gynecology has been more appealing to obstetricians. It can be hard to get papers written from psychology or sociology perspectives into mainstream biomedical journals, many nursing journals are not indexed by Medline and medical contributions can be unwelcome in some social science publications. The reader or researcher has to become adept at searching multiple databases for the important literature in this area. Many clinical services are becoming more joined-up, but the literatures have lagged behind.

We hope the book will stimulate debate in the wider community and at an individual level encourage practitioners to engage in reflective thought about their own practice. We recognize the different historical and cultural contexts in the various parts of the world (and in different parts of the same country) in which our authors work. There is also variety in the configuration of both maternity and mental health services in different countries. No one solution will fit all. We wish to capitalize on the strengths of this variability and hence have allowed our authors to write and set out their chapters in very different styles and using different language.

We have avoided the use of the acronyms 'PND' (postnatal depression) and 'PPD' (post partum depression) for the reasons outlined in the emergent themes of Chapter 11 of *Why Mothers Die 1997–1999* (Lewis and Drife 2001). In the UK, 'PND' has become a generic term for almost any mental disorder arising in the postpartum, instead of being restricted to non-psychotic unipolar illnesses. Consequently, some women with a history of psychosis have been identified in pregnancy as having had a much less severe illness and the opportunity for preventing recurrence missed.

Screening instruments

The Edinburgh Postnatal Depression Scale (EPDS) was developed and validated following dissatisfaction with standard instruments for detecting depression (Cox, Holden and Sagovsky 1987). Standard rating scales appear to have reduced sensitivity and specificity in the postpartum period (Harris *et al.* 1989). The EPDS is a 10-item pencil and paper test that takes very little time to complete and the original validation was carried out on Scottish mothers at six weeks postpartum. It originally consisted of 13 items, but during the validation process it was found that reducing to 10 items did not decrease its effectiveness. The items lost were 'I have enjoyed being a mother' and two irritability items. Response categories are scored 0, 1, 2, or 3 according to the severity of the symptom. Items 3 and 5–10 are reverse scored. The total score is calculated by adding item scores together. A cut-off of 12/13 identified all women with definite major depression and two of the three women with probable major depression. The total sample size was 63 women. There were, however, false positives and, in a more recent French study (sample size 87), three women with major depression were not detected using a 12/13 cut-off. The authors of this study suggested that the EPDS is better at detecting women with anxious and anhedonic symptoms but not those who present primarily with psychomotor retardation (Guedeney *et al.* 2000). Lowering the cut-off to 9/10 was suggested as a means of reducing the failure rate, but this is likely to be over-inclusive in some settings.

Since this first study there has been a proliferation of translations (only some of which have been validated), validation studies in different countries and cultures and also in non-childbearing populations (Appendix 2). The EPDS has been shown, along with other instruments, to have unsatisfactory psychometric properties when used in the first week postpartum (Lee *et al.* 2003). Matthey (2004) has calculated that a four point change in the EPDS score indicates a clinically significant change and suggests that this could be used as an outcome measure in treatment trials.

There have also been variations in the way the scale is presented and completed. Some of these, particularly those used in the qualitative studies described in this book, can be found in Appendix 1. Using the EPDS in any form other than that in the 1987 validation paper, and not including the full reference, breaches copyright. Two of the authors of the 1987 validation have since then produced two books. The first was an edited text outlining the uses and abuses of the EPDS (Cox and Holden 1994) and more recently they authored an updated guide to the EPDS (Cox and Holden 2003), which contains copies of some of the translations.

In the US, Cheryl Beck developed the Postpartum Depression Screening Scale (PDSS), a 35-item instrument, from qualitative work; this process is described in Chapter 12. Others have concentrated on devising predictive indices in an attempt to identify during pregnancy those women most likely to become depressed after delivery, although not all tested these indices against standardized diagnostic interviews or recognized diagnostic criteria. Work also continues in comparing the performance of the EPDS and PDSS and other standard measures (for example, the Beck Depression Inventory, the General Health Questionnaire) in various pregnant and postpartum populations and in comparisons between instruments. References for these studies can be found in Appendix 2.

Who should screen?

Which professional is best placed to undertake screening obviously depends on which professionals are in contact with women during pregnancy and into the postpartum period. This varies from country to country. For example, in the UK, women who are deemed to be obstetrically 'low risk' are managed by shared care between midwives and their general practitioner (GP), will make very few visits to a hospital based antenatal clinic and may not see an obstetrician. Provided their delivery is uncomplicated, they will be delivered by a midwife and after a stay in the maternity unit of between 6 and 48 hours they will return home. A community midwife carries out postpartum care, with the health visitor usually taking over at around ten days after delivery. Although midwives can remain involved until 28 days postpartum, the impetus for this is usually the woman's physical rather than mental health needs. Postpartum women have a postnatal check at around six weeks postpartum, carried out by their GP. A small minority of women whose delivery was particularly complicated have their postnatal check undertaken by an obstetrician.

Hence, the midwife is most likely to be the professional best placed to screen during pregnancy and the health visitor in the weeks and months after birth. In countries such as the US and Austria for example, where the majority of antenatal and intrapartum care is carried out by obstetricians and there are very few midwives, the focus must shift to how these doctors can become involved in screening.

The UK health visitor is a qualified nurse or midwife who has undergone further training in health promotion, child health and education. Each family with a child under the age of five has a named health visitor who can advise on everyday concerns such as feeding, sleeping, behaviour problems and parenting in general, but who also assists with special needs, and may run immunization programmes, child development checks and parenting classes. Holden and colleagues demonstrated in a small randomized controlled trial that after a short training, health visitors could deliver an intervention based on Rogerian non-directive counselling which comprised eight 'listening visits' and that this was an effective intervention for non-psychotic unipolar postnatal depression (Holden, Sagovsky and Cox 1989). The role of the health visitor in this area of work has since increased dramatically. Health visitors in most areas now have had some form of training, although the quality and quantity of updates and supervision is very variable. In countries where mothers regularly take their children to well-child clinics, the paediatric nurses and paediatricians who run these services are likely to be well placed to screen for maternal depression. But as Lisa Segre and Michael O'Hara discuss in Chapter 7, resistance can come from both mothers and health professionals.

Women's voices

We have been hearing women's voices regarding the experience of postnatal depression for some time (e.g. Brown *et al.* 1994; Wheatley 2001). Recent studies have focused on women from ethnic minority communities and the developing world (Rodrigues *et al.* 2003; Templeton *et al.* 2003). We are now beginning to hear what women think about being screened for postnatal depression. Two of the chapters in this book are devoted to qualitative studies describing the experience of women. In another UK study, Shakespeare, Blake and Garcia (2003) interviewed 39 women around a year after they had been screened using the EPDS as part of routine clinical care. Twenty of the women had found screening unacceptable; two had deliberately avoided being screened and had very negative views. Others felt that they would rather have talked than merely answer questions and some appear to have been unprepared or poorly prepared. Those who were screened at home found the process more acceptable than those who were screened in the baby clinic. A third had little feedback and women were very aware of not wanting to be labelled as depressed, seen as a bad mother or risk having their baby taken away. Given the widespread nature of screening in UK primary care, we need to listen to these voices and consider how to respond.

The book begins with a description of the process by which the UK National Screening Committee (NSC) assessed screening for postnatal depression against its criteria. Tessa Leverton then addresses the dilemma of being asked to develop services for postnatally depressed mothers by her employer, with the backing of many organizations but at the same time aware that the NSC advises against using the most widely used and researched instrument. The following six chapters describe local solutions and systems that aim to improve the care of women with perinatal mental disorders in five different countries. All of these systems merit evaluation or research. In Chapter 9, Abi Sobowale and Cheryll Adams tackle the problem of screening where a questionnaire or scale cannot be used and describe their solution. Margaret Oates (Chapter 10) outlines the need to screen during pregnancy for women at risk of severe mental illness. Chapter 11 examines the role of the midwife. In Chapter 13 Jo Green focuses on the problems surrounding screening with the EPDS in research settings. Walter Barker (Chapter 14) provides a more philosophical view of the role of the health visitor in screening and the book concludes with the privileged last word from two groups of service users.

Appendix 1 contains the Edinburgh Postnatal Depression Scale with its variations and Appendix 2 is a compendium of references for the EPDS, PDSS and other measures used in depressed perinatal populations. Appendix 3 reproduces the guidelines for the use of the EPDS as part of an assessment, issued by the Community Practitioners' and Health Visitors' Association (CPHVA) following the NSC report.

Chapter 1

Screening: The Role and Recommendations of the UK National Screening Committee

Judy Shakespeare

Introduction

'Screening' is a word that has sometimes been loosely used, but the National Screening Committee (NSC) in the UK has a specific definition:

> A public health service in which members of a defined population, who do not necessarily perceive that they are at risk of, or are already affected by a disease or its complications, are asked a question or offered a test to identify those individuals who are more likely to be helped than harmed by further tests or treatment to reduce the risk of disease or its complications. (National Screening Committee 2000, pp.27–28).

In the UK the NSC has the task of providing advice about established and newly proposed screening programmes and aims to evaluate these against specified criteria (see Box 1.1). The criteria were developed from the earlier work of Wilson and Jungner (1968). The NSC views screening as a process of risk reduction, balancing the benefits to those diagnosed correctly against the possible harms of a positive screen for those who do not have the disease (false positives) or a negative screen for those that do have the disease (false negatives).

In May 2001, I prepared a briefing document for the NSC considering screening for postnatal depression against the criteria. This was discussed at a workshop in July 2001, revised and posted on the NSC website in October 2001 (Shakespeare 2001). The NSC made recommendations in response to this document that I will discuss later in this chapter.

For this chapter I have updated and abbreviated the 2001 review. I did this by searching Medline and PsycINFO from 1966 to October 2003, CINAHL from 1982 to September 2003 and the Cochrane Library for Issue 4, 2003 using the keywords 'postpartum/postnatal depression'. I did not search in languages other than English and have not looked for evidence from grey literature, except for government reports in the UK. When there was no evidence relating to postnatal depression, I sought evidence about the management of depression in primary care from systematic reviews and secondary sources, particularly the Cochrane Library. This review does not claim to be systematic and it does not address the 'Condition' and the 'Test' sections in detail, as these have been covered in the Introduction. The structure of the review follows the NSC criteria described in Box 1.1.

Box 1.1 The NSC criteria for appraising the viability, effectiveness and appropriateness of a screening programme

Ideally the following criteria should be met before screening for a condition is initiated.

The condition

1. The condition should be an important health problem

2. The epidemiology and natural history of the condition, including development from latent to declared disease, should be adequately understood and there should be a detectable risk factor, disease marker, latent period or early symptomatic stage

3. All the cost-effective primary prevention interventions should have been implemented as far as practicable

4. If the carriers of a mutation are identified as a result of screening the natural history of people with this status should be understood, including the psychological implications

---

The test

5. There should be a simple, safe, precise and validated screening test

6. The distribution of test values in the target population should be known and a suitable cut-off level defined and agreed

7. The test should be acceptable to the population

8. There should be an agreed policy on the further diagnostic investigation of individuals with a positive test result and on the choices available to those individuals

9. If the test is for mutations the criteria used to select the subset of mutations to be covered by screening, if all possible mutations are not being tested, should be clearly set out

The treatment

10. There should be an effective treatment or intervention for patients identified through early detection, with evidence of early treatment leading to better outcomes than late treatment

11. There should be agreed evidence based policies covering which individuals should be offered treatment and the appropriate treatment to be offered

12. Clinical management of the condition and patient outcomes should be optimised by all health care providers prior to participation in a screening programme

The screening programme

13. There must be evidence from high quality Randomised controlled Trials that the screening programme is effective in reducing mortality or morbidity

    Where screening is aimed solely at providing information to allow the person being screened to make an 'informed choice' (e.g. Down's syndrome, cystic fibrosis, carrier screening), there must be evidence from high quality trials that the test accurately measures risk. The information that is provided about the test and its outcome must be of value and readily understood by the individual being screened

14. There should be evidence that the complete screening programme (test, diagnostic procedures, treatment/intervention) is clinically, socially and ethically acceptable to health professionals and the public

15. The benefit from the screening programme should outweigh the physical and psychological harm (caused by the test, diagnostic procedures and treatment)

16. The opportunity cost of the screening programme (including testing, diagnosis, treatment, administration, training and quality assurance) should be economically balanced in relation to expenditure on medical care as a whole (i.e. value for money)

17. There must be a plan for managing and monitoring the screening programme and an agreed set of quality assurance standards

18. Adequate staffing and facilities for testing, diagnosis, treatment and programme management should be made available prior to the commencement of the screening programme

19. All other options for managing the condition should have been considered (e.g. improving treatment, providing other services), to ensure that no more cost-effective intervention could be introduced or current interventions increased within the resources available

20. Evidence-based information, explaining the consequences of testing, investigation and treatment, should be made available to potential participants to assist them in making an informed choice

21. Public pressure for widening the eligibility criteria for reducing the screening interval, and for increasing the sensitivity of the testing process, should be anticipated. Decisions about these parameters should be scientifically justifiable to the public

(www.nsc.nhs.uk/pdfs/criteria.pdf)

The condition

In summary, postnatal depression is an important health condition, whose epidemiology and natural history are understood. The risk factors for its development are known, but they are unhelpful in reliably predicting development of the disease. Most available evidence has failed to show that prevention or early intervention, even in high-risk women, is possible. For more detail, see the NSC website (Shakespeare 2001).

The test

The Edinburgh Postnatal Depression Scale (EPDS) is the test most frequently advocated as a screening test for postnatal depression. The characteristics of the EPDS as a screening tool have been discussed in the Introduction.

There is very limited evidence about the acceptability of the EPDS, especially in routine clinical practice. A recent systematic review of routinely administered questionnaires for depression and anxiety in community settings reported that no study examined patient views of usefulness or acceptability (Gilbody, House and Sheldon 2001). A qualitative study in Oxford (where there is a policy of universal screening) showed that just over half of the women interviewed (sample size: 39) found screening with the EPDS less than acceptable, whatever their postnatal emotional health (Shakespeare, et al. 2003). The main themes identified were problems with the process of screening and, in particular, the venue, the personal intrusion of screening and stigma. The women interviewed had a clear preference for talking about how they felt, rather than filling out a questionnaire.

There was no agreed policy on the further diagnostic investigation of individuals with a positive test result until the NSC had made recommendations about screening for postnatal depression. However, the Community Practitioners' and Health Visitors' Association (CPHVA) have subsequently recommended that health visitors should use the EPDS as 'part of a full and systematic mood assessment of the mother supporting professional judgement and a clinical assessment' (Coyle and Adams 2002). The clinical assessment should be made using the DSM-IV criteria for major depressive disorder (American Psychiatric Association 1994), in line with evidence from primary care psychiatry (Weel-Baumgarten et al. 2000). At present, the choices available to women with postnatal depression will depend on the resources available locally and the ability of the woman and her primary care team to access these resources.

The treatment

Only results from systematic reviews or randomized controlled trials (RCTs) have been included in this part of the report.

Pharmacological treatments

ANTIDEPRESSANTS

A Cochrane review (Hoffbrand, Howard and Crawley 2001) found only one trial that met their criteria (Appleby et al. 1997). In this study, 87 women with postnatal depression were randomized to double-blind therapy with fluoxetine or placebo, plus either one or six sessions of cognitive-behavioural counselling. At 12 weeks, all the groups had improved, but the benefit was significantly greater with fluoxetine than placebo, and with six sessions rather than one session of counselling. Combining fluoxetine with six sessions of counselling gave no additional benefit. This study excluded breast-feeding mothers. More than half of the depressed women approached refused to take part (women were reluctant to be randomized to the possibility of medication) (Whitton, Warner and Appleby 1996) and there were significant losses to follow up (30%). In addition, the follow up was short and no outcomes for infants were reported.

HORMONAL THERAPY

A Cochrane review (Lawrie, Herxheimer and Dalton 2001) included only one small RCT in which oestrogen patches in severely depressed women were associated with a greater improvement in depression scores than placebo (Gregoire *et al.* 1996). The use of oestrogen in postnatal women is limited because of the risk of thrombo-embolic disease and a contraindication in breast-feeding mothers.

Psychological/psychotherapeutic treatments

A comprehensive literature review has examined published studies identified between 1964 and 2000 (Boath and Henshaw 2001). They identified five RCTs of psychological or therapeutic interventions for postnatal depression; two examined non-directive counselling visits (Holden, Sagovsky and Cox 1989; Wickberg and Hwang 1996); one a cognitive-behavioural counselling technique (Appleby *et al.* 1997), one a group cognitive-behavioural technique (Meager and Milgrom 1996) and one an interpersonal psychotherapy intervention (O'Hara *et al.* 2000). All the studies showed an improvement in depression in the intervention groups compared with controls. However, all had significant methodological flaws: sample sizes were often small, randomization was inadequate, some women also received antidepressants, the Hawthorne effect[1] could have affected outcomes, and the interventions were poorly described. There were also high withdrawal rates, unblinded assessors, the same profes-

---

1   The Hawthorne effect can be defined as changes in behavior resulting from attention participants believe they are getting from the researchers, and not the variables manipulated by the researchers.

sional carrying out intervention and control interventions, and selection bias. In addition, none of the studies sought outcomes for infants.

Since 2000, two further trials have been reported. One reported a brief psycho-educational group intervention for postnatal depression (Honey, Bennett and Morgan 2002). Forty-five women attending mother and baby clinics in Gwent, Wales, who scored 12 on the EPDS within the first 12 months after delivery were referred to the study by their health visitor. They were block randomized to the intervention (consisting of eight weekly meetings with educational, cognitive-behavioural and relaxation components) or routine primary care. At three and six months the women in the intervention groups had mean EPDS scores significantly lower than those in the control group. However, this study also had methodological flaws: there was no independent assessment of depression, the EPDS mean was still above a level consistent with probable depression in the intervention group, a Hawthorne effect was possible, compliance with the intervention was unclear, and no infant outcomes were sought.

In a recently reported study, 194 women with postnatal depression were randomized to routine primary care or to one of three interventions: non-directive counselling; cognitive-behavioural therapy or psycho-dynamic psychotherapy (Cooper *et al.* 2003; Murray *et al.* 2003). A specialist or a specially trained generalist provided treatment in the woman's home weekly between 8 and 18 weeks. Mothers were assessed immediately post-intervention, at 9, 18 and 60 months. By 18 weeks there was a significant impact on maternal mood for all treatment groups, but by nine months the control mothers were as well as the treated mothers. Treatment did not reduce subsequent episodes of postnatal depression. The mother–child relationship and child outcomes were examined at 4.5, 18 and 60 months. Early intervention was of short-term benefit to the mother–child relationship and infant behaviour problems, but these benefits were not sustained at 60 months.

Combining antidepressants and psychological therapies
The only significant trial has been discussed above under 'Antidepressants'.

Postnatal support
COMMUNITY SUPPORT WORKERS

A randomized controlled trial (RCT) of the costs and effectiveness of community support workers visiting low-risk mothers in the first four weeks after birth showed no health benefits compared with traditional midwifery support and no savings to the health service over the six months after their introduction (Morrell *et al.* 2000).

INVOLVING THE PARTNER

A small RCT conducted in Canada allocated 29 women with postnatal depression either to a control group receiving seven psycho-educational visits, or to a group that also involved the partner (supported group) (Misri *et al.* 2000). Relative to the control group, the supported group showed a significant decrease in depressive symptoms, and relative to the supported group, the general health of the partners in the control group deteriorated. This trial is of limited value because of the small sample size, selected from a population who were attending a reproductive mental health programme, an unblinded assessor and a short follow-up period.

PEER SUPPORT

A recent pilot RCT of telephone peer support has been reported from British Columbia (Dennis 2003). Forty-two women with an EPDS score >9 (possible postnatal depression) were recruited at eight-week immunization clinics. They excluded women on antidepressants, those with recent or chronic depression or other psychiatric disorders. The intervention group were paired with a peer volunteer and the control group received standard community care. The volunteers, who had all suffered and recovered from postnatal depression, received a four-hour training session. They contacted new mothers in the intervention group within 48 hours. The outcome data were collected by telephone using blinded research assistants. There were significant differences in probable major depressive symptomatology (EPDS >12) after four and eight weeks, with high maternal satisfaction and acceptability of the intervention. A larger trial is needed with adequate power to demonstrate the significance of these promising pilot results.

The mother–infant interaction

There is limited evidence that promoting a positive mother–infant interaction may improve psychological outcomes for the mother and the child. A small RCT of mothers with postnatal depression (Onozawa *et al.* 2001) showed that massage improved the mother–infant interaction and maternal depression.

Another approach is to tackle an infant management problem. An RCT in a middle-class area in Australia used a behavioural approach to a perceived infant sleeping problem (Hiscock and Wake 2002). One hundred and fifty-six mothers of infants aged 6 to 12 months who reported severe sleeping difficulties were recruited. The intervention was a meeting with a community paediatrician (H. Hiscock) on three occasions at two-week intervals to discuss 'controlled crying'. The control group received a mailed description of normal sleeping patterns in infants aged 6 to 12 months. The primary outcome measures were an EPDS score and maternal report of a persisting infant sleep problem (yes or no), mailed to the mother. Postnatal depression was associated with a maternal report of infant sleeping problems. At two months there was a significant improvement in infant sleep problems in the intervention group, but not at four months. Depressed mothers (EPDS $\geq$ 10) did significantly better in the intervention group than the control at both two and four months. This study is difficult to interpret because: the attention and amount of contact was not controlled so that a Hawthorne effect is possible, the EPDS was the proxy outcome measure of postnatal depression used, the cut-off point used was inappropriate and the follow up was short.

Complementary therapies

There is no information about the use of St John's Wort in postnatal depression, particularly in breast-feeding mothers, so it should not currently be recommended (Klier *et al.* 2002).

Research in progress or planned

The PONDER study in Sheffield has been commissioned by the National Health Service Research and Development Health Technology Assessment (HTA) programme to compare two counselling interventions: non-directive counselling and cognitive-behavioural counselling delivered by health visitors in their usual clinical setting (Morrell 2003). An HTA project *Antidepressant Therapy in the Treatment of Postnatal Depression* has been approved, subject to changes, following an HTA Commissioning Board meeting (2002). Neither of these studies will report their findings before 2007. A large study in five states in Australia, the *BeyondBlue Postnatal Depression Program*, aims to screen 975,000 women for antenatal and postnatal depression over a three-year period between January 2002 and December 2004 and to examine a variety of interventions (*BeyondBlue* 2003).

Conclusions about treatment

Despite methodological flaws, there is evidence that treatments for postnatal depression are effective for the mother. On the other hand, the evidence is limited in several respects: that early treatment leads to better outcomes for the mother or infant than later treatment, that one treatment is superior to another, that the results are achievable in routine primary care, and that there are beneficial outcomes for infants (or other family members). It is hoped that current and future studies will address this.

Treatment for a mother with postnatal depression can be effective only if she accepts and complies with treatment. Counselling is more acceptable to women than antidepressants, which are viewed as addictive and unsafe in breast-feeding (Whitton et al. 1996). This view of antidepressants is also true for other depressed patients (Churchill et al. 2000; Priest et al. 1996). It seems logical to offer depressed women a choice between a brief counselling intervention by health visitors and antidepressants. By promoting patient choice, concordance with treatment is likely to be greatest (Chilvers et al. 2001).

The screening programme

At present, there is no evidence from RCTs that screening reduces mortality from postnatal depression and limited evidence that it reduces morbidity. The *BeyondBlue* study, in progress in Australia (2003), should be able to answer this question. There is some evidence from general primary care that screening can reduce morbidity. A meta-analysis has demonstrated that screening and feedback can improve the outcome of depression in general primary care psychiatry. However, this only happens when they are coupled with system changes to ensure adequate treatment and follow up (Pignone et al. 2002). The type of system changes are quality improvement approaches: staff education, institutional commitment and investment in the intervention, screening with recall and follow up by nurses, direct training of therapists with effective treatments, direct patient education and audit and feedback. When these methods were used, there was a 10 to 13% reduction in relative risk and a 7 to 9% absolute decrease in the prevalence of persistent depression (measured at 12 months). This translates into a number needed to screen of 110 to produce one additional remission after six months of treatment. Whether this represents a worthwhile health economic benefit is debatable. These system changes have never been tried in postnatal depression trials, which have focused on treatment modalities, rather than changes in the process of care.

Evidence is lacking that a screening programme for postnatal depression would be acceptable to the general public. There is some evidence that women may find a diagnosis and treatment for depression unacceptable: they do not want to be labelled as depressed and do not consider that they are 'depressed' (Small et al. 1994). There is evidence that health visitors find screening acceptable (Seeley, Murray and Cooper 1996).

There is a lack of evidence about the relative risks and benefits for physical and psychological outcomes of screening for postnatal depression. Screening for postnatal depression is unlikely to cause physical harm, but there are always psychological costs attached to any type of screening (Marteau 1989). No psychiatric screening programme has been evaluated in this way, but it is likely that the psychological costs would be at least as great as in other conditions. There is some evidence that women who are not screened within a local screening programme may have a higher than normal risk of postnatal depression, perhaps because they evade screening (Leverton and Elliott 2000).

At present, the health economic costs of screening for postnatal depression are unknown, but the PONDER and *BeyondBlue* studies should lead to estimates.

Although there are often local policies, there are no national agreed quality assurance standards for managing and monitoring a screening programme for postnatal depression. Screening with the EPDS would identify more patients and create an expectation of care when resources are already inadequate and overstretched. In the UK, postnatal depression is managed predominantly by health visitors in primary care, within their usual caseload. There is some evidence that they are already overburdened, especially in deprived areas (Shakespeare 2002). The National Service Framework for Mental Health, which required all areas to have agreed protocols for postnatal depression by April 2001 (Department of Health 1999a) has probably exacerbated the pressure on health visitors, as the work had been largely dumped on their doorstep. At present the availability of specialist secondary care resources for perinatal women, including community psychiatric nurses, psychologists, psychiatrists, and mother and baby facilities, is variable throughout the UK and in many areas it is patchy or absent. The Royal College of Psychiatrists has produced a report drawing up a blueprint for perinatal services (Oates 2001). Following the Department of Health (DOH) investigation into the death of the psychiatrist Daksha Emson (DOH press release 4 August 2003), the Government has included mother and baby units into the remit of the group looking at the commissioning of specialist mental health services, the report of which was due to be produced early in 2004. This means that perinatal mental health may have reached the Government's agenda.

The training of health visitors is critical to the success of screening and it needs to be backed up with supervision and adequate support from local secondary care services (Elliott *et al.* 2001). Training programmes for screening and managing postnatal depression are available in the UK, but evidence about their effectiveness is limited.

Ethically, the introduction of screening for postnatal depression could increase health inequalities. The test relies on the ability to read and understand idiomatic English. Women from ethnic and more disadvantaged backgrounds may not be able to complete the EPDS. If screening is introduced to an area, options other than an EPDS should be available to assess a mother's level of distress. This means that translation facilities and multicultural counselling services need to be readily available; this is not currently the case in most districts.

There may be pressure to introduce antenatal screening, earlier postnatal screening or repeated tests after birth. A systematic review of antenatal screening (Austin and Lumley 2003) and the Scottish Intercollegiate Guidelines Network (2002) advice on postnatal depression and puerperal psychosis have both concluded that there is no evidence to introduce this at present.

Despite the lack of evidence, the EPDS has already been implemented in most parts of the country (Tully *et al.* 2002).

Recommendations of the NSC

The NSC issued initial recommendations in 2001 that screening for postnatal depression was not justified. This was based on:

> the evidence being weak in many areas, in particular, the lack of evidence about the validity of the EPDS as a screening tool, uncertainty about the most effective treatment when treating women with, or at risk of postnatal depression and uncertainty about the magnitude of the effects, both beneficial and harmful, of screening for postnatal depression.
>
> At present the NSC does not recommend that screening for postnatal depression is introduced except in a research context with the research protocol having been reviewed externally and internally and with the protocol having been approved by an ethics committee. Where screening programmes are being offered they must be backed up by high quality specialist psychiatric services. (National Screening Committee 2001)

The NSC decision caused considerable consternation. As a result, resources for the treatment of postnatal depression by health visitors were withdrawn in some areas. The CPHVA and others lobbied the NSC and the guidance was subsequently modified:

> Until more research is conducted into its potential for routine use in screening for postnatal depression, the National Screening Committee recommends that the Edinburgh Postnatal Depression Scale (EPDS) should not be used as a screening tool. It may, however, serve as a check list as part of a mood assessment for postnatal mothers, when it should only be used alongside professional judgement and a clinical interview.

The professional administering it should have training in its appropriate use and should not use it as a pass/fail-screening tool. Practitioners using it should also be mindful that, although it has been translated into many different languages, it can pose cultural difficulties for the interpretation, particularly when used with non English speaking mothers and those from non-western cultures. (National Screening Committee 2001)

Very different conclusions appear to have been reached elsewhere. A paper from Australia has concluded that:

Screening for...postnatal [depression] is likely to be useful because of the high prevalence of depressive disorders...and evidence that depression can be effectively treated. Early intervention may also have substantial benefits for the woman's partner, infant and older children. We have argued that the case *for* screening outweighs that *against*. (Buist *et al.* 2002, emphasis in original)

The Australian paper addressed the case for antenatal and postnatal depression and it is the justification upon which the huge *BeyondBlue* research study is based. I believe the paper sets the background hypothesis for their study, so does not contradict the NSC recommendations, which are based on available evidence. Australia is effectively doing a three-year research programme – exactly what the initial recommendations of the NSC had suggested.

That the evidence is lacking to justify a national screening programme does not mean that treating postnatal depression is unimportant or ineffective. There is ample evidence that an increased awareness amongst professionals about postnatal depression can help them to detect and manage the disease, provided they are adequately trained, and with resources and support from specialist secondary care services. Ethically, this is very different from screening, as expressed by Cochrane and Holland (1971, p.30):

We believe there is an ethical difference between everyday medical practice and screening. If a patient asks a medical practitioner for help, the doctor does the best he can. He is not responsible for defects in medical knowledge. If, however, the practitioner initiates the screening procedures he is in a very different position. He should, in our view, have conclusive evidence that screening can alter the natural history of disease in a significant proportion of those screened.

The NSC reviewed its position on screening for postnatal depression in March 2004 and made no change to its position. It will be reviewed again in 2007.

Chapter 2

Advantages and Disadvantages of Screening in Clinical Settings

Tessa Leverton

Introduction

I am a child and adolescent psychiatrist in inner London. I started work in Westminster Surestart for half a day a week a year ago. Surestart is a UK government funded initiative to 'deliver the best start in life for every child by bringing together: early education, childcare, health and family support' (www.surestart.gov.uk). Statutory services and the voluntary sector work together with the local community to design and implement a local plan to achieve preset national targets (Roberts 2000). After initial meetings with project workers and other local stakeholders, it was agreed that I focus on working with the team to improve services for women with postnatal depression in the local Surestart area. I am actively involved in a multidisciplinary, multiagency steering group developing and piloting an integrated care pathway for postnatal depression (Campbell *et al.* 1998).

My previous experience includes research on the prediction and prevention of postnatal depression (Elliott *et al.* 2000) and the strengths and limitation of the Edinburgh Postnatal Depression Scale (EPDS) (Elliott and Leverton 2000; Leverton and Elliott 2000). Clinical experience gained over almost 20 years as a child and adolescent psychiatrist has taught me the vital importance of early relationships and the significance of parental mental health for families (Leverton 2003).

I am also the mother of three children and so have some experience as a service user. When I was booking into the antenatal clinic of a teaching hospital before the birth of my second child, the midwife suddenly started to ask me personal questions with no explanation. She enquired about my relationship with my partner (and others), previous psychological issues and whether I had a psychiatric history. New to the clinic and the computerized booking system, she made no eye contact as she struggled to scan in my answers. I recognized the questions very well as they were part of my antenatal research questionnaire to screen for vulnerability to postnatal depression (Elliott *et al.* 2000). I did not know why she was asking these questions, who would have access to the replies and how the information might be used. As the interview continued, I began to feel increasingly uncomfortable and wondered how some of the mothers known to me through my clinical practice might respond to these questions, bearing in mind the complexity of their lives and their disillusionment with statutory services.

This experience brought home to me how vital it is to explain what you are asking and why. For *this* interviewee there was a world of difference between answering personal questions having consented to participate in a research project or as part of a computerized clinical record or because additional services may be offered. The relationship (or lack of it) between the interviewer and interviewee also contributes to the amount of information which feels 'safe' and appropriate to share. My experience that day has influenced my thinking and practice ever since.

In this chapter I will discuss the growing popularity of screening for psychological problems with children and families. Postnatal depression is rightly considered a priority area and there is considerable enthusiasm to identify women who are suffering and offer appropriate services. The evidence base has lagged behind the recommendations of statutory bodies and some clinical practice, creating a dilemma for those seeking to start new services. I will consider the advantages and disadvantages of screening for postnatal depression using the EPDS with particular reference to my present post with a Surestart project. The practical issues that need to be considered when screening for postnatal depression are outlined, and I conclude with suggestions for further research that would really help clinicians working in this area to improve services for new mothers.

The clinician's dilemma

Practitioners (e.g. the Community Practitioners' and Health Vistors' Association [CPHVA]) and service users (Aiken 2000) have expressed concerns that services for postnatal depression are variable in the UK.

Over the past few years there has been an avalanche of recommendations concerning early identification and treatment of postnatal depression from statutory agencies and charities: *Bright Futures* (Mental Health Foundation 1999), *Every Child Matters* (Department for Education and Skills 2003), *Getting the Right Start; National Service Framework for Children, Young People and Maternity Services; Emerging Findings* (Department of Health 2003), *National Service Framework for Mental Health* (Department of Health 1999a), Scottish Intercollegiate Guidelines Network (SIGN) (2002), Surestart (Department for Education and Skills 2002). Some organizations specifically advocate screening for postnatal depression: *Bright Futures* (Mental Health Foundation 1999), Health Advisory Service (Finch, Hill and Clegg 2000), Scottish Intercollegiate Guidelines Network (2002).

The National Screening Committee has reviewed the situation in detail against explicit criteria and concluded that in the current state of knowledge there is insufficient evidence to recommend a national screening programme for postnatal depression (Chapter 1).

There is a mismatch between the many authoritative recommendations to improve services for women with postnatal depression and the existing evidence base as interpreted by the National Screening Committee. Many areas in the UK already have agreed protocols for the identification and management of postnatal depression across agencies in the form of integrated care pathways (Campbell *et al.* 1998).

All the integrated care pathways that I have seen have used the EPDS as a screening tool. As noted above, clinical practice has moved beyond the published research. I am not aware of anyone advising areas that do have existing (functioning) care pathways to abandon these, but there is a problem in areas *without* any agreed pathways to know whether or not to use the EPDS to try to improve the care of women who suffer from postnatal depression. Clinicians striving to improve services and address the concerns of parents and practitioners have a problem deciding the best course of action while waiting for published research to catch up with statutory recommendations.

Screening for psychological problems in children and families

In the UK there is a growing emphasis on the early identification and appropriate intervention with children who have signs of psychological difficulties: *Bright Futures* (Mental Health Foundation 1999), *Framework for the Assessment of Children in Need and their Families* (Department of Health 2000a), Health Advisory Service 2000a, *National Service Frame-*

work for Children; Emerging Findings (Department of Health 2003), *Making a Difference for Children and Families* (Department for Education and Skills 2002).

Screening for child and adolescent mental health symptoms has been recommended in the UK to form part of the comprehensive *Assessment of Children in Need* conducted on children referred to social services departments (Department of Health 2000a). It is particularly interesting that this recommendation implies that the responsibility for screening for psychological problems in children and young people has begun to move from health professionals to other disciplines (e.g. social workers and teachers) in other agencies. The *Framework for the Assessment for Children in Need and their Families* is a comprehensive package for statutory assessment designed for social workers to complete with children and families referred to their service (Department of Health 2000b). It includes the *Family Pack of Questionnaires and Scales* comprising eight standardized assessment questionnaires, which address a range of concerns including: emotional and behavioural symptoms in children 4 to 16 (Strengths and Difficulties Questionnaire [SDQ], Goodman 1997), adolescents (Birleson 1980), and adults (Irritability, Depression and Anxiety Scale [IDA], Snaith *et al.* 1978). There are detailed practical guidelines as to how to use the questionnaires appropriately and even a training pack (Cox and Walker 2000) for staff unfamiliar with the use of questionnaires in this way.

Although the use of these questionnaires is recommended, it is not clear how far they are now incorporated into routine practice. Recently published research considering social services 'core assessments' of 68 children in 24 areas found the questionnaires and scales were rarely used (Cleaver and Walker 2004). In my experience, in both an urban and inner city area, social workers do not often feel confident to use these questionnaires with families and often do not do so. It is unusual for social workers to have been trained to use the questionnaires and scales. There are also some social workers (and others) who do not feel comfortable with the action of 'putting numbers on people's misery'. Even when such questionnaires are used, it is not always clear how much explanation and preparation has been undertaken. The interpretation and feedback of the resulting scores to the family and others needs careful consideration.

What services should be offered to women with postnatal depression?

When I arrived in Westminster in 2003 there was no local care pathway for postnatal depression, no perinatal psychiatry service and some variation in local health visitors' training and clinical practice. Some health visitors used the EPDS and some offered listening visits. 'Identifying, caring for and supporting mothers with postnatal depression in a culturally sensitive way' was both a local priority and a target for Surestart nationally. There were already many interested local practitioners and considerable groundwork had been done, for example, in mapping local services and producing a summary for reference on a laminated card for local professionals.

When our local multiagency, multidisciplinary steering group was considering how to improve the services to new mothers who might be depressed in an evidence based way, we were mindful of the published research on possible methods of screening for postnatal depression, the strengths and disadvantages/limitations of the EPDS and some of the myths that surround the use of this tool (Elliott and Leverton 2000).

The key issues are considered below.

How could you screen for postnatal depression in clinical practice?

There is no literature on using a brief interview or a few standard questions, as has been used in primary care (Arroll, Khin and Kerse 2003) or other non psychiatric settings (Whooley et al. 1997) to screen for postnatal depression. The literature focuses on using the EPDS.

What are the advantages of using the EPDS?

The scale is short, with just ten items designed to cover dysphoria and anhedonia rather than the somatic symptoms of depression. The first two questions refer to positive aspects of life ('being able to laugh and see the funny side of things' and 'looking forward with enjoyment to things'), which seems to make it easier to begin completing the form. In our area a significant minority of indigenous women have literacy problems. Our basic skills advisor from the local adult education department advises that the questions on the EPDS need only reading levels at Entry 3, i.e. the national standard for reading for 11-year-olds. A recent publication from the Department for Education and Skills would indicate that nationally 5% of adults age 16 to 65 would have a literacy standard below Entry level 3 (www.dfes.gov.uk/research). Thus, 95% of the UK English-speaking adult population should at least be able to read and understand the EPDS.

There are many versions of the EPDS for women for whom English is not a first language (although not all of these have been validated using a standardized psychiatric interview). There is an evidence base to suggest that women find the EPDS gives 'permission to speak' and welcome the chance to focus on their feelings (Holden 1994). These women may not have sought help from anyone else, despite being in contact with primary health services. Some women may find it easier to express their distress using a questionnaire. In the Lewisham study, we found eight women who appeared low at interview but did not 'open up' and acknowledge depressive symptoms to the researcher in the psychiatric interview (Leverton and Elliott 2000). When we subsequently reviewed the interviewer's transcript and clinical vignette with the contemporaneous EPDS score, we found six of these women had an EPDS score above the threshold 12/13. It seems therefore that the EPDS may give some women the opportunity to express their low mood on paper if not face to face.

The addition of screening using the EPDS has been found to increase the detection of depression in clinical practice (Evins, Theofrastous and Galvin 2000). The EPDS has been shown to be valid and reliable as a screening tool although these figures will, of course, vary depending on the prevalence rates of depression in the study sample (Eberhard-Gran *et al.* 2001; Leverton and Elliott 2000, Chapter 1 this volume).

What are the disadvantages and limitations of using the EPDS to screen for postnatal depression?

The EPDS is a screening tool and not a diagnostic test. A high score is not synonymous with clinical depression and a low score does not necessarily rule this out. The EPDS cannot replace a clinical interview. Recent work has suggested that the EPDS performs better with women who have depression with anxiety and anhedonia and will miss women with retarded depression (Guedeney *et al.* 2000). The EPDS does not have questions regarding somatic symptoms of depression, a deliberate decision as these symptoms can be hard to assess in postnatal women (Cox 1986). There is a growing awareness that in some cultures somatic symptoms are very important, acceptable indicators of psychological distress and so the absence of these symptoms may be an important omission from the EPDS. The EPDS is not entirely specific for depression and will pick up other disorders. In our Lewisham study, two women with phobic neurosis, one with paranoid psychosis and one woman in the manic phase of manic depressive psychosis all scored above the 12/13 cut off on the EPDS (Leverton and Elliott 2000). Although designed to screen for depression, the EPDS does also pick up women with anxiety symptoms and in clinical practice there can be considerable overlap between these conditions in new mothers (Browvers, van Baar and Pop 2001; Green 1998; Leverton and Elliott 2000; Pop, Komproe and van Son 1992; Ross *et al.* 2003).

The instructions at the beginning of the EPDS ask 'How you have felt in the past seven days', not just how you feel today. This timescale has the advantage of not missing women whose dysphoria has not reached diagnostic criteria, but in clinical practice may pick up many women with transient distress. In our study (Leverton and Elliott 2000), ongoing life stresses (e.g. having your mother in law come to stay 'to help with the new baby') resulted in more than one woman scoring above the threshold on a number of symptoms – but only for the duration of the visit! The fact that the EPDS provides a 'snapshot' of a woman's mood during one week means that it cannot be used to rule out postnatal depression over many months nor to pick up postnatal depression immediately after delivery (Lee *et al.* 2003). The EPDS was designed and initially validated on a sample of English-speaking women in Scotland. The ways in which women experience mood and other changes in the postnatal period vary from place to place and culture to culture. The notion of 'testing' using a questionnaire is not a universal one. In Western cultures we are to some degree 'socialised into a culture of taking tests which starts from primary school' but for others the experience may be 'bewildering' (Laungani 2000, p.92). There are now many translations (not all validated) and new pictorial adaptations to address some of these concerns (Chapter 9).

None the less, there will still be women who prefer not to disclose their feelings to an outsider (or anyone), perhaps fearing that if they were to disclose how they felt, their baby might be removed (McIntosh 1993). Some women do not wish to have their sad or unhappy feelings labelled/medicalized as postnatal depression (Hill and Revill 2004). There will also inevitably be women who prefer to talk over how they are feeling rather than underline phrases on a questionnaire.

A recent study of Syletti/Bengali-speaking women in London and Bangladesh found that the women apparently 'often preferred' to be asked the questions by the research worker rather than complete the translated (paper) version of the EPDS (Fuggle *et al.* 2002).

When setting up any screening programme, it is also important to be aware that there will always be some women whom health visitors find it difficult to contact to *ask* them to complete a questionnaire. These hard to reach women are more likely to be clinically depressed. In our Lewisham study the women whom the health visitor did not see at three months postnatal had four times the rate of postnatal depression when interviewed by a research psychiatrist as compared with those women the health visitor did see (Leverton and Elliott 2000).

How should we proceed in our district?

There appeared to be three possible options:

1.   To defer any service provision until the published research had caught up with the statutory recommendations.

2.   To design, obtain funding and ethical committee approval to conduct a comprehensive controlled *research* trial comparing standard screening tools (EPDS, General Health Questionnaire [Goldberg 1972] and Beck Depression Inventory [Beck 1978]), with clinical interview to identify which women are suffering from postnatal depression and offer them evidence based treatment. In order to answer all the outstanding research questions posed by the National Screening Committee, the outcomes for the women and their families would need to be compared with the outcome for women in an inner city area (matched for a range of important characteristics including education, socio-economic status and ethnicity) where there was neither screening nor treatment available for postnatal depression.

3.   To provide a basic service as a *pilot* (at minimal extra cost), offering both screening for postnatal depression with the EPDS (followed by a clinical interview if appropriate) by trained health visitors and the option of non-directive counselling (listening visits as per Holden, Sagovsky and Cox 1989) if required from the Surestart health visiting team (to avoid placing a great burden on community health visitors). This service could be summarized in the form of an integrated care pathway that included advice as to where to refer women for further help if appropriate. Some simple records could be kept to audit the project and to inform future service developments.

The pros and cons of the three options can be summarized as below.

OPTION 1

Pro:

- This avoids using resources for any practice that does not have a strong evidence base. Health visitor workload will not increase as no new demands will be made.

Cons:

- The current situation with considerable practice variation will continue.

- The needs of distressed mothers will not be better met than at present.

- New health visitors will be unsure how best to proceed.
- The stated objective of Surestart will not be met.

OPTION 2

Pro:

- We will attempt to answer the outstanding research questions for this locality and then develop practice based on strong evidence.

Cons:

- This approach will take time.
- It may be hard to identify a suitable comparison area.
- There is no obvious source of funding for the project.
- Even if we could carry out this project, any results will apply to this area *now*. The demographic and other characteristics of the area are changing so fast that in a few years the results may no longer be an accurate basis for service development.

OPTION 3

Pros:

- This is a feasible project.
- We can capitalize on the local support (from professionals and users) to develop services.
- This will meet one of Surestart's stated objectives.
- There are some funds to 'pump prime' this development from Surestart.

Cons:

- This is a limited project and cannot answer research questions.
- There will be some burden on health visitors to screen women and complete questionnaires.

We chose Option 3 as being the most practical approach. Since there is no perinatal psychiatry service locally to provide comprehensive back-up services, it made sense to trial the new care pathway just in the Surestart ward as we are fortunate to be in the catchment area of an adult psychiatrist who is interested in the needs of patients as parents with a supportive community mental health team. This approach addresses 'the objective of ensuring that clinical practice is based on the best *available* evidence integrated with clinical expertise and patient preference leading to the best possible patient care' (Geddes *et al.* 1998, p.5). The CPHVA recommendation that 'In the absence of a failsafe screening tool the EPDS despite its imperfections has considerable value if properly used with its weaknesses acknowledged' was also influential (Coyle and Adams 2002, p.395).

Option 3 also meets the recommendations of the *National Service Framework for Mental Health* (Department of Health 1999a), the *Emerging Findings* from the Children's National Service Framework (Department of Health 2003), the SIGN Guidelines (SIGN 2002) and the objectives of our host organization, Westminster Surestart. The service user who had joined the steering group made it clear that services needed improving without delay, thus Options 1 and 2 were simply not appropriate (even if Option 2 were ever funded).

Putting theory and research into practice

Some of the difficulties outlined above in using the EPDS can be overcome in practice. It is now well recognized that health visitors and other professionals need training before using the EPDS (Coyle and Adams 2002; National Screening Committee 2003).

Training the trainers

A number of training courses exist in the UK to 'train the trainers', enabling whole districts to be trained by local professionals (e.g. Keele and Reading, details below). We were fortunate to obtain funding to attend both trainer training courses. The training courses have some similarities but also some significant differences (a detailed description of these is beyond the scope of this chapter). Both provide considerable information, teaching materials and reading lists on postnatal depression. The courses are residential and offer a great chance to network and debate the issues at length. The issues involved in using the EPDS are well covered and suggestions made as to how to use this tool in the best way.

The Reading training covers the impact of postnatal depression on the child and the clinical interview as recommended by the CPHVA (using symptoms for depression from the American Psychiatric Association *Diagnostic and Statistical Manual for Psychiatric Disorders* [APA 1994]. The Keele training takes more of a workshop format and assumes considerable basic knowledge (assessed on the application form). The emphasis is on raising questions and issues to consider when planning services. It is essential that representatives from adult mental health services attend the trainer training with health visitors and others. Close attention is paid to the processes and strategic approach required to develop services.

There is some evidence to show that training health visitors in the appropriate use of the EPDS and non directive counselling skills can reduce overall medium range (but not high) EPDS scores over time (Elliott *et al.* 2001). Both training courses cover treatment approaches and the evidence for non directive listening, although I was interested that neither really included how to train staff to carry out listening visits nor how to follow up training to establish if listening visits are actually being provided by front line staff (quality control). I consider that attending both training courses was useful to gain a full picture of the issues and comprehensive training materials.

The Keele course has been running for ten years and there is some published outcome research following up previous attenders to see if they implement service changes.

Local management support is critical as it can be difficult for trained trainers to use their skills to provide local education and service development (Elliott *et al.* 2003).

What are the key areas to address in local training courses?

Clearly, training health visitors (and others) in the appropriate use of the EPDS needs to cover the evidence base for the EPDS, the strengths and limitations of this approach to screening for postnatal depression and the practicalities of how to do this in a sensitive way. It seems helpful to include role-plays and experiential learning as well as didactic teaching and video demonstrations. Preparing to give the EPDS in an empathetic manner in a suitable setting (with privacy) is now recognized to be extremely important. Of course, any woman has the right to decline to complete the EPDS and this must be respected while still leaving the possibility for her to talk about her feelings to the health visitor.

Careful discussion of the best way to educate women about postnatal depression is vitally important since the extensive lay literature available can be very confusing and anxiety inducing (Martinez *et al.* 2000). Health visitors need the confidence to continue to exercise their own judgement and experience and not to dismiss their own views if the EPDS score is not as they expect. In our Lewisham study, we found a combination of health visitor judgement and EPDS score to be the *best* predictor of clinical depression at six weeks postnatal using a standardized psychiatric interview (Leverton and Elliott 2000). The woman should be able to complete the questionnaire on her own (although it can be read to her if she has literacy difficulties) and health visitors should be wary of being drawn into clarifying and discussing the meaning of items before the women completes the scale, as in doing this the reliability and validity of the test may change (discussed in Laungani 2000). Once the woman has completed the EPDS, time should be taken to go through the items, the score and to discuss whether any further support is necessary and who is best placed to provide this.

There is a recommendation from the CPHVA that health visitors should be trained to carry out a clinical interview for depression (Coyle and Adams 2002). The Reading trainer training advocates using an interview based on DSM-IVR criteria for health visitors to use to clarify the picture if a woman is depressed prior to referral to a GP (Seeley 2001). Training will need to cover the precise action to be taken if a women is depressed and/or suicidal and refuses to consult her GP. There may be situations when a health visitor needs to be confident in contacting the GP against the woman's wishes, but in her interest (but of course keeping her informed). There is a need to jointly make a clear and explicit plan of action if a women scores above the chosen threshold and/or scores positive on question 10 (regarding self-harm) (Cox and Holden 2003, pp.56–57). The plans need to be written down and a copy given to the mother to keep. A locally agreed care pathway can provide a helpful framework here (Campbell et al. 1998).

As a child and adolescent psychiatrist, I stress the importance of asking a woman about any thoughts she may have about harming the baby. These are not uncommon in postnatal depression (in one study, 41% of clinically depressed mothers of children aged up to three years had thoughts of harming their child as compared with 7% of control mothers), cause enormous distress to mothers and warrant careful exploration since a minority of mothers will go on to harm their children (Jennings et al. 1999).

General practitioners and adult psychiatrists vary in their knowledge (and level of interest) in this area so they will also need information, training and consultation to support a district initiative (Aitken and Jacobsen 1997). It is particularly important to involve GPs (Hearn et al. 1998), and disconcerting that some early initiatives for community management of postnatal depression appear to bypass them (Jebali 1991).

Simply agreeing a care pathway and providing training in the appropriate use of the EPDS and non directive counselling is not sufficient to ensure that health visitors continue to provide appropriate care for new mothers who may be depressed (Shakespeare 2002). There is a need for ongoing support/consultation from mental health services and training will need to be repeated for new staff and updated regularly since research in this area is advancing all the time. Even if these supports are in place the heavy workload, staff turnover and high vacancy rates may preclude routine screening and offers of counselling (see Chapter 3). As yet there is a limited evidence base for screening in some cultural groups, and in areas with a high percentage of women from ethnic minorities health visitors may not offer screening and treatment to all (Shakespeare 2002).

All care pathways/clinical guidelines should be subject to regular review and revision to ensure they are effective, up to date and being implemented (Thomson, Lavender and Madhok 1995).

Future directions in screening for postnatal depression

Clinical practice in the detection and management of postnatal depression is at an interesting stage of development. There is widespread recognition that postnatal depression is an important condition with implications for mothers, children and families. All professionals who come into contact with mothers and babies are encouraged to identify mothers who are depressed and ensure they receive appropriate evidence based support. However, there is a lack of clarity about the best way to identify mothers with postnatal depression and the limitations of the widely used EPDS have been well described by the National Screening Committee. There is a growing recognition of the need to provide appropriate and sensitive screening for depression for women from other cultures and exciting new approaches are being piloted. Despite the many existing publications, there is still a real need for research in this area. As a clinician who strives to deliver person centred care, I would like to know if women could be offered a *choice* of whether to complete a questionnaire or to have a conversation using screening questions to describe how they are feeling. In my current practice, it would also be useful to know whether the *whole* Surestart team (including parent volunteers) could be trained to screen new mothers sensitively for postnatal depression and provide support.

'Training the trainers' courses in the UK

Keele University: contact Lynda Clewlow, Course Administrator, email: lyndaclewlow@yahoo.com; tel: (+44)1782 555084

Reading University: contact Sheelah Seeley; details at www.pndtraining.co.uk

Chapter 3

One Bite of the Cherry: A Resource Dilemma

Sheelah Seeley and Ann Girling

Introduction

The term 'one bite of the cherry' refers to a primary care service provision crisis that occurred in Cambridge, UK in 1997. The use of clinical audit demonstrated a sharp fall in the identification of postnatal depression following substantial financial disinvestments. Families who had been well known to their health visitors now had much more restricted access to the new child and family nurses and therefore limited opportunity to be screened for depression postnatally and none antenatally. This disappointing outcome had implications for maternal and infant well being and what follows is the history of, and primary care response to, this resource dilemma.

Background

Ten years ago, primary care in Cambridge and health visiting in particular had a very different profile to that observed today. Most health visitors undertook antenatal visits to first-time mothers, and other mothers referred by professional colleagues who assessed those women to be in need of support or specific intervention during pregnancy.

Following the primary birth visit at 10 to 14 days postnatally, weekly or sometimes fortnightly visits were routine for several months where required.

In short, health visitors set out, and were able, to get to know the women in their care and a working alliance was established. Importantly, this time spent raised the health visitor's awareness of each woman's personal and family health and social history, her relationships and circumstances. Additionally, the women understood the health visitor's role and her/his concern for each woman's own well being as well as the health of her family. The establishment of this relationship is crucial to effective work with mothers and their families. Much of the health visiting literature is concerned with the centrality of this relationship (e.g. Houston and Cowley 2002; Normandale 2001; Twinn 2000; Worth and Hogg 2000).

In addition, the health visitor's local knowledge often enabled the women to establish networks. The women knew their health visitor. In January 1993, born out of Lynne Murray's recently completed Cambridge treatment trial (Cooper and Murray 1997), and with strong support from management, the first compulsory training courses for health visitors in the detection and management of postnatal depression were set up in Cambridge. Arranged over six half days these focused on:

- education about depression

- the impact of postnatal depression on families and infant development

- the value and use of active reflective listening

- some techniques derived from cognitive behavioural theory as applied to the treatment of postnatal depression and

- the administration and interpretation of the Edinburgh Postnatal Depression Scale (EPDS).

SS (first author of this chapter) had extensive experience of use of the EPDS in the research context. She recognized its limitations if used as a checklist and relying on the score as the trigger to provide intervention. The training therefore included the use of the EPDS with additional mood assessment using three questions: extent of low mood over the past two weeks, loss of pleasure or interest in previously enjoyed activities and feelings of uselessness or guilt. This encouraged identification of false positives and negatives on the EPDS – those women scoring above 'cut-off' who were not depressed and vice versa.

When it came to offering the EPDS at four to six weeks, the health visitors were well aware of its limitations as well as its strengths and the women were well appraised of its purpose, felt confident enough to be honest, and trusted the health visitor to be a good listener. Health visitors were encouraged to arrange time-limited, contracted home visits with mothers found to be in need and accepting of this support, referring on to secondary services those requiring more specialized treatment. All health visitors in post in 1993 completed the training. The high level of commitment from health visitors was reflected in screening levels of over 90% from within a few months of commencement of this service (Seeley, Murray and Cooper 1996). Just under 10% of new mothers were assessed as in need of support visits. From a survey of women delivering at the Cambridge maternity hospital, the rate around this time was 13% (Cooper et al. 1996).

At this time, health visitor caseloads were about 400 children under five years, which then would have probably been just about the national average. Prior to this training it was not known what was the health visitor detection rate for postnatal depression. However, in 1992, a case notes survey incorporating a health visitor interview found that of the 25 depressed women identified by researchers on the Cambridge treatment trial (using the EPDS and the Structured Clinical Interview for DSM-IV (SCID: First et al. 1996) their health visitor recognized 14 of them to be emotionally unwell. Additionally, of the 25 well women the health visitors believed eight to be depressed. Combining false positives and negatives, this was a misdiagnosis rate of 38% (Seeley et al. 1996).

The 1993 evaluation showed a postnatal depression rate of 9.7%, and intervention to be effective at alleviating depressive symptoms and improving the mother's perception of her relationship with her baby (Seeley et al. 1996).

The financial squeeze on the health services started around the early 1990s; local community health resources were being routinely cut by about 3% year on year. Then came the bombshell – disinvestment. In 1997/98, by order of the commissioning authority, a reduction of 27% to the school nursing and health visiting budget was imposed. In an attempt to accommodate this reduction, an experimental service model was devised.

Health visiting and school nursing were combined to provide a 0 to 16 child and family service. Staff from both professions were now expected to work right across the age range. All interventions had to have an evidence base. However, much of the effective work carried out by health visitors does not fit with the medical model of health and the positivist research agenda. There was therefore a limited evidence base to fall back on. Consequently, the majority of routine contacts were lost, as was one third of nursing staff. The number of open access baby clinics was reduced; some operated only by appointment. Of those that were left, some were now run by volunteers, others by nursery nurses, school nurses and *maybe* health visitors. Health visitor input to antenatal and postnatal classes ceased. In fact, formal health education was abandoned entirely.

An inevitable result was that health visitor/school nurse contact with pregnant and recently delivered mothers dropped dramatically, thereby rendering the development of a trusting relationship nearly impossible. Despite this loss of so many aspects of the traditional health visiting service to mothers and families, one important service remained. Due to the unassailable strength of the evidence for intervention, the locally established and structured approach to the detection and management of postnatal depression was to continue. The major consequence of this was that the number of new births per child and family nurse (i.e. former health visitor or school nurse) increased dramatically. Although by reducing other routine contacts there was more time released to accommodate this, it still meant increased numbers of women per nurse. A caseload could now be of the order of 1000 children between zero and five years old. Therefore, the opportunities for the child and family nurses to get to know the women and their families were curtailed and, indeed, the women did not feel that they knew the person charged with their postnatal care.

Child and family nurses surveyed at inception of the new service and one year later estimated that, compared to other aspects of the job, postnatal care had been most affected. A similar survey of local GPs revealed that 88% felt that postnatal care had been compromised (Durdle Davis and Cowley 1999).

At this point, many in primary care realized cases of postnatal depression were being missed. An audit of postnatal depression rates illustrated a 6.7% detection rate as compared to 9.7% in 1993. As a response to this disappointing audit finding:

- guidelines were developed for detection and management of postnatal depression, and implemented across the whole children's service

- mandatory training was instituted for new child and family nurses and new in post health visitors

- top-up training was offered to health visitors five years after their original training.

A three-day training course was delivered by SS and Dr J. Bray, senior psychiatric nurse tutor, at Homerton School of Nursing. Although similar to the original course, there was now more emphasis on the detection of postnatal depression, making a mood assessment using the EPDS and, where indicated, a clinical interview.

The clinical interview used here is derived from First *et al.* (1996) Structured Clinical Interview for DSM-IV – the major depressive episode module. The interview focuses on the two screening questions from DSM-IV for major depression – low mood and loss of interest or pleasure in previously enjoyed activities. The first two statements on the EPDS also focus on those two issues. For clinical depression, one or other of these must be present for at least two weeks more of the time than not. Where a woman responds positively to either of these screening questions, further enquiry is carried out using the other DSM-IV items defining depression – seven in all. A recent study supports the use of these two verbally asked questions as a screen for depression (Arroll, Khin and Kerse 2003).

A survey of nurses' working practice following the training indicated increased confidence in approaching maternal mental health issues, both in detection and management. Despite the greatly reduced access to postnatal women described here, a further audit in 2000 showed a detection rate of 11%. There has been no subsequent audit.

Conclusion

Despite having limited access to the women, perhaps one or two meetings, the postnatal depression screening programme set up here, part of which included training health visitors and school nurses in making a mood assessment, produced a detection rate near to that found in research where the 'gold standard' of structured clinical interview for DSM-IV for depression was used. Research needs to be conducted to ascertain whether those identified in this manner as depressed actually are.

The Community Practitioners' and Health Visitors' Association (CPHVA) have endorsed this approach in their response to the National Screening Committee (Coyle and Adams 2002). Research is still needed to address most of their recommendations. A research study in Reading confirms the importance of training. This showed that health visitors who had not been trained in detection or intervention for postnatal depression using the EPDS did not enhance detection of postnatal depression. Those health visitors using it were no more able to pick up depressed women than those health visitors not using it (Murray, Woolgar and Cooper 2004), i.e. 10% of depressed women as compared to 9.1%.

Chapter 4

Two Bites of the Cherry: One Solution?

Philip Boyce and Caroline Bell

Introduction

Currently, there is often little done to address the emotional needs of women during pregnancy, despite the improvements in physical care during the last ten years. For example, in Australia 60% of women in Victoria were visited by a domiciliary nurse in 2000 compared to 24% in 1994 (Brown, Darcy and Bruinsma 2001). A growing recognition of the need for comprehensive care (including emotional support) for women in the perinatal period has led some services to introduce screening programmes for psycho-social problems and distress. Controversy has emerged as to whether these programmes may be premature given the current lack of knowledge regarding the psychological outcomes of those screened, the cost-effectiveness of screening, and the level of consumer satisfaction.

There are a number of fundamental questions that need to be considered when implementing a screening programme.

1. What are we screening for?

2. When should we screen?

3. What are the consequences of the screening?

4. Who should do the screening?

5. How should the screening be co-ordinated?

Each of these questions will now be considered.

What are we screening for?

At different times over the perinatal period, screening would appear to have a rather different focus. Currently, a variety of types of screening occurs in antenatal clinics. The aim of screening during the antenatal period is to identify women at potential *risk* of developing subsequent depression. Screening in the immediate postnatal period (i.e. immediately after delivery) also places the emphasis on identifying women at high risk of developing subsequent difficulties. Identifying those women at potential risk provides an opportunity to implement preventative and prophylactic strategies to reduce the risk of frank difficulties developing. A number of key vulnerability factors have been identified as increasing a woman's risk for developing postnatal depression. These include poor social support, particularly emotional support, and, to a lesser extent, practical support from her partner in caring for the baby (Boyce 1994), and a lack of other sources of practical support. Other vulnerability factors include having a personality style characterized by over-sensitivity and anxiousness, and obstetric factors such as early discharge from hospital (Hickey *et al.* 1997), a traumatic delivery or caesarean section (Boyce and Todd 1992). Identifying those women who have these risk factors is important in the antenatal and early postnatal periods, if their risk of going on to develop depression is to be reduced.

Screening in the later postnatal period on the other hand is generally more concerned with *case identification*, with a view to implementing treatment and/or protection, as opposed to the identification and reduction of risk. The screening process then becomes more about identifying women who are displaying actual symptoms of depression. One method of increasing the recognition of postnatal depression is to use a screening tool for the disorder that can be administered at routine clinic visits. Such screening should focus on higher-risk women (e.g. those lacking social support or with an anxious/worrying personality style), as general screening programmes tend not to be effective. The Edinburgh Postnatal Depression Scale (EPDS) has been developed as such a screening tool, and studies (e.g. Evins *et al.* 2000) have found that its use increases the detection rate of postnatal depression. This is a user-friendly ten-item scale that can be completed by women in a few minutes. A score of 12 or more suggests a high probability of a woman suffering from major depression. In an Australian study, Boyce, Stubbs and Todd (1993) found that women who scored greater than 12 met diagnostic criteria for major depression (sensitivity = 100%, specificity = 95.7%, positive predictive value = 0.69, likelihood ratio = 23.1). Such a screening tool could be routinely used in early childhood clinics or when a woman attends her postnatal check up at six to eight weeks postpartum.

While a lot of effort is often put into screening and identifying women at risk of developing postnatal depression and anxiety, it is also important to be aware of other mental health problems during the perinatal period. For example, it is crucial to identify women at risk for developing a psychotic illness, an issue that is discussed in detail in Chapter 10 (this volume).

When should we screen?

As noted above, screening in the antenatal and early postnatal period is largely concerned with identifying those women who are not currently presenting with symptoms, but who are at greater risk of developing subsequent depression. To reduce the risk of some women developing symptoms, preventative strategies (such as teaching stress management or providing increased support) could be implemented during this time. Screening throughout the postnatal period would also seem to be indicated for those women identified antenatally as having several of the risk factors for postnatal depression (such as reduced support). Consequently, to maximize the prevention of distress and to target interventions effectively, screening during the antenatal and early postnatal periods would seem to be very important, particularly for those higher-risk women.

Currently, perinatal screening is most commonly conducted at six to eight weeks postpartum, with the primary aim of detecting actual cases of postnatal depression. An unpublished study in Australia investigated the efficacy of this. The study was conducted in an area where it was policy for women to be screened by community health services for postnatal depression. The women in the study were screened by a member of the research team using the EPDS, and a cut-off score of ≥12 was used to indicate depression was present. We found that of 163 women screened, 16 (9.82%) met criteria for postnatal depression. Of these women, only 20% had been identified by the community health screening process. Forty per cent of the women with depression had been screened by community health but it had not been identified, and the other 40% had not been screened by community services at all. Thus, having a screening policy is not sufficient in itself to ensure that women at risk or women who are already depressed are identified and appropriately managed. To be effective, screening must be accessed by the women for whom it is intended, and it must be linked with a coherent management strategy so that women who are identified as potential cases will be comprehensively assessed and offered appropriate intervention and follow up. This is discussed more fully below.

Given the impractical nature of screening large numbers of women routinely, we have begun to investigate the efficacy of initially screening in the immediate postpartum period, while the women are still on the maternity ward (Boyce 2003). The aim is to identify women who score highly on the EPDS and who are therefore regarded as at very high risk of developing subsequent difficulties. In addition, factors such as a previous history of depression or relationship problems are investigated to aid in the identification of high-risk women.

In the study (full details of which can be found in Boyce 2003), women were screened in the immediate postpartum period (two or three days after the birth) using the EPDS. The women (n = 403) were then divided into either a high-risk (EPDS ≥12) or low-risk (EPDS ≤12) group. We found that women in the low-risk group had a significantly lower risk of subsequently developing postnatal depression. Thirty-three per cent of women in the high-risk group were later identified as cases of depression (EPDS ≥12), compared to only 6% of the low-risk group. Based on this, we suggest that women in the high-risk group should be followed up more assertively, i.e. have a further comprehensive postnatal screen at six to eight weeks, and then an appropriate management plan put into place if they are identified as cases of depression.

Such targeted screening programmes, where women identified (either antenatally or early postnatally) as high-risk are then more assertively followed up, may be a more cost-effective strategy.

What are the consequences of the screening?

If the effort is being made to screen antenatally or in the early postnatal period, this should have appropriate implications. If a woman is identified as high-risk for depression, measures should be taken to modify that risk (e.g. implementing prevention strategies). Identifying a woman as high-risk should also act as a cue for increased surveillance and follow up by the clinicians involved during the antenatal and postnatal periods, and potentially the use of prophylactic intervention. If they show signs of depression then appropriate treatment could be implemented.

Once women are identified as low or high risk for subsequent difficulties, different interventions are indicated. Appropriate interventions for women in the low-risk category may be the provision of educational packages (e.g. about how to recognize postnatal depression). This would ensure that they have some contact with services, to enable them to seek appropriate help and support should they require it. One strategy may be to provide them with copies of the EPDS to complete themselves at six to eight weeks, along with information regarding services that they can contact should they score highly or have any concerns. However, Cox and Holden (2003, pp.63–64) have recommended that the EPDS only be used as an adjunct to a clinical interview. Women in the high-risk group are those who we would suggest require more assertive follow up if difficulties are to be prevented or minimized. This could include a further detection screen at six to eight weeks postpartum, with an appropriate management plan being implemented for those identified as cases of depression.

Who should do the screening?

The EPDS is a quick and simple self-report measure, and is the most widely used screening scale internationally. It has been validated for use both antenatally and postnatally. With appropriate training, it can be administered by a variety of professionals in both primary and secondary care. Screening using the EPDS would not therefore necessarily involve visits to specialists, but instead could be conducted at home by e.g. health visitors, or in the GP's surgery during a routine antenatal or postnatal appointment. As these professionals are often already overstretched, this increased workload would have implications for resource levels within primary care services. It is possible that women in the high-risk group may be less likely to make contact with or visit specialist health services (e.g. as a result of poor motivation in the context of a low mood). Conducting the screening at home or during a routine appointment may therefore make identification of risk and subsequent follow up and/or intervention more accessible to these women. It may also be possible for the screening to occur over the telephone or by postal questionnaire (although there are likely to be difficulties with depressed women responding to postal surveys).

Such indirect methods of screening require a co-ordinated approach to ensure that these high-risk women are actually contacted at six to eight weeks postpartum. This requires effective co-ordination between the various services involved such as early childhood nurses, midwives, health visitors, GPs, mental health services and so on. Management protocols are also required if women are to be appropriately managed depending on their identified level of risk and/or caseness. Training in identifying the risk factors described above and in administering the EPDS (and more importantly interpreting the result) is likely to be required for some health professionals (e.g. GPs, midwives) whose main focus would usually be the woman's physical (and not psychological) health. These professionals may represent the first contact with health services for some women. It is therefore crucial that these professionals are aware of what signs to look for and what action they should take in the event that a woman presents who appears to be at risk of developing difficulties.

How should the screening be co-ordinated?

In clinical practice, a potential problem with running an integrated service is a lack of co-ordination between antenatal and postnatal screening, and the services conducting them. In some services in Australia the hospital records may be separate from the community records, and different (separate) records may be held for the infant and the mother. In Australia, women also do not always consistently see the same GP, whereas in the UK the GP can act as the co-ordinator of the mother's care. In such situations, where there is a lack of integrated records, women identified during the antenatal or early postnatal period as being at risk may not be monitored closely enough by the relevant professionals. They may therefore go on to develop clinical problems, leading to adverse outcomes not only in terms of their mental health, but also in terms of the mother–infant relationship. Similarly, women identified as being cases of postnatal depression may not be offered the appropriate treatment and support if there is a lack of co-ordination between those services responsible for identification, and those responsible for intervention (where they are not the same service). Thus, one of the major challenges we face when thinking about implementing a comprehensive and effective screening programme is the entire process of co-ordination. Effective co-ordination between the various health services with whom a woman is involved in the perinatal period is essential if any screening programme is to lead to effective outcomes.

Summary

Screening at different times during the perinatal period has different aims and potential outcomes. These are summarized in Table 4.1 below.

Targeted screening allows for the identification of women who are either at low or high risk of developing postnatal depression, and suggests different management strategies in each situation (see Figure 4.1). Such targeted screening provides an opportunity for health service resources to be used with optimum efficiency at a time when women's contact with health professionals is at a peak (Cox and Holden 2003, pp.50–52).

An effective screening programme needs: to have clear aims; to have appropriate management programmes in place; and to be properly co-ordinated.

Table 4.1 Screening for postnatal depression

Time	Aim	Outcomes
Antenatal	Screen for risk	Modification of risk Surveillance and follow up Potential case identification Antenatal intervention and prophylaxis
Immediate postpartum (within 72 hours of delivery)	Screen for risk	Assertive follow up Communication between services 6–8/52 screen for detection and management
Postnatal (6–8/52)	Screen for detection	Management/treatment of postnatal depression

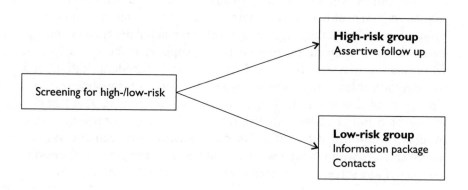

Figure 4.1 A targeted screening programme

Chapter 5

The EPDS as a Tool for Identifying New Onset Depression Within the First Postpartum Year

Kathleen S. Peindl

Finding new approaches to help identify women at risk of an onset of major depression during the first postpartum year is essential for all clinicians who care for these women. Several studies show that women who have experienced a previous confirmed diagnosis of postpartum depression have an 80% chance of a recurrence of depression in the year following birth (Bell *et al.* 1994; Davidson and Robertson 1985; Peindl, Wisner and Hanusa 2004; Philipps and O'Hara 1991; Robling *et al.* 2000). Recent and consistent findings also indicate that both women and their children are adversely affected by episodes of major depression that occur during the first postpartum year.

With an increased risk of suffering from major depression in the year after birth, clinicians need screens to help them identify depression so that treatment is started in a timely manner.

Concerns arise about the use of screening tools because they are not diagnostic instruments. Screening does lead to false positives (women scoring high on the screen but that are not clinically depressed). Several other questions are also relevant when using screening instruments. Will the screen increase the clinicians' awareness of depression and the possible need for treatment? If it does increase awareness, at what time should the screening process take place? Is it useful as a tool for identifying women at risk of developing an episode of major depression over the course of a year? Finally, will the Edinburgh Postnatal Depression Scale (EPDS) have enough sensitivity to monitor symptoms in the first postpartum year or, put another way, will there be a meaningful change in scores on the EPDS to monitor women's emotional health over time? This chapter will attempt to answer these questions.

Screening for depression at the first visit: evidence for its use

In relationship to timing of the screen, screening for depression at the first postpartum visit with a valid and reliable instrument is not routinely performed in obstetric practices in the US, even though evidence strongly suggests that if screening is performed, more women are identified as depressed and referred for treatment. The reason for screening during the first postpartum visit is twofold: 1. to identify women who are currently depressed and 2. to identify women who may be at increased risk of an onset of major depression in the first postpartum year, especially women who have experienced a previous episode of depression.

In the following studies, investigators reported that rates of recognition of depression increased after using the EPDS during the first postpartum visit. Moreover, more women were referred and received treatment after the screening process. None of these studies (by virtue of design) followed women after their first visit to examine if the scores on the EPDS helped identify women at risk for an episode of major depression in the first year after birth.

Rates of recognizing postpartum depression without screening

Studies clearly indicate that neither postpartum nor later maternal depression is routinely identified in clinical practice. Holden (1996) reported a 60% failure rate for identifying postpartum-onset depression among health visitors who visited new mothers weekly. Investigators who reviewed medical charts in Olmsted, Minnesota found the rate for a diagnosed episode of postpartum depression was 3.7% (Bryan et al. 1999) compared to a community rate of 10 to 15% worldwide. Moreover, maternal depression is not identified in some psychiatric settings. Among mothers who brought their children for treatment or evaluation for depression, 14% of the mothers had major depression and only 31% of the depressed women were receiving treatment (Ferro et al. 2000). Pediatric health care providers also failed to recognize severe symptoms of depression in mothers who were bringing their children for care. In this study, only 29% of maternal depression was identified (Heneghan et al. 2000). In primary care, where women often seek treatment for depression, 50% of all cases are not recognized (Yonkers and Chantilis 1995). Despite an increased awareness of postpartum depression, the illness is still under-diagnosed for a variety of reasons. One is the timing of probable onset of the illness; symptoms of depression can be mistaken for normal changes during the period after birth. Another is increased demand on clinicians to see many patients so that women who may not be able to express their feelings go unnoticed.

Rate of recognizing postpartum depression with screening

Reports from three separate studies show increased rates for identifying cases of postpartum depression with routine use of the EPDS. In Olmsted, Minnesota, routine screening with the EPDS was instituted for a period of one year (Georgiopoulos et al. 2001). The rate of diagnosed depression among postpartum women in the county increased from 3.7% (women identified without EPDS screening) to 10.7%, an almost 189% increase in detection of postpartum depression. In another study, the EPDS was compared to standard practice in a residency training clinic. Among 391 women screened over a one-year period, 35.4% were identified as having depression when the EPDS was used compared to 6.3% recognition of depression during routine standard care (Evins et al. 2000). Barnett et al. (1993) finished a study of 100 women who came to a mothers' residential facility where their infants were receiving care. The women completed the EPDS; 39% scored above the cut-off for probable depression, but only one woman was previously identified as having depression prior to her infant's admission to the facility. Hearn et al. (1998) found that after using the EPDS in a primary care facility, there was an almost three-fold increase in the rate for recognizing depression.

Screening improves treatment

Screening is a way to help clinicians identify, in this case, postpartum women who *may* be suffering from major depression. Depressive episodes linger without treatment. O'Hara (1987) reported that 25 to 50% of diagnosed, untreated postpartum depression lasted up to six months. In a study conducted by Cox, Murray and Chapman (1993), at least 50% of the women had not recovered from depression by one year postpartum. With screening, there may be an increased awareness by clinicians and patients so that the patient will be referred to or receive treatment. In the Olmsted studies, Georgiopolulos *et al.* (2001) found that among women who completed the EPDS, of the 10.7% diagnosed with depression, almost one-quarter received treatment. In another study conducted in a community sample, the authors specifically asked clinicians if screening with the EPDS increased their awareness of postpartum depression. Eighty-three per cent of the clinicians reported an increased awareness and 92% referred patients for treatment (Schaper *et al.* 1994). Studies do show that screening does lead to better awareness and treatment of postpartum depression.

Monitoring symptoms with the EPDS over time: evidence of increased recognition of depressive symptomatology

Rather than being used as a one-time screening tool, the EPDS can be used to monitor symptoms over the course of one year. Using the EPDS over time demonstrates that scores on the EPDS are consistently high in some groups of women, low in other groups of women, and some women have scores that fluctuate over the course of a year. Clinicians who use the EPDS and monitor women over the first year after birth need to have some sense of the meaning of these patterns of scores so that they can further evaluate women for treatment.

High levels of depressive symptoms (and not just cases above the diagnostic threshold) are associated with decreased maternal functioning and poor outcomes for children (Luoma *et al.* 2001). This evidence gives substance for use of the EPDS as a monitoring tool for depressive symptoms in the first year after delivery. The following studies show the EPDS as a sensitive monitor of depressive symptoms over time.

Postnatal EPDS score patterns

When the EPDS is used multiple times across the postpartum period, certain patterns emerge from the scores for women both with and without a history of major depression. What these patterns mean in terms of diagnosis and need for treatment has only been evaluated in two studies (Peindl *et al.* 2004; Yonkers *et al.* 2001). However, one of these investigations studied a population of women who had suffered from a previous episode of depression.

Women screened with the EPDS over time clearly have specific patterns of scores. One way to examine patterns is to determine which women score low on the EPDS across postpartum time points (low-low), which score consistently high across time points (high-high) and which women have scores that fluctuate over time (high-low, low-high). Several studies with a follow-up design incorporated multiple measures of the EPDS to assess depressive symptoms in the postpartum. In the first study, women completed the EPDS at three time points during the first month postpartum (Yonkers *et al.* 2001). The results indicate that 28% of the women scored above the threshold score of 12 across two time points (high-high) indicating probable major depression. Moreover, of the women who completed the diagnostic interview at the third time point, 78% met criteria for major depression according to DSM-IV.

Wickberg and Hwang (1997) used the EPDS to examine postpartum symptoms at two time points (8 and 12 weeks). The following patterns of symptoms (using a cut-off of 11/12 on the EPDS) emerged – high-high: 4.5%, high-low: 3.8%, low-high: 8.0% and low-low: 83.7%. The majority of women scored low across both time points and approximately 12% showed symptom variations. In another study, women completed the EPDS scale during pregnancy and at eight weeks and eight months postpartum (Evans *et al.* 2001). A similar pattern emerged from the data for the women who completed the EPDS at all four time points. 2% remained in the high-high group, 7.0% were in the high-low group, 2.0% had low-high scores and 89% had low scores across the four time points. Again, the majority of women who scored low on the EPDS had low scores to almost a year postpartum. About 10% had symptom fluctuations and 2% scored consistently high. Luoma *et al.* (2001) found that 69% of the participants always scored <13 of the EPDS, 22% scored >13 at least once and 9% scored >13 at least twice when the EPDS was completed during the last trimester of pregnancy to six months postpartum.

In light of these findings, it is clear that monitoring is important for assessing depressive symptoms even though the majority of women will score low on the EPDS and will continue to score low across the postpartum period. However, without intervention, about 12% of women will continue to score high after completing the EPDS. Dennis (2004a) examined the likelihood of scoring high on the EPDS at four and eight weeks postpartum based upon scores at the first week after delivery. Those mothers who scored >9 on the EPDS at week one postpartum were 30.3 times more likely and 19.1 times more likely to score high at postnatal weeks four and eight. If they scored >12 on the EPDS at week one then they were 11.6 times more likely to score >12 at four weeks and 6.9 times more likely to score >12 at eight weeks postpartum.

Differentiating patterns of symptoms based on EPDS scores shows evidence of some mood change present in the postnatal period but, more importantly, they show the need to determine which groups of women are in need of treatment i.e. have a diagnosis of depression or functional impairment. Three thoughts on EPDS score patterns emerge. First, the EPDS can be used as a monitoring instrument to examine these patterns. Second, there may be a specific pattern of EPDS scores that suggests a risk of experiencing an episode of depression as defined by a gold standard diagnostic assessment. Third, some women would benefit from monitoring symptoms on more than one occasion. Only one study has examined patterns of EPDS scores and then determined which group of women was suffering from depression by a diagnostic interview (Peindl *et al.* 2004).

Prediction of depression during the first postpartum year with the EPDS

A trial was conducted to examine patterns of symptoms as reported by women using the EPDS over a 20-week postpartum period. Moreover, an episode of recurrent major depression was determined according to Research Diagnostic Criteria (RDC) as it occurred within the first 20 weeks and up to one year postpartum.

Design of the trial

Women were followed weekly for 20 weeks postpartum and then bimonthly until 12 months as part of a double-blind randomized clinical trial that determined the efficacy of nortriptyline versus placebo for the prevention of recurrent postpartum depression (Wisner *et al.* 2001). Eligible women were <35 weeks pregnant, aged 18 to 45 years, and had at least one episode of postpartum depression according to RDC.

During pregnancy we monitored participants for psychiatric illness and only women who remained free of depression (Hamilton Rating Scale for Depression [HRS-D] <15) and were physically healthy continued in the study. During the last week of gestation, women were randomized to either drug or placebo. Within 24 hours after birth, the new mothers started the medication. Every week, the women were assessed for depression with the 17-item HRS-D. Any woman who scored >15 on the HRS-D was reinterviewed within two weeks with the Schedule for Affective Disorders-Change and for severity with the HRS-D. Approximately 25% of the women suffered a recurrence. Verkerk *et al.* (2003) also showed a 25% recurrence rate for postpartum depression among a high-risk group of women.

During the 20 weeks of the trial, women completed the EPDS weekly. We were able to determine the specific scores on the EPDS that were associated with an onset of depression according to RDC. We graphed the score patterns in relation to three groups of women:

1. never recurred over one year,

2. recurred within 20 weeks postpartum, and

3. recurred within one year postpartum.

Both sensitivity and specificity were calculated for the EPDS with RDC used as the gold standard. We also examined how many cases of true depression were identified over the course of a year by scores on the EPDS completed at four weeks postpartum. Finally, we developed an algorithm for use of the EPDS in primary care practices.

Three patterns of mean scores on the EPDS emerged as shown in Figure 5.1. Women who scored <5 on the EPDS (low-low) were more likely to have no recurrence. Women who scored 5 to 9 (fluctuation: high-low or low-high) were more likely to recur after the 20-week trial and women who continuously scored >9 or increased scores (high-high) recurred within the first 20 weeks.

The women who experienced a recurrence within the first 20 weeks postpartum scored higher on the EPDS across the time period. Those women who recurred in the first year also scored higher than women who never suffered a new onset of major depression. After examining the patterns, we determined that scores at week four postpartum could be used to predict a new episode of depression. Table 5.1 (p.66) shows the number of cases of depression correctly identified according to RDC criteria by a specific range of scores on the EPDS at week four postpartum.

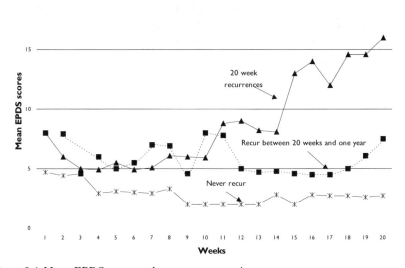

Figure 5.1 Mean EPDS scores and recurrences over times

Table 5.1 Cases of postpartum depression identified by RDC and the EPDS over the first postpartum year

EPDS score at week 4	Number of women	Number of recurrence in 1–20 weeks	Cases identified (%)	Number of recurrence in 1 year	Cases identified (%)
0–1	18	1	6	2	11
2–4	8	1	13	3	38
5–9	14	5	36	7	50
≥10	10	6	60	8	80
Total	50	13	26	20	40

Table 5.1 shows that we could identify 80% of the women who became depressed over the first postpartum year by a score on the EPDS of greater than or equal to 10. While the data is from women who were at risk for having a postpartum recurrence of depression and the sample size is small, it supports the utility of using the EPDS to monitor and to follow up certain groups of women. We developed the algorithm shown in Figure 5.2 for use in primary care.

This model was constructed from data on women who had a previous episode of postpartum depression and it needs to be tested in a clinical setting with patients both with and without a history of depression. However, and more importantly, the model presented here shows that the EPDS is not completed in isolation but is part of a comprehensive mental health follow-up for postpartum women. It emphasizes a plan in which all postpartum women are screened and outlines strategies for continuous monitoring if necessary. Education about signs and symptoms of depression, both for the clinical staff conducting the screening and postpartum women, is essential for the success of any screening program. The screening and monitoring is part of a postpartum educational plan for emotional wellness. Without screening, only a fraction of the true numbers of postpartum depression will be identified. This chapter provides evidence to support the use of the EPDS at the first postpartum visit, and to identify women at this visit in need of further monitoring over the first postpartum year.

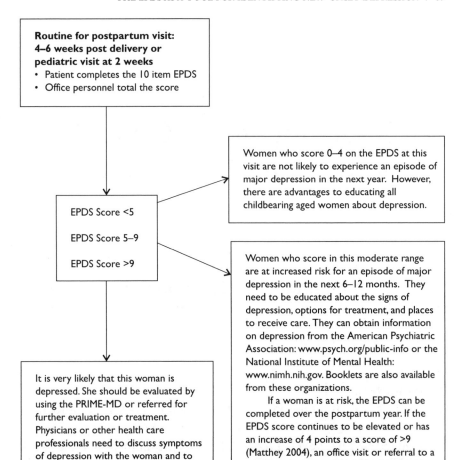

Figure 5.2 Practical guidelines for use of the EPDS as a screening tool for depression in women who received a diagnosis of depression in the year after the birth of a previous child

Chapter 6

Screening in the Context of Integrated Perinatal Care

Bryanne Barnett, Patricia Glossop, Stephen Matthey and Helen Stewart

Introduction

In 1997, South Western Sydney Area Health Service established a network to link all relevant services offered to mothers from conception through the first five years of their child's life: the mother–infant network (MINET). After consent has been obtained, wherever the parent or child consults in the health system, information from other clinical encounters should be readily available. Operating on the principle that attention to psychological and social well being should routinely be part of the comprehensive health care that any consumer has the right to expect, it was further decided that mental health would be accorded appropriate interest in all health consultations with parent or child over that period.

One strand of this plan, the Integrated Perinatal Care (IPC) program, aimed to integrate aspects of mental health with routine physical health care provision during pregnancy and the following two years. Universal assessment, to avoid both stigma and missed opportunities, at least three times over the course of the pregnancy and the first 12 months postpartum was recommended, with the first assessment occurring at the time of the initial (booking-in) visit.

IPC derives from child and family psychiatry and, therefore, takes a broad developmental view of the parents, child and family. It does not focus narrowly on identifying or predicting antenatal or postnatal mental illness, such as depression, in the mother and then providing psychiatric treatment for that individual, but focuses on prevention and early intervention for the family. It does not focus on high-risk families only, but aims to acknowledge all levels of risk and offer appropriate information, additional appointments or referral. It is not perceived or described as 'screening', but as the routine and universal provision of good clinical care. Avoiding use of the word 'screening' also avoids endless debate regarding the theoretically desirable criteria for implementing screening projects. The program is to be implemented in all health regions in New South Wales and has also been trialled elsewhere in Australia.

IPC now forms an essential part of the infrastructure for Families First, the New South Wales (NSW) Government's health promotion and early intervention strategy to support parents in giving their children (from conception to eight years) a good start in life. Families First is delivered by area health services, departments of community services, education and training, housing, disability, ageing and home care, in partnership with parents, community organizations and local government. Different levels of support and linkage to services are provided according to assessed level of need. For example, high-risk families might be provided with professional home visitation beginning antenatally and sustained over the following two years. All families will receive postnatal home visits, the number varying according to perceived need. Volunteer home visiting is also available. Accurate assessment of the support required is clearly of fundamental importance. Evaluation of the quality and effectiveness of IPC and related initiatives is integral to the Families First concept.

Translating evidence-based strategies from research into clinical practice is neither simple nor straightforward. In this chapter, the complex process of integrating systematic, psychological and social information-gathering into the routine antenatal clinic interview will be described and discussed.

Integrated Perinatal Care (IPC)

The project was fortunate to be able to take advantage of a political climate where parenting, pregnancy and the early years of children's lives were being recognized at state and federal levels in Australia, as well as internationally, as being crucial for optimal individual development (McCain and Mustard 1999; Olds and Kitzman 1990; Perry et al. 1995; Schore 1994). Routine postnatal screening for depression using the Edinburgh Postnatal Depression Scale (EPDS) was already in place in many clinics in South Western Sydney and around New South Wales in general. The MINET and postnatal depression working groups provided local structures for further exploration, including formal support at senior and middle management levels.

A focus on promotion, prevention and early intervention in the National Mental Health Plan (e.g. Commonwealth Department of Health and Aged Care 2000) ensured financial support for four years from the Centre for Mental Health of the NSW Health Department. This funding provided a project co-ordinator to oversee implementation locally and around the state, a midwife/nurse educator to work alongside the antenatal clinic staff at each hospital as they started to implement the assessment and triage process, a part-time research officer to collect, analyze and report on data, and three clinical staff to accept referrals and provide supervision. Other tasks, such as provision of the education programs and oversight of the research aspects, were undertaken by permanent staff of the Infant, Child and Adolescent Mental Health Service (ICAMHS).

The first assessment occasion is at the booking-in visit or whenever the woman first presents at the hospital. The antenatal assessments are particularly important for early linking of high-risk families to sustained home visiting programs. All perinatal assessments include the EPDS. It is a useful measure of distress, including anxiety, as well as a proven screening tool for depression (Chapter 13, this volume).

At major hospitals in New South Wales, the booking-in consultation involves a computerized interview, OBSTET, collecting general medical and obstetric history to provide a database for planning of subsequent obstetric care. It already includes questions on issues such as 'sexual assault' and 'mental illness', but without indicating precisely what these mean or how the questions should be introduced or responses managed. No evaluation of the process had occurred, since it was simply seen as appropriate clinical practice. Additional questions addressing a range of psycho-social issues suggested in the literature to affect parenting capacity (see below) were formulated in consultation with midwives, GPs and child and family health nurses and tested in the antenatal clinic at Campbelltown Hospital. The local teaching hospital at Liverpool then offered to be the primary site for formal implementation and evaluation.

The aim of the expanded clinical assessment is to identify a much broader range of problems (or their antecedents) than depression or anxiety *per se*, whether antenatal or postnatal. These problems include: chronic, current or potential mental illness and psycho-social difficulties; anxiety, depression, psychosis, alcohol and other substance abuse; personality disorders, bereavement, lack of social support, domestic violence, chronic or acute physical ill-health; other adverse life events, and adverse childhood experiences, such as emotional, physical or sexual abuse: all the things that research and clinical practice suggest might make life difficult for families to develop and function satisfactorily.

The semi-standardized assessment process is intended to ascertain whether vulnerability is present or possible – it is not intended to assess the details of the problem in depth; usually the interviewing health practitioner will not have sufficient time or training for the latter. There is no cut-off point – threshold is zero – in this assessment. Scores over nine in total on the EPDS or any score on the self-harm question mandate further assessment, usually, but not necessarily, by the midwife. The clinical response to the overall consultation includes a spectrum of possibilities from 'flag this for future consideration' to 'immediate referral'. Prior identification of referral pathways and available resources is essential.

If the respondent answers any of the general questions in a 'positive' fashion, or scores over nine on the EPDS, or more than zero on question 10 of the EPDS, it is then incumbent on the interviewer to ask for more information, make decisions and offer whatever help is deemed relevant. It is important to remind anxious interviewers that women are not in any way compelled to divulge information – it is their choice whether they respond, lie or refuse. There is nowadays a general consent to consultation that is signed by all patients attending the hospital. The obstetric unit has an additional consent and information form indicating that questions will be asked at the booking-in interview in order to offer the best possible help during the pregnancy and afterwards.

After the initial consultation, if the woman or the midwife has any concerns, and if the woman wishes, further appointments are set up with the midwife, social worker or other appropriate service, e.g. the Perinatal and Infant Mental Health Service (see Figure 6.1, p.73). A letter is sent to the woman's GP, stating what her EPDS score was and whether there were any psycho-social aspects of concern. If the woman does not have a family doctor, she is encouraged to seek one promptly. Appropriate management strategies, including linking to other services, are put in place. After due discussion, private patients of consultants have been included in the program and feedback procedures established.

Following community consultation and specialized staff training, extending the program into our non-English speaking and indigenous communities is now underway. Education modules have been provided for interpreter services. Many translations of the EPDS are now available, although not all have been validated or suitable cut-off points on the scale determined (Cox and Holden 2003, pp.21–25 and 41–70). A user-friendly version of the EPDS is being trialled in our Department for Indigenous and Torres Strait Islander Women.

As with any intervention program, thoughtful, competent interviewing or assessment is obviously a critical component. These fields of inquiry are familiar to professionals working in child and family psychiatry, but may be 'outside the comfort zone' of many midwives or early childhood nurses. Not only is the integrated consultation going to be longer, but a more sensitive, 'counselling-oriented' stance is required. Apart from the EPDS, the assessment is deliberately not a paper and pencil process and the staff member is expected to engage with the woman, and any other relatives or friends who may be present, conveying a message that the service cares about her personally. The interviewing professional needs to know *why* it is important to ask these questions, *how* to ask the questions in order to elicit meaningful responses (including the possible need for the woman to be unaccompanied during part of the consultation), and *what* to do with the responses when they arrive. This includes knowing how to close off discussion in a tactful, positive manner when 'opening Pandora's Box' threatens interviewer or client. Education, clinical support and supervision, inbuilt feedback mechanisms (e.g. to staff, funding bodies etc.) must precede and accompany the implementation of routine psycho-social assessment. This includes acknowledgement that health professionals themselves may experience these problems and need support or treatment.

Accordingly, basic and advanced training modules were developed to cover these issues. These had to be modified according to staff work arrangements, e.g. some clinics preferred four separate half-day modules, while others preferred two full-day programs. Appropriate prior learning was recognized and the program evaluated. Funding was available to replace nurses undertaking recognized education programs, but not other staff. The NSW Health Department has now supported publication of a formal training manual including IPC and home visitation training modules (available from the authors), and a CD-Rom is in preparation so that material will be readily available at all times to ward staff. Additional workshops have been offered according to special requests from nursing and allied health staff. These include: perinatal mental health, general individual and group counselling skills, specific stress and depression group leadership, attachment theory and practice. Regular supervision from specialist mental health staff is provided and is now appreciated, although initially regarded with some caution by nursing staff unfamiliar with this concept.

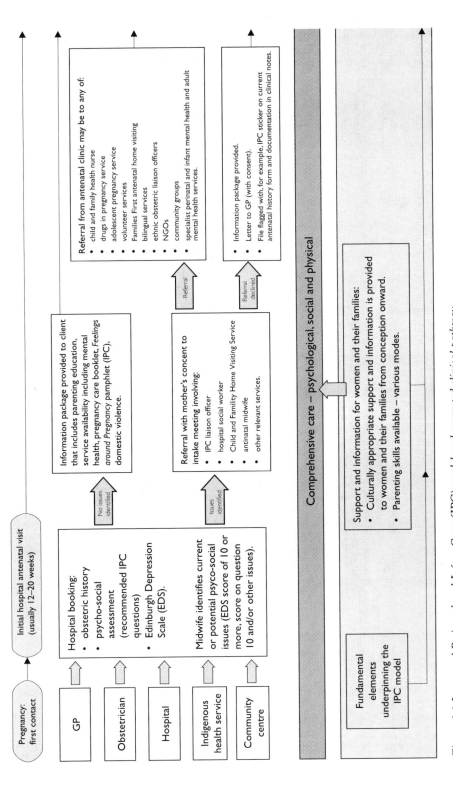

Figure 6.1 Integrated Perinatal and Infant Care (IPC) model and suggested clinical pathway. South Western Sydney Area Health Services. Reproduced with permission

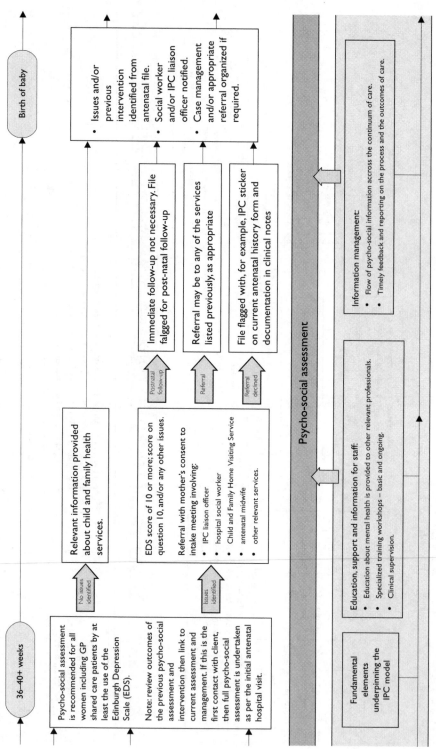

Figure 6.1 continued

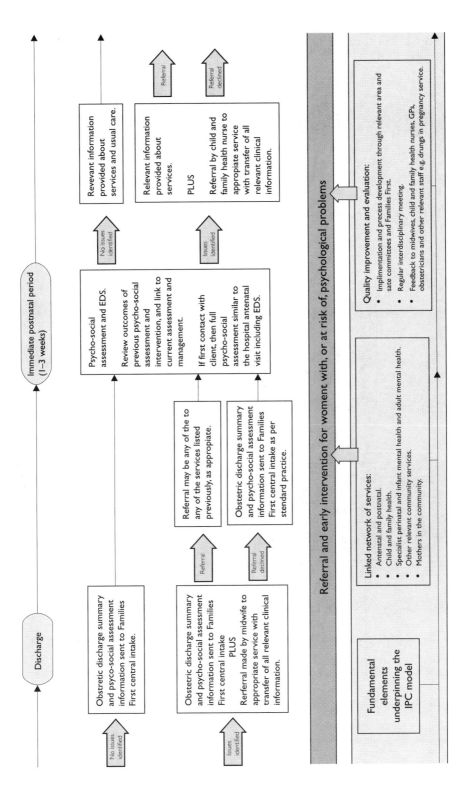

Discharge

Immediate postnatal period (1–3 weeks)

No issues identified

Obstretric discharge summary and psyco-social assessment information sent to Families First central intake.

Issues identified

Obstretic discharge summary and psyco-social assessment information sent to Families First central intake
PLUS
Rerferral made by midwife to appropiate service with transfer of all relevant clinical information.

Referral

Referral may be any of the to any of the services listed previously, as appropiate.

Referral declined

Obstetric discharge summary and psyco-social assessment information sent to Families First central intake as per stardand practice.

Psycho-social assessment and EDS.

Review outcomes of previous psycho-social assessment and intervention, and link to current assessment and management.

If first contact with client, then full psycho-social assessment similar to the hospital antenatal visit including EDS.

No issues identified

Revevant information provided about services and usual care.

Issues identified

Relevant information provided about services.
PLUS
Referral by child and family health nurse to appropiate service with transfer of all relevant clinical information.

Referral

Referral declined

Referral and early intervention for woment with, or at risk of, psychological problems

Fundamental elements underpinning the IPC model

Linked network of services:
- Antenatal and postnatal.
- Child and family health.
- Specialist perinatal and infant mental health and adult mental health.
- Other relevant community services.
- Mothers in the community.

Quality improvement and evaluation:
- Implimentation and precess development through relevant area and sate committees and Families First.
- Regular interdisciplinary meeting.
- Feedback to midwives, child and family health nurses, GPs, obstetricians and other relevant staff e.g. drungs in pregnancy service.

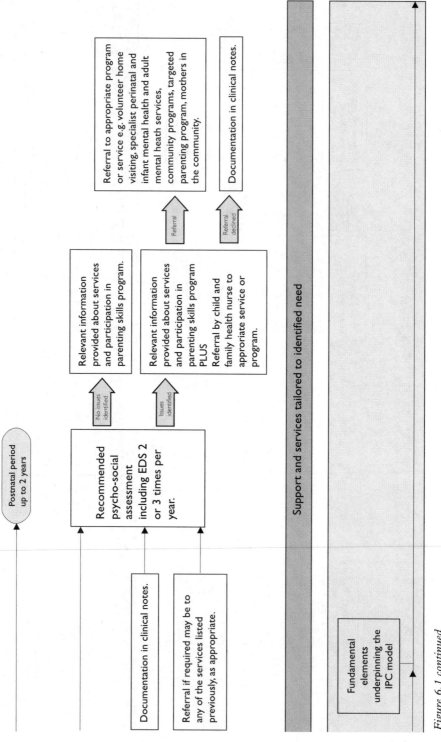

Figure 6.1 continued

Evaluation

The questions have been piloted, evaluated and refined. The original set of 31 questions covered a variety of psycho-social variables (Box 6.1) and this set has been reduced to 12 (Box 6.2, p.78), which are now integrated into the computer interview format (OBSTET). Comparison of placing the set of questions en bloc or interspersing them throughout the interview as seems appropriate is currently in progress in a crossover design using two hospitals. The midwives will be asked which mode they prefer and how long the new consultation takes.

Box 6.1 Possible variables for detection of a broad range of psychological and social risk factors (presaging parenting problems) in the perinatal period

- Age less than 18 years
- Adverse obstetric history, including infertility
- Lack of social support from partner, family and others (including no partner)
- Late or minimal antenatal care
- More than usual ambivalence about the pregnancy, especially if termination was/is contemplated
- Dysfunctional partnership, including domestic violence or other abuse
- Poor relationship with her own parents, especially her mother
- Low self-esteem, high trait anxiety, perfectionist or dependent traits
- Previous mental health problems of any kind, especially if pregnancy-related
- Current anxiety or depression, acute or chronic
- Family history of mental illness
- Bereavements (recent or otherwise significant), including miscarriages, terminations, stillbirth, sudden infant death
- Alcohol, smoking or other substance abuse (woman or partner)
- Adverse childhood experiences, including neglect, witnessing or experiencing any type of abuse
- Experience of harsh, coercive parental discipline
- Refugee or recent migrant (especially if non-English speaking)
- Recent or long-standing life stresses, including health, housing, financial, employment, isolation and related difficulties.

Box 6.2 Final variables for detection of psychological and social risk factors in the perinatal period

- Expected availability of practical support
- Expected availability of emotional support
- Recent major stressors, changes or losses
- Personal rating of self-confidence
- Personal rating of anxiety and obsessionality
- History of feeling anxious, miserable, worried or depressed for more than two weeks. If yes, was that related to a previous pregnancy or birth?
- Past or current treatment for emotional problem
- Emotional, physical or sexual abuse in childhood
- Alcohol or drug (including cigarettes) use
- Domestic violence
- Earlier or current involvement with child protection agencies
- Edinburgh Postnatal Depression Scale: total score and response to question 10.

Details of the earlier evaluation are reported in a separate publication (Matthey *et al.* 2002, 2004) and in a manuscript submitted in 2003 for publication by Matthey *et al.*: *Acceptability of Routine Antenatal Psychosocial Assessments to Women from English and non-English Speaking Backgrounds.* These reports may be summarized as follows.

1. Responses to the original 31 questions and the EPDS from 562 women indicated that:

   - 29% scored 10 or more on the EPDS, while13% scored 13 or more
   - 11.9% lacked emotional support from both partner and their own mother
   - 26% tended to worry a lot or be perfectionist
   - 28.3% had a history of anxiety or depression
   - 8% hit their partner and 3% reported that their partner hit them
   - 14.4% had 6 or more (out of a possible 10) psycho-social risks for parenting adjustment.

It was noteworthy that questions purporting to elicit these data were already part of the OBSTET computer interview, but frequently did not do so. For example, only 9% reported a 'psychiatric history' in the original

OBSTET interview while 28.3% reported depression or anxiety problems in response to the additional questions. Only four women conceded domestic violence on OBSTET interviewing, while 17 reported this when answering the new questions.

2. Telephone interviews during the week following the antenatal consultation with a sample (n = 104) of the women indicated that:

    - 80% considered the additional questions were reasonable and acceptable
    - they did not mind the length of time spent on the interview and were pleased that someone was taking such a careful, personal interest in them
    - objections to the lengthy consultation were often a result of the time the women had had to wait prior to the actual interview
    - 7% considered the questions unacceptable
    - in some instances the objection was to the questions already asked in the original computer interview (the original interview had never been subjected to any form of evaluation)
    - in some instances the objections were due to puzzlement about why some questions would be asked, e.g. concerning their own childhood, or to the questions (e.g. about losses) bringing back unhappy memories
    - no one suggested additional questions
    - all were very pleased with the rapport created by the midwife.

3. Telephone interviews at five to eight weeks postpartum (n = 65) indicated that:

    - 75% of the women recalled the antenatal interview and questions
    - 43% thought the consultation had been helpful
    - a further 23% thought that asking the questions was a good idea although not directly helpful for them. The consultation had raised their awareness of relevant issues, offered an opportunity to express their feelings and made them feel supported
    - 9% had subsequently sought help for issues raised and had benefited from that

- the remaining 34% considered the questions had not been helpful or unhelpful. Many offered the explanation that the questions may have been less relevant since they were not first-time mothers.

4. Interviews with a sample of the midwives (n = 14) indicated that:

    - despite acknowledging the benefits of asking the additional questions, some were concerned about the extra time required (between 10 and 40 minutes) and the addition to their workload
    - some (but not all) of the midwives noted that the new questions included items already asked in the original computerized interview set of questions. (During the pilot-testing of the program, no changes to the original booking-in interview were permitted, so there was some overlap, although the items were worded very differently.)

5. Following the introduction of the new set of questions:

    - referrals for psycho-social intervention doubled
    - approximately 37% of the women were deemed to merit referral
    - about 50% of these declined the additional support offered
    - of the 50% accepting referral, around 25% were seen for less than four sessions of counselling or other intervention and 17% for more than four sessions
    - the other women were given information about other services (33%), referred to other services (14%) or continued to have telephone contact with the IPC clinical team
    - a further 13% of the women were 'flagged' for postnatal follow-up, e.g. because of anticipated lack of support, but not considered to require current referral
    - workload for social work and mental health staff increased: estimated to be around 30% in the short term.

Discussion

Antenatal clinics provide many opportunities for health promotion. Nevertheless, because of the lack of human and other resources, many of our antenatal (and postnatal) clinics are anything but parent-friendly. Partners feel uncomfortable and unwanted. Often women have to bring other children with them, and rarely is there a room where the latter can play happily for a while. The women may wait for hours and then have a very brief or impersonal interview.

If there is a delay, that opportunity should be used to offer educational material, including videos (in various languages) to demonstrate strategies for self-care and parenting, or to provide entertainment for the children, or talk to other family members such as fathers and mothers-in-law to involve them positively in the process. This opportunity is often missed. There are many things about being friendly towards and respectful of a woman and her family that still require attention.

We have described here a mode of enhancing job satisfaction for antenatal clinic staff as well as parents, but it is not a simple matter and there are many issues and consequences to be addressed, for example, increased upstream workload. Also, many physical and mental health questions are intrusive, so sensitivity as well as competence is required of the interviewer. Especially at the first antenatal interview, friends or other family members may be present, so some questions (e.g. previous obstetric history, the marital relationship or family violence) may need to be reserved for later consultations. In some clinics, a letter indicating the requirement for the woman to be alone for part of the consultation now accompanies the letter sent out with details of the first appointment. As evidence supporting routine screening for domestic violence remains inadequate, further research on this important aspect will begin in Sydney in 2004.

Several discrete paper and pencil self-report forms already exist for specific detection of problems such as postnatal depression, high risk of abusive parenting and so on. These have a different goal as well as a different process. Commitment to facilitating engagement and enhancing job skills and satisfaction for the professional requires that assessment (screening) is carried out through personal interviewing. Before staff are expected to undertake this task, they need to feel confident that resources are available for the clients and themselves at every stage in the process.

The suggested psycho-social questions do not constitute a free-standing screening instrument or a self-report measure. Questions may be asked in a block or interspersed throughout the interview and we are currently comparing the effectiveness and acceptability of these two modes. The self-reported EPDS is included. Staff are trained to interpret all results and make triage decisions. A weekly multidisciplinary team meeting discusses appropriate referral for non-urgent situations (see Figure 6.1, pp.73–6) and ensures feedback to staff in the clinic.

Conclusion

Several points must be emphasized as contributing to the successful implementation of any radical change in health practice:

- Support at all levels from senior management to front-line clinicians must be sought and cultivated throughout the process.

- Resistance to change must be expected and planned for at every step.

- The process will be untidy and slow.

- Basic and ongoing training, support and supervision of primary care staff are essential.

- Resources must be in place and referral pathways developed before implementation.

- The enthusiasm and commitment of the initiating team must be contagious if the intention is that the nature and quality of care will change.

- The changes must be so embedded that they remain after the architects have gone.

- One measure of successful implementation might be that no one remembers the architects or that things were ever done in any other way.

Chapter 7

The Status of Postpartum Depression Screening in the United States

Lisa S. Segre and Michael W. O'Hara

Major depression is a serious health problem in the US that affects men, women and children, both directly and indirectly. It is one of the leading causes of disability in the world and is the second leading cause of hospitalization for young women of childbearing age in the US (Jiang et al. 2002; World Health Organisation [WHO] 2001). It also has a significant economic cost to the American economy (Pignone et al. 2002). Despite the importance of early identification and treatment of depression, it is often overlooked in primary care settings and many depressed adults do not receive even minimally adequate treatment (Pignone et al. 2002). To address these problems, a number of studies have been undertaken over the past ten years to evaluate the effectiveness of screening for major depression in primary care settings (Pignone et al. 2002). This work has resulted in new recommendations from the US Preventive Services Task Force (2002) that depression screening be incorporated into routine primary health care.

A major question for a depression screening program is whether screening leads to improved detection of depression, to improved treatment, and most importantly, to improved health outcomes (i.e. reduction in depression). The research literature suggests that screening that includes only the provision of feedback to the clinician does not necessarily result in improved health outcomes (Pignone *et al.* 2002). For example, Williams *et al.* (1999) tested the effect of providing immediate feedback to clinicians based on the results of the Center for Epidemiological Studies Depression Scale (CES-D) versus a single question about depressed mood with no clinician feedback. Thirty-nine per cent of screened patients were identified by clinicians as depressed versus 29% of non-screened patients, a non-significant difference. There were no differences in rates of treatment or depression diagnoses at three months post-screening. In sum, giving the clinician feedback alone was insufficient to affect clinician behavior or patient outcomes.

In an example of a comprehensive approach to screening, Wells *et al.* (2000) combined screening and a quality improvement program in a study that included 46 primary care clinics. In addition to screening, practices were asked to schedule a patient visit within two weeks. Practices in the screening condition were also provided with education materials, assistance in treatment maintenance, and access to nurse-led medication follow-ups or to cognitive-behavioral therapy. At 12 months post-screening, patients in the intervention group were significantly more likely to have received adequate treatment for depression and were significantly less likely to be depressed than patients in the control condition. Based on this study and other research that demonstrated the beneficial effects of screening, the US Preventive Services Task Force (2002) recommended 'screening adults for depression in clinical practices that have systems in place to assure accurate diagnosis, effective treatment, and follow-up' (p.760). This recommendation is Grade B, meaning that the Task Force found evidence that screening improves health outcomes and that the benefits outweigh the harms. An A recommendation is stronger because of more evidence of effectiveness and a better risk–benefit ratio. Blood pressure screening for adults would be an example of this.

The depression screening recommendation applies to all adults including pregnant and postpartum women. Unfortunately, there is no evidence that pregnant and postpartum women were included in any of the studies that led to the depression screening recommendations of the Task Force. Moreover, there have been no controlled studies of the effectiveness of depression screening (as far as we can tell) in pregnant or postpartum women in the US or Europe or anywhere else in the world. The lack of controlled research on the effectiveness of screening undermines the credibility of current screening efforts with pregnant and postpartum women and should be remedied. Despite these limitations, a number of perinatal depression screening efforts have emerged in public and private clinical settings as well as in the context of research-based programs. These programs will be discussed next.

Private sector perinatal depression screening programs

Many providers of health insurance contract the provision of mental health services to a behavioral health care company. One of these collaborations, between Humana Incorporated, a for-profit health plan, and Magellan, a large behavioral health care company, resulted in the development of a widely used perinatal depression screening program. In this program, new and expectant mothers are mailed relevant educational material and the Edinburgh Postnatal Depression Scale (EPDS) to complete and return by mail. Women with elevated scores are contacted by a Magellan Health Care manager for further evaluation and possible referral. From its inception in March 1999 until July 2000, 1,000 postpartum packets were mailed with a 40% EPDS return rate. Over 50% of the positively screened women accepted treatment referrals (Gemignani 2001). Magellan currently offers pregnancy and postpartum depression screening to all of its contract insurance providers, who serve approximately 60 million Americans.

Although Magellan's screening program is reaching a significant number of American women and increasing early identification, certain problems remain. First, relying on women to independently complete and return the EPDS by mail may well contribute to poor return rates. In addition, returning the EPDS and obtaining an elevated score creates a mental health file for the participant. The presence of such a file may jeopardize the woman's chance of obtaining reasonably priced insurance at a later date. This realization may also prevent some depressed women from participating.

Public sector perinatal depression screening

Healthy Start is a nationwide, federally funded program (Maternal and Child Health Bureau) for families with young children (conception to age two years) living in communities with high levels of infant mortality. The goal of Healthy Start is to reduce infant mortality and infant morbidity by improving mothers' utilization of primary care services. There are 96 Healthy Start programs throughout the US.

In 2001, the federal Maternal and Child Health Bureau funded eight of these sites to develop and implement perinatal depression screening and referral programs, including the Des Moines, Iowa Healthy Start program to which we provide consultation. Since its inception three years ago, case managers administer the EPDS to all clients within 30 days of enrolment. Because these clients represent an at-risk population, depression screenings are conducted frequently during pregnancy and after delivery until the woman's child reaches the age of two years. Clients scoring above 11 are referred to a mental health professional for further evaluation and, if necessary, treatment.

Ongoing case manager training was introduced concomitantly with the introduction of screening. Case managers have diverse educational backgrounds and vary in their knowledge of and experience in mental health care. This training provides basic information about depression including epidemiology, symptoms, course, effects, assessment, and treatment. Another goal of training is to improve case manager compliance in screening and referral. Screening represents an additional task for case managers who are already heavily burdened with paperwork. Some case managers were initially skeptical about the relative priority of depression screening with respect to helping their clients with other pressing problems, such as substance abuse, physical abuse, and poverty. The need to screen *all* clients and the frequency of the screenings has also been questioned by case managers. Some case managers preferred to use the EPDS only to confirm their clinical observations, and felt awkward administering the EPDS to women who do not seem depressed. Furthermore, case managers sometimes felt that additional screenings were unwarranted when previous screenings were normal and the client did not *appear* to be currently depressed. Finally, the logistics of depression assessment were unfamiliar, particularly to case managers without specific mental health training. To overcome these sources of resistance, several specifically targeted training workshops were developed. Over the past three years, the percentage of Healthy Start clients that are screened has steadily increased.

Research-based screening programs

The US Preventive Services Task Force (Harris *et al.* 2001) has established a three-stage framework for evaluating the effectiveness of screening, including: 1. improved detection, 2. increased referral or treatment utilization, and 3. reduced morbidity. Thus, while effective screening should ultimately result in reduced morbidity, the framework also allows for evaluating screening effectiveness on the basis of improved detection, referral, or treatment utilization alone.

Does screening lead to increased detection? Studies comparing the detection rates of routine clinical evaluation and depression screening scales found that screening scales detected significantly more depressed women (Fergerson, Jamieson and Lindsay 2002; Morris-Rush, Freda and Bernstein 2003). Bryan *et al.* (1999) conducted a retrospective chart review of postpartum women who received standard clinical care and found that depressive symptoms were noted in 3.7% of the records. In a follow-up study of the same population, 11.4% of the EPDS scores were elevated (Georgiopoulos *et al.* 1999). Thus, significantly fewer women were identified by routine clinical evaluation than by EPDS screening. When physicians were given EPDS scores prior to the woman's six-week postpartum visit, physicians' detection rate increased (Georgiopoulos *et al.* 2001).

Does improved detection of postpartum depression lead to increased referral and/or treatment utilization? After providing physicians with EPDS scores, Georgiopoulous *et al.* (2001) reviewed the charts of women with and without elevated EPDS scores to determine whether knowledge of an elevated score affected physicians' referral. Follow-up appointments were suggested for 45.3% of the women with elevated EPDS scores as compared to 2.9% of women without elevated scores. Of the women who sought treatment, 49% received a prescription for antidepressant medication, 78% received counseling, and 39% received both counseling and prescriptions for antidepressant medication.

Using the US Preventive Services Task Force (Harris *et al.* 2001) framework for evaluating the effectiveness of screening, it is clear that perinatal depression screening research is limited to measuring effectiveness in the first stage, that is, improved detection. These studies indicate that the use of depression screening tools in primary care settings improves detection. In terms of intermediate screening outcomes, the results of the one available study suggest that detection increases physicians' referrals and that physicians make treatment available to many referred women. None of the studies measured reduced morbidity as an outcome of screening. Additional outcome research in the area of perinatal depression screening is needed and can be informed by the research methodology used in screening studies of major depression.

Other studies address issues that lie outside the scope of the Task Force model. For example, is it feasible to incorporate perinatal depression screening programs into primary care health services? In the US, a woman's contact with maternal health settings typically includes prenatal care, delivery, and one six-week postpartum visit; thus determining specific opportunities for screening. The results of several studies indicate that screening was easily incorporated into prenatal care visits (Marcus *et al.* 2003) as well as the six-week postpartum visit (Morris-Rush *et al.* 2003; Roy *et al.* 1993). For example, in the study conducted in ten obstetric clinics in Michigan, 90% (or 3472) of the women completed the EPDS while waiting for their prenatal care appointment thereby indicating that most women are amenable to being screened in this setting (Marcus *et al.* 2003). Similarly, only one of the 308 women approached in the hospital after giving birth refused to consider completing the EPDS at six weeks postpartum (Roy *et al.* 1993). However, in the same study, only 60% of these women returned the EPDS by mail, indicating that compliance is maximized when screening tools are completed in the clinic.

After prenatal care and the postpartum visit, a woman generally has more frequent contact with pediatric health services. These visits offer new opportunities for screening. Results regarding the feasibility of screening for postpartum depression in pediatric health care settings are mixed. In a study of five Washington State pediatric clinics, mothers were screened for depression: 89% completed the screening instrument, thereby indicating their receptivity to being screened at well baby visits. In contrast, researchers implementing a similar program in San Diego encountered significantly more patient and clinician resistance (Tam *et al.* 2002). Three pediatric clinics were asked to distribute the EPDS and the Beck Depression Inventory (BDI) to parents during well baby visits. Although two pediatric clinics agreed to participate, the third declined, on the basis that the staff doubted their ability to talk to a mother who was crying, and were even more uncomfortable with the idea of talking to a woman with suicidal thoughts. They were also concerned about being held legally responsible for ensuring that a depressed mother received treatment. Despite the co-operation of the other two pediatric clinics, recruitment was unsuccessful. The authors speculate that the low participation rates can be attributed to stigma and concern about being labeled an unfit mother.

In terms of feasibility, this pediatrician resistance raises concerns about pediatricians' willingness to screen mothers in a health care setting that typically focuses on the infant's well being. Olson *et al.* (2002) surveyed a national sample of randomly selected pediatricians regarding their perceptions of their role in identifying and managing maternal depression. Of the 508 pediatricians that responded, 57% believed it was their responsibility to recognize maternal depression, with 58% indicating that they made their diagnosis based on their overall impression alone. Thirty-seven per cent indicated that they used their overall impression and inquired about one or two symptoms to assess depression, 4% used formal diagnostic criteria, and none used a screening instrument.

The results of these feasibility studies indicate that perinatal depression screening can be incorporated into primary health care. Logistically, the staff is able to do the screening in the context of a routine visit and women are receptive to this screening, particularly in maternal health care settings. Some resistance to screening in pediatric clinics was found, thereby indicating special problems that might be encountered in this setting. The feasibility of screening in pediatric settings might be significantly improved by the introduction of screening instruments. Further, concerns expressed about ability to talk to depressed women might be effectively addressed by providing pediatric staff with brief and focused training on discussing elevated scores and making referrals. Screening in pediatric settings remains relatively unexplored and is an area that is ripe for future research.

In summary, we have described the perinatal depression screening programs currently being implemented in the US and summarized available research on perinatal depression screening. While the use of a screening tool is generally feasible in primary care settings and associated with increased detection, two general categories of questions remain. The first pertains to the optimal format for perinatal depression screening programs. Among maternal health and pediatric clinics, which are the best settings for screening? Since compliance is not perfect in any of these settings, what should be done to screen women who are not utilizing health services? These women may indeed represent a significant portion of the depressed women who are too fatigued or unmotivated to keep their appointments precisely because of their depressive symptoms (Leverton and Elliott 2000). Therefore, these women cannot be ignored. In these settings how will a mental health related file affect the mother's relationship with her primary care providers and will such a file raise her insurance fees? Continued program development research is needed.

The second set of unaddressed questions returns us to the opening of this chapter: does screening lead to improved detection of depression, to improved treatment and, most importantly, to improved health outcomes (i.e. reduction in depression)? While improved detection is evident in the perinatal context, there is no available evidence regarding improved utilization, treatment, and outcome. Research on all three types of outcome is needed before the cost associated with screening can be justified and perinatal depression screening can be widely implemented as an evidenced based program.

Chapter 8

Screening in Developing Countries

Dominic T.S. Lee and Tony K.H. Chung

About four-fifths of the world's six billion people are living in developing countries, but mental health research in developing countries is rare. Postnatal depression is no exception. Previous studies in developing countries suggest that postnatal depression is not uncommon (Cox 1983), and in some countries the rates of postnatal depression were found to be comparable to those reported in the West (Chandran *et al.* 2002; Kumar 1994; Patel, Rodrigues and de Souza 2002; Rahman, Iqbal and Harrington 2003). Recent studies also showed that in low-income countries postnatal depression adversely affects infant growth (Patel *et al.* 2004). Yet there has been little discussion as to how services could be provided for depressed mothers in the developing world.

Developing countries often have unique social, economic and political problems that require different policy solutions from those offered by conventional developed countries. Poverty, natural disaster, structured violence, political instability and lack of infrastructure can all hinder the delivery of health care to those who are in need. This chapter reviews the barriers to care and screening for postnatal depression in the context of developing economies. The strategies that can be considered in overcoming these care and screening barriers are also discussed. The chapter ends with an agenda of postnatal depression research for the developing world.

Barriers to care

There has hitherto been no study on the naturalistic detection and treatment rates of postnatal depression in developing countries. However, for a variety of reasons, the problem of 'hidden morbidity' is likely to be more severe in developing countries. First, depression is not an indigenous folk concept in many non-Western cultures (Manson 1995). Hence, when the mothers are depressed, the psychological distress as well as the other depressive symptoms are commonly construed under other paradigms, such as possession or personality changes. Not uncommonly, the family or friends may rationalize the distress as a response to the hardship of motherhood or long-standing intra-familial discord. Even when the diagnosis of postnatal depression is proposed, the mother or family may resist mental health contact, due to the immense stigma entailed. In many societies, having a close relative with mental illness may hinder an individual from securing a job or even marriage. Many mothers with postnatal depression understandably avoid psychiatric consultation for the future of their children.

There are also structural factors that hinder access to treatment. Many developing countries do not have affordable and accessible primary health care, like the GP system in the UK. Besides, GPs in developing countries are generally unfamiliar with the management of mental health disorders. Hence, when a depressed mother presents to the GP with insomnia, headache, backache or wound pain a few weeks after delivery, postnatal depression is not commonly considered.

Last, even when a diagnosis of postnatal depression is made, and the mother and family are willing to receive treatment, psychiatric referral can be difficult. With few exceptions, there is a general lack of psychiatrists in developing countries (Shinfuku 1998). Hence, long waiting lists in the public mental health services or expensive fees for the private sector are the rule. Both of these can deter the already ambivalent mother and family from pursuing the necessary treatment.

In Hong Kong, the operational statistics of the Prince of Wales Hospital[1] showed that only 9% of women with postnatal depression were referred to the psychiatric service, and by the time these mothers reached the psychiatric service, many had already been depressed for months. It was also not uncommon to see depressed mothers presenting to the clinic

---

1   The Prince of Wales Hospital is a university-affiliated hospital with a catchment of 1 million people of diverse socio-economic status.

with more than a year's history of depression. By then, many husbands and families had become indifferent to the depressive illness. Even with rigorous pharmacological and psychotherapeutic inputs, these women had poor chance of complete recovery.

Barriers to screening

It can be argued that postnatal depression screening programmes are even more pressingly needed in developing countries where there are more hurdles along the pathway to care. Yet the barriers to service often also constitute barriers to screening. In societies where depression is not a common word used to express distress, the health care providers and policy makers may not understand what postnatal depression is about. Even when they are aware of the concept of depression, they may argue that a depression screening programme would be likely to medicalize psycho-social problems.

Likewise, the issue of stigma may deter mothers and families from using the screening programme even when available. The establishment of any screening programme also relies on an effective infrastructure, such as mother and child health clinics or a health visitor service, to deliver the screening instrument. Unfortunately, few developing countries can afford such level of care. Even mother and child health programmes can be difficult for financial or geographic reasons. Lastly, postnatal depression screening programmes may threaten the already stretched psychiatric services. It is not uncommon that public mental health services in developing countries are so thinly staffed that they can only focus on severe mental disorders, like schizophrenia or other psychotic conditions. To such services, non-psychotic depression may not be viewed as a priority.

Technical support and leadership are also important in establishing a screening programme. Self-report, paper and pencil questionnaires are commonly used to identify postnatal depression in screening programmes. Yet expertise in psychometrics and transcultural psychiatry may not be available in developing countries to assist in the translation and validation of screening scales, like the Edinburgh Postnatal Depression Scale (EPDS). Last but not least, overcoming the above mentioned barriers would require leaders who can engage a wide array of players, from policy makers, funding agents, obstetric services, mental health services, primary care providers, social services, media and, when available, self-help programmes in the community. This requires good understanding of the needs as well as the fears of different sectors, not to mention persistence, passion, and sometimes a charismatic persona.

Overcoming the barriers

Before embarking on a discussion of the strategies to overcome the barriers mentioned above, it is important to appreciate that there is no single solution that is applicable across societies. The level of economic development, structure of the health care system, as well as the local culture should all be taken into account in designing a postnatal depression screening programme. The following discussion should in no way be construed as a ready-made recipe. Rather, the authors want to use the Hong Kong experience as a case study to illustrate how some of the barriers can be overcome. More importantly, the authors want to highlight the outstanding issues and propose a future research agenda.

Hong Kong is now a special administrative region of the People's Republic of China. The city has a population of 6.5 million, with more than 95% being Chinese. As a former British colony, Hong Kong has been a hub where East meets West. The city is modern, Westernized and cosmopolitan, but at the same time, many Chinese customs and traditional values continue to be practised and observed. Like many other developing economies, Hong Kong spent only 4% of its GDP on health care.

There is a well-developed maternal and child health (MCH) programme that provides perinatal and infant primary care. The public obstetric service, which is free at point of delivery, provides care for about 65% of the 4–50,000 deliveries in Hong Kong per annum. A typical obstetric department in Hong Kong delivers around 4000 to 5000 babies each year. There has been a slow but progressive decrease in the birth rate over the past five years. The same period also witnessed a dramatic increase in the demand for public mental health services. The latter was the combined effect of the economic recession, increased public education, lessened stigma, and above all the improved quality of the service. Thus, while the already overstretched public mental health services are supportive to territory-wide postnatal depression screening, the psychiatrists are also understandably concerned about the consequent workload. Given an incidence rate of 11%, about 5500 postnatal depressions are anticipated each year, 100 new cases per week (Lee et al. 2001).

This arithmetic, however, had not taken into account the fact that not all women who scored above the cut-off would agree to further assessment. Previous studies in the US and UK showed that as many as 50% of high scorers would decline further management even though they had agreed with screening in the first place (Appleby et al. 1997). In Hong Kong, at the Prince of Wales Hospital, it has also been our experience that around 50% of women identified as potential cases by the EPDS decline further assessment. Thus, the actual caseload for the hospital – with nearly

4500 deliveries annually – has been around 250 cases per year, five cases per week.

More importantly, not all of the 250 high scorers would need to be attended by a psychiatrist. Indeed, many Hong Kong Chinese mothers are daunted by the prospect of seeing a psychiatrist. Apart from their concern at being labelled by their families and employers as mad, many mothers also misconstrued the psychiatric consultation as an indication of the seriousness of their condition. In view of this, at the Prince of Wales Hospital, the psychiatrist would assess only the most severe postnatal depression. Midwives and psychiatric nurses were trained to assess and counsel the less severe cases. As a rule of thumb, we find that high scorers with few or fleeting suicidal ideas can be looked after by the midwives. High scorers who fulfilled the criteria of major depression, or who have serious suicidal/infanticidal risk would need to be assessed and treated by a psychiatrist. High scorers who are not severe enough to warrant a diagnosis of major depression, but nonetheless have significant suicidal or infanticidal ideas can first be assessed by a trained psychiatric nurse, who can work closely with the psychiatrist to develop a further management plan. Often, repeated assessments over a few weeks provide a better understanding of the treatment needs of such women. Operated in this manner, the screening programme requires a psychiatrist's input of no more than a session per week. When there is no emergency case, we find that it is sometimes even possible for the psychiatrist to come to the obstetric clinic once a fortnight. Hence, once the psychiatrist had provided the necessary training for the midwives and psychiatric nurses, the actual demand on the mental health service is not as substantive as the simple arithmetic would suggest.

When the Prince of Wales postnatal depression screening programme commenced in 1998, there was concern about the high scorers who declined to return for further assessment. Indeed, these cases could be anxiety provoking for the midwives who are responsible for the screening. In response to their concern, a meeting was arranged among all team members to review and discuss the philosophy and science behind the screening programme. After thorough discussion, a consensus was reached that it would be important to respect the individual wish of the mothers, even if they were suspected to have postnatal depression. Besides, the screening team recognized that there were alternate resources, such as religious organizations, alternative medicine practitioners, self-help groups and social services that the women might choose to use. Hence, when there is no immediate risk to the mother or the infant, the screening programme would respect their wish not to come back for further assessment, even if their EPDS score is high.

However, if the women score positive on question 10 of the EPDS ('the thought of harming myself has occurred to me'), the midwives would call the mother to clarify her mental state and social situation. If significant suicidal ideation is found, the case would be passed onto the psychiatric nurse or the psychiatrist on an urgent basis. In any case, all suspected cases who did not return for assessment were given the contact number of the screening programme as well as the numbers of any other relevant resources. Occasionally, after a few weeks or even months, as the postnatal depression continued to deteriorate, the mothers or their family members would change their mind, eventually agreeing to assessment and treatment.

It is also important to appreciate that there are different ways of screening for postnatal depression. Apart from paper and pencil questionnaires, it is also possible to sharpen the awareness of the obstetricians and primary care physicians. In Hong Kong, an overwhelming majority of women would return to the MCH for postpartum follow-up and infant vaccination. These clinical contacts provide invaluable opportunities to screen for postnatal depression. Over the past few years, the MCH has been organizing a series of training courses for their medical and nursing staff, equipping them with the knowledge and skills to assess and counsel women with postnatal depression. A noticeable effect of the training programme has been an increase in detection and referral of postnatal depression from the MCH. Since the MCH is still conducting training for the staff, it is too early to assess if it will have a long-lasting effect. Nevertheless, the MCH staff training programme is a cogent reminder that systematic screening with a paper and pencil questionnaire is not the only means to improve the detection and treatment of postnatal depression. Sharpening clinical awareness with a training programme is an effective alternative that is commonly forgotten.

Future directions

It cannot be overemphasized that the Hong Kong experience is used here merely to illustrate how some barriers to detection and treatment can be overcome. It is by no means a perfect solution. However, the authors sincerely hope that the Hong Kong experience can be used to demonstrate that improved detection and treatment of postnatal depression should not be perceived as a luxury by the health care providers and policy makers of developing countries. With careful planning and effective leadership, it is possible to improve the detection and treatment of postnatal depression within a limited budget.

More research is needed to evaluate the model above. Indeed, developing countries have a very different research agenda. In contrast to developed countries, the category of depression is often not an indigenous concept in many developing countries (Manson 1995). Yet in this age of globalization, DSM or ICD depression is increasingly marketed as the idiom of distress in all continents. With modernization and Westernization, mothers in developing countries are increasingly likely to be exposed to the concept of depression. They may also be under pressure to resort to the category of depression to express their psycho-social distress, particularly if health care providers choose to use postnatal depression as the accepted terminology in clinical contacts. Yet the socio-emotive experience and psychopathology of distressed mothers in developing countries can be very different from those of their Western counterparts. How should the perinatal mental health professionals respond to this tension? Should we search for the indigenous equivalent of postnatal depression first? Should we not endorse or even advocate for the category of postnatal depression, but pay special attention to the local idioms of distress? Or should we simplify the confusion by spearheading a DSM/ICD operational approach to depression, educating the population to use the symptoms listed in the operational criteria? These questions – that have no simple answers – will continue to confront professionals involved in postnatal depression research and service in developing countries. Unfortunately, these questions cannot be addressed with the methodology commonly used in biomedical research.

In the same vein, it is legitimate to ask if screening for postnatal depression should be diagnosis or problem based. Many postnatal depression screening services in developed countries begin with establishing a diagnosis. This is then followed by an assessment of the bio-psycho-social aetiologies, based on which a treatment plan will be formulated. Yet in the developing world, if the category of depression is non-indigenous, not widely used, and even stigma attracting, must the intervention begin with establishing a diagnosis? If the ultimate treatment is going to be problem based, is it possible to bypass the diagnostic step? What would be the merits and risks of a problem based approach to the screening and treatment of postnatal depression? Since this issue is also relevant to many screening services in the West, research is clearly in order.

Furthermore, the kind of mental health services available in developed countries are unlikely to be affordable to the developing world. Small public mental health budgets, a shortage of mental health professionals, and expensive private services mean that a substantive part of the assessment and treatment of postnatal depression would need to be conducted outside the mental health services. Midwives, nurse counsellors, social workers, self-help groups, non-governmental organizations, advocacy groups, traditional medicine practitioners, and even folk healers can all play a pertinent role in improving detection and treatment. There cannot be an ideal model for every developing country, but future research should deliberate on how these practitioners and mental health workers can be integrated into a graded model, in which there are different levels of care for women with different psycho-social problems and different degrees of psychopathology. The best model is likely to be sensitive to the indigenous culture and to adapt to the local health care system. With rigorous and systematic evaluation, some of these models can become demonstration projects for other developing countries.

Last, it is important to note that improved detection does not automatically improve outcomes. Not all women detected will agree to treatment intervention, and not all women treated will fully recover. Assuming that a half of the women detected will not agree to treatment, and about a third of women treated do not fully recover, the current screening and treatment model can only bring about complete recovery in a third of all cases. These figures are likely to be even less favourable in developing countries.

Hence more research is needed, in both developed and developing countries, to clarify why women with postnatal depression decline treatment. Furthermore, current research has overemphasized the detection and treatment of high-risk groups. This approach has been shown to be less effective than public health measures targeted at the overall population, a principle commonly known as the 'prevention paradox' (Rose 1985). Future research should refocus the effort on public health interventions that would improve the psychological well being of the whole postpartum population. This is particularly relevant in developing countries where health care resources are scarce.

There are other uncharted areas that deserve better attention. Of pressing importance is the conspicuous absence of rural psychiatry in the discussion. Unlike developed countries, a great proportion of the population in the developing world are living in rural areas. Little research, however, has been conducted to understand what issues are at stake among rural women. What does it mean for a rural mother to be 'depressed' after delivery? How does her illness experience differ? How should 'postnatal depression' be conceptualized, discussed, and best managed? How can intervention be provided in rural areas with few staff and resources? It is only with these basic understandings that we can go further to consider screening for postnatal depression.

Conclusion

We have outlined the unique challenges and obstacles faced by health care workers who want to work toward improving the psychological well being of postnatal women in developing countries. Some obstacles are easier to overcome than others, but there is by no means a simple solution that is applicable to all developing countries. It is also important to appreciate that many obstacles to improving the detection and treatment of postnatal depression are also applicable to psychiatry at large in developing countries. Postnatal depression workers should hence work alongside the larger effort of the mental health profession to reduce stigma, improve funding, educate the public, and above all engage with the policy makers to understand that mental health care is an investment that will strengthen the population as a whole.

Chapter 9

Screening Where There is No Screening Scale

Abi Sobowale and Cheryll Adams

This chapter discusses how health professionals can respond to the challenges of detecting the possible presence of perinatal depression where it is inappropriate to utilize the published screening scales.

Whilst the use of screening scales such as the Edinburgh Postnatal Depression Scale (EPDS) is increasingly common there are many countries and populations where such tools can not be or are not used. The obvious reasons are those of language barrier, access and comprehension. The challenges of a language barrier are obvious. The challenge of universal access to screening is widely present internationally as most countries do not have a health visiting, community nursing or midwifery service that can provide access to all mothers as it does in the UK. Discussion on improving access is largely beyond the scope of this chapter. The challenge of a lack of literacy to complete a scale or variation in cultural understanding of the concepts it includes, may be less conspicuous but can lead to even greater isolation or confusion for those women for whom it applies if health professionals do not employ alternative approaches.

There is a growing availability of translated versions of the EPDS and many have undergone validation trials (see Appendix 2). However, although these studies usually support the value of the translated scale for detecting postnatal depression in the population it is targeting, most studies have involved small numbers of women and have not addressed the complexities of establishing screening programmes for large numbers of women outside the research context. Also, more attention may be given to translating linguistically rather than culturally, and this could cause considerable misinterpretation of the language if the translated meaning and idiom in different ethnic groups isn't carefully checked. Furthermore, there is considerable academic debate regarding the need to address the mental health needs of non-Western women from a cultural, individual, social and environmental perspective (Helman 2003; Laungani 2000) rather than just applying a translated version of a scale such as the EPDS, which was initially developed to suit the specific needs of British women.

Many non-Western women refer to somatic rather than mental health symptoms when suffering from depression and may not recognize depression with a specific word in their language. For example, there is no recognized word for depression in Punjabi; the word used, 'phagull', spans the spectrum of mental illness and is interpreted by the community as meaning the person is 'mad'. Commonly described symptoms of depression by Punjabi women include: total back pain, tingling feelings, inability to rest, and a weak or heavy heart (Day 2001). Indeed such is the potential stigma of mental illness in many non-Western cultures that any attempt to screen women for the signs of depression must be treated very sensitively.

Many authors have explored the features of postnatal depression in non-Western populations and most have concluded that its incidence will in part be related to similar factors to those well known in the West, for example poor support, in particular the lack of a supportive partner, but others such as disappointment in the sex of the baby can also be significant. There would seem to be clear benefits for professionals who are not members of a particular ethnic minority language speaking group in trying to understand women's mental health needs from within the woman's individual and cultural situation, rather than by applying the professionals' own norms and training. That is, by using a broad, holistic, women centred approach. Indeed the need for such an approach was made clear at a recent conference (Adams 2003, pp.14–17) in respect of non-Western women living in England who are juggling not only the challenges of their own cultural norms when they start a family, but also those of the country where they are now living. Mothers speaking at the conference made the following points:

> Muslim women are not allowed to do much work for 40 days after giving birth. In this society, where everything is fast and furious – especially if the woman is working – it is very difficult for them to take the time off. (p.14, Urdu-speaking mother living in Sheffield)

Family support is one of the biggest problems for the Somali community living in the UK. Back home there was an extended family: aunties, grandmothers, parents who used to give all the practical as well as moral support. Young mothers having children in the UK find it really difficult: family support is nil and mothers find it really hard particularly if they are struggling with depression or mental health problems. (p.15, Somali mother living in Sheffield)

Box 9.1 Risk factors for Punjabi women living in England

- Being a new bride.
- Being a recent immigrant to Britain.
- Living in an unfamiliar environment.
- Experiencing unfamiliar antenatal care.
- Poor housing.
- Unemployment.
- Having difficulties in adjusting to the husband's family.
- Lack of choice in birth management.
- Lack of information and poor communication.
- Lack of access to interpreters on the postnatal ward in hospital.

(Day 2001, p.24, reproduced with permission)

Knowledge of perinatal depression in populations where screening scales have not been used may be scanty, indeed it may not be formally recognized at all. However, this does not mean it doesn't exist or that its implications are likely to be of any less concern than in Western populations. What it does mean is that there is a need for professionals to be trained in understanding recognized cultural norms as well as individual, social and environmental factors for any population of expectant and new mothers, and to be able to explore with these women what the factors may be that have influenced the development of their depression. Knowledge of such risk factors in the absence of a suitable screening scale will be very helpful in supporting clinical judgement to explore further the possible presence of depression.

Challenges

The challenges for professionals to be considered where there is no suitable screening scale can be summed up as:

- awareness of risk factors

- language barrier

- understanding of cultural norms

- the diversity of norms within and between cultures

- understanding individual's concept of 'health' or 'illness'

- finding suitable communication channels; this may apply to a mother with learning difficulties as well as to a non-English speaking mother

- understanding health professionals' own prejudices

- the need for flexibility as populations and circumstances are often constantly changing

- effective use of interpreters or link workers

- the conflicting effect of screening results versus professional judgement

- arranging suitable access

- understanding the conflicts individuals face between their ethnic culture and that of the community where they live

- for ethnic minority women the challenge is that the range of postnatal depression symptoms recognized in Western countries is completely alien to those commonly associated with their status as mothers, thus causing confusion, apprehension and sometimes denial due to the association of postnatal depression with severe mental illness.

Solutions

A number of solutions are now available.

Translations of the EPDS

We have already discussed the use of translated versions of the EPDS. Cox and Holden (2003, pp.21–25) explore this option in more depth. Copies of available translations are included at the end of their book.

Self-screening with the EPDS or another scale

One possible way to improve access is the provision of self-screening facilities. The EPDS is now available for use in some countries on the Internet (e.g. the US) or may be distributed via leaflets as in Australia. The authors believe that these approaches should be used with caution due to the potential for misinterpretation or distress when a trained professional is not available to interpret the results or initiate a programme of management.

Posters providing self-screening using a symptom list

In response to a request from a mother who had suffered postnatal depression but been diagnosed only after the birth of her second child, the Community Practitioners' and Health Visitors' Association (CPHVA) in the UK has developed a series of posters encouraging mothers to self-refer. These are in six languages (English, Urdu, Arabic, Bengali, Chinese and Somali) and list the symptoms of depression. The symptoms listed were agreed during an extensive consultation exercise with focus groups of mothers who had had or were suffering with postnatal depression across the UK and vary somewhat from the list based on DSM-IV (American Psychiatric Association 1994) originally suggested to these women.

It is suggested that the posters are displayed in doctors' surgeries and clinics and other places visited by mothers with young babies. They encourage those who recognize the symptoms to self-refer to their doctor, health visitor or midwife. Feedback has been very encouraging.

Figure 9.1 Chinese poster providing self-screening for depression. Reproduced with permission of the Community Practitioners' and Health Visitors' Association (2003)

How are you feeling? booklets (CPHVA 2003)

These were developed following an extensive investigation of available resources for use with ethnic minority women living in the UK. This included a preliminary evaluation of a new Punjabi postnatal screening questionnaire (Adams and Sobowale 2003; Sobowale 2002). Consultations with local ethnic minority women in Sheffield, and community organizations supporting them revealed that there was limited or no understanding of postnatal depression and mental health issues amongst the ethnic minority population. Following the consultation, the women gained an insight into postnatal depression, and pointed out the 'need to talk' and to discuss their feelings with their health visitors. Sheffield therefore identified the need to devise a different, culturally specific way of identifying depression in its ethnic minority women. This needed to be an alternative tool to a questionnaire that was versatile and could be used with different language groups. Such a screening model needed to encourage discussion of those moods and feelings associated with psychological distress to help the early recognition of perinatal depression. Furthermore, the tool needed to not be solely reliant on the literacy and English language skills of the women but provide an avenue for expressing emotional distress. The final 'picture booklets' were the result of collaboration between health visitors, link workers, local ethnic minority women, and local community organizations in Sheffield. A collective decision was made to develop a visual aid depicting potential social, cultural and emotional expressions of stress and physical symptoms.

The *How are you feeling?* picture booklets were initially developed for women with English as a second language but are now being extended for use with other women such as those with learning disability and those who are illiterate. The booklets support the assessment of mental, some social and physical health needs and are available in Urdu, Bengali, Somali, Chinese, Arabic and English.

The illustrations in the booklets are designed to trigger discussion and help health workers together with their clients recognize the signs of emotional distress that may help the early detection of mood disturbance in pregnancy and/or following childbirth. There are also illustrations of physical symptoms as they may be related to emotional causes or they may be occurring in isolation.

The development of each booklet has given consideration to the linguistic and cultural needs of the clients, consulting them at every stage. They agreed on the illustrations, the words, the interpretation, translation and the cover photograph.

Figure 9:2 Bengali poster providing self-screening for depression. Reproduced with permission from the Community Practitioners' and Health Visitors' Association (2003)

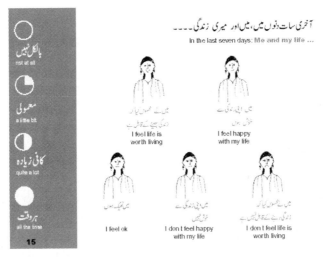

Figure 9:3 Urdu poster providing self-screening for depression. Reproduced with permission from the Community Practitioners' and Health Visitors' Association (2003)

The aim of the pictures is to help guide the client's thought process, encouraging her to think about her feelings now and in previous days and encourage her to verbalize her moods, emotions and general health as she explores the illustrations with the health worker. If used appropriately, the booklet will trigger discussion and promote recognition of those signs of psychological distress and should help the recognition of perinatal depression, help to target interventions appropriately, and help to improve the client's service experience and clinical outcome.

The simple and engaging illustrations were deliberately chosen to reflect the multifactoral aetiology of postnatal depression. The artist based the illustrations on general information about postnatal depression, symptoms of depression, available screening tools and information gathered from women at local baby clinics and in their homes. They depict accepted symptoms of postnatal depression incorporating important points for discussion such as:

- antenatal or postnatal state

- psychological state

- social interactions/activities, interests or pleasure

- low/depressed moods/irritability

- sleep disturbance

- coping

- help and support

- home duties

- anxiety and depressive states

- feelings about self

- appetite disturbance

- physical symptoms

- available support.

The emphasis is on the illustrations but the accompanying non-wordy captions elucidate the meaning of the illustrations and help the health worker to facilitate the discussion accordingly. The successful use of the booklet is reliant on allocation of adequate time to talk, interview skills, effective communication, knowledge of postnatal depression and under-standing of the cultural and personal circumstances of the individual client by the health worker.

Who can use the booklets?

The booklets have been designed for use by a variety of health and support workers, e.g. nurses, midwives, doctors, psychologists, health visitors and by non-professionals with a knowledge of postnatal depression such as link workers, interpreters and support workers who currently work with ethnic minority populations in the UK. The booklets do not replace professional judgement, clinical interviews and assessments or support for the clients in line with local policies. When used by a non-professional, he or she should report back to the professional who has the ultimate responsibility for the client.

Where the health professional has an understanding of her client's culture, speaks her language and is knowledgeable about postnatal depression, using the picture booklet should pose no problems. As a clinician, she should have some idea of the client's mental health state using her professional judgement. However, when she combines that impression with a discussion of moods and feelings by going through the booklets, applies assessment skills and captures the non-verbal cues, she should be able to reach a better agreement as to the client's mental health.

On the other hand, where the health professional is knowledgeable about mental health issues, has a limited or no knowledge of the client's cultural beliefs and does not speak the language, she will require the services of a link worker, an interpreter or similar to inform the client of the aim of the contact and to facilitate discussion of the moods and feelings to enable the recognition of postnatal depression.

When the booklet is being used by an ethnically matched and language specific non-professional worker, she should have a good understanding of postnatal depression and have good interpersonal skills. The cultural relevance and her language skills will make her a better person to introduce the booklets. It must be remembered, however, that most link workers, support workers and home visitors have limited training, limited or no knowledge of mental health issues, and a lack of core health service and medical knowledge.

The booklet is useful at any stage during pregnancy and following childbirth at a time set aside for the purpose. It is anticipated that service providers will have protocols in place and that the implementation of the picture booklets should fit into a local care pathway such as recommended by the National Service Framework for Mental Health (Department of Health 1999a). This requires the development of protocols for the management of postnatal depression spanning early identification and management of postnatal depression in primary care through to more specialist care for those who need it.

The use of interpreters or link workers

The use of go-betweens such as interpreters or link workers can be very helpful in supporting the use of existing screening scales but has some inherent problems. The interpreter may misinterpret the actual meaning the health professional is trying to convey if the words are not directly transferable. If the interpreter is a family member they may not choose to interpret accurately. Any communication between a health professional and members of some ethnic groups will be difficult if a mental illness is alluded to, particularly in the presence of other family members.

Link workers work directly as part of the health care team and are members of relevant language groups. They are trained to work directly with the health professional and can provide cultural understanding as well as translation, hence generally they will have a better understanding of the purpose of the communication. Surestart schemes in the UK, which target particularly poor communities, have made very successful use of link workers to improve communication with non-English speaking families.

Box 9.2 Specific service requirements

These include

- local strategies for the detection and management of perinatal depression, which include measures to support the perinatal mental health needs of all mothers

- training of professionals on cultural issues including transcultural communication

- training and development of bilingual non-clinical workers; multidisciplinary training should be encouraged

- an improved organization of bilingual services in terms of recruitment, training, development, management and negotiation of roles (transformational leadership)

- provision of a variety of postnatal depression patients' information materials to include written, audio and visual information on symptoms and available help and services in relevant languages

- use of translated posters, such as those discussed to provide information about postnatal depression to the target population and encourage women to self-refer

- services that reflect governmental policies.

Recommendations for service development to meet the needs of ethnic minority mothers living in the West

In any multicultural society, recognition should be given to cultural and religious beliefs in the planning of services, therefore health providers should be aware of different backgrounds and images of illness and avoid stereotypical assumptions or generalizations. The under-representation of trained ethnic minority practitioners in the workforce in the UK has paved the way for developing non-clinical bilingual workers in primary care to work closely with the primary care team in the area of mental health.

Where to access the posters and booklets

CPHVA Postal Bookshop
6 Bourne Enterprise Centre
Wrotham Road
Borough Green
Kent TN15 8DG
UK
Tel: (+44)1732 88642
Fax: (+44)1732 886686
Email: cphvabooks@mcmslondon.co.uk or via the CPHVA website: www.amicus-cphva.org

Chapter 10

Screening for Women at Risk of Serious Mental Illness

Margaret Oates

The Confidential Enquiries into Maternal Deaths

The last two Confidential Enquiries into Maternal Deaths (CEMD) 1997–1999 and 2000–2002 (Department of Health 2004; Lewis and Drife 2001) in the UK recommend that all women should be asked at booking clinic about their previous psychiatric history in a sensitive and systematic way. Those women identified with a previous history of serious psychiatric disorder should be seen by a psychiatrist during their pregnancy and a written management plan, shared with the woman, her family and the maternity services, should be in place prior to delivery. The CEMD also recommends that women who have suffered from an episode of severe mental illness, following the birth or at other times, discuss with their psychiatrist and obstetrician their plans for future childbearing with regard to the risk of recurrence following childbirth.

These recommendations are informed by the key findings of the CEMD. Psychiatric disorder in general, and suicide in particular, were found to be the leading cause of maternal death. The majority of the suicides were suffering from a serious mental illness; half were being treated by psychiatric services. Half of all suicides had previously been admitted to a psychiatric unit.

The overwhelming majority of the suicides died violently, were older and more socially advantaged than other maternal deaths and a third were professionally qualified. Over half of them died within three months of childbirth. Their illnesses were of sudden onset, deteriorated rapidly and their deaths appear to have taken all by surprise.

Some of the findings of the CEMD, particularly the violent methods of death and the socio-demographic profile of the suicides, were new. However, the findings reflecting the high risk of recurrence of previous mental illness following childbirth were not. It has been known for over 30 years that there is an increased rate of recurrence of affective psychosis following childbirth. The sudden onset and rapid deterioration of these postpartum conditions has also been known for many years.

Despite this long-established knowledge, it is of concern that in very few cases had the previous psychiatric history been elicited at booking clinic. In even fewer cases had any proactive management plan been put in place prior to delivery. In no case was a woman admitted to a mother and baby unit either during the index maternity or at any time.

The CEMD found therefore that half of the suicides that occurred over the six-year period might not have happened had the women's substantial risk of recurrence been identified early in pregnancy and acted upon.

Screening for serious mental illness

The purpose of screening and therefore its justification (see Chapter 1) is ultimately the prevention or amelioration of a disorder which would otherwise pose a significant risk to the health and safety of the person. For screening to be justified, this condition should either be preventable before it is symptomatic by some form of intervention, or be treatable in its prodromal or early phases, or early awareness of the condition, on the part of professionals and the patient, can alter the prognosis and reduce morbidity and mortality. In order to justify screening, there should be some markers of the condition present in the pre-symptomatic phase that have a sufficiently high predictive value to justify screening large populations. Severe mental illness following childbirth fulfils all of these criteria.

Risk of recurrence

Puerperal psychosis, severe postnatal depressive illness, bipolar illness, schizoaffective disorder and severe depressive illness recur in up to a half of all women who have previously suffered from such an episode. The risk appears to be particularly high in those who have suffered from an episode with its onset after a previous childbirth and in those who have been ill within the last two years (Kendell et al. 1987; Wieck et al. 1991).

Family history

Although there have been many attempts over the years to identify other risk factors for puerperal psychosis, the only one apart from a previous psychiatric history that emerges with a strong positive predictive value is a family history of bipolar disorder (Kendell, Rennie, Clarke and Dean 1981). This has been estimated to be as high as a one in three risk. More recently, there has been evidence to suggest that a family history of postpartum severe affective disorder is also a risk factor for developing a severe illness following delivery (Jones and Craddock 2001).

Onset and severity

The illnesses are of early onset: 50% have presented by day 7, 64% by day 16, 76% by day 30 and virtually all by 90 days postpartum. They also have distinctive symptomatology and are more severe than similar illnesses at other times and rapidly deteriorate (Dean and Kendell 1981).

Special needs

Without prior planning, speedy and appropriate response to these conditions is difficult and considerable risks may be faced by both the woman and her infant. Admission to a general psychiatric unit without the baby would appear to increase the risk of both suicide and prolonged morbidity. It is recommended (Department of Health 2002; Department of Health 2003; Lewis and Drife 2001; Royal College of Psychiatrists 2000) that women who need to be admitted to a psychiatric unit should be admitted to a specialist mother and baby unit. This may require admission to another area.

At best, awareness of the risk prior to the event would allow for preventative intervention. At the very least, contingency planning and frequent supportive monitoring and surveillance would make it possible to intervene at the earliest possible stage and to arrange appropriate care.

Asking questions of women in early pregnancy about previous psychiatric history and family history can be achieved relatively simply with a feasible and achievable amount of training for the midwives who will ask the questions.

Screening for other conditions

A previous history of mild to moderate depressive illness, mixed anxiety and depression also predicts a risk of recurrence following childbirth (Cooper and Murray 1995). This is probably true also for severe anxiety disorders with panic attacks and obsessional compulsive disorder. These conditions are more common than puerperal psychosis and very severe postnatal depression, and are no less important. However, they do not necessarily require the interventions of secondary psychiatric services, nor do they have the characteristic early, rapid onset and sudden deterioration found in serious mental illness. This allows more time for watchful waiting and early identification.

Case finding

Questions about mental health in the early pregnancy assessment should also include current mental health problems, not only those about previous and family psychiatric history. The prevalence of all psychiatric disorders at conception is the same as at other times. The whole range of psychiatric disorders may therefore be present in women in early pregnancy. Mild to moderate depression and anxiety are common in pregnancy, as common as postnatally and as common as at other times. Some of these conditions will continue following delivery. A small number of women will suffer from chronic schizophrenia and current bipolar disorder. Their management and medication during pregnancy will require liaison between psychiatric and maternity services. Therefore, screening for a previous history of psychiatric disorder must also take place alongside questions about current mental health problems (case finding). The same need for a differential response on the part of midwives and maternity services will be required.

How to screen

Throughout the UK, women are assessed by midwives and obstetricians in early pregnancy in order to determine the risks associated with their pregnancy and the care that they will then receive. This assessment is recorded in a standardized way and includes not only questions and examinations about current health but also about previous obstetric and medical history and family history. All these written assessment schedules in the UK include a section for current and previous mental health problems and for a family history of these problems. However, there is not necessarily any further guidance on how these questions should be asked and what further action needs to be taken. Following the recommendations of the last CEMD (Lewis and Drife 2001) the Clinical Negligence Scheme for Trusts (CNST 2002) required all maternity trusts to implement screening for previous history of psychiatric illness. Some trusts have implemented systems for this and use protocols, flow charts and care pathways to assist midwives (see Chapter 11; Oates 2003).

The assessment in early pregnancy already covers many areas of health and takes a considerable amount of time. The contact with the midwife and obstetrician in early pregnancy has other equally important functions of establishing a good working relationship for the future. Screening for psychiatric disorders has to play a part in this but cannot overwhelm other equally important areas of enquiry nor be too time consuming. Milder mental health problems are extremely common and are at least as common in early pregnancy as at other times. Without further guidance, midwives may well find that merely asking the question, 'Have you ever had any problems in the past with postnatal depression or mental health problems?' will produce a positive response in as many as 10% to 15% of women. Referring all such women to mental health services will not only be unnecessary in many cases, but may also overwhelm services. Any screening schedule introduced must therefore assist the midwife and obstetrician to identify those women with a previous history of serious mental illness (bipolar disorder, schizoaffective disorder, severe unipolar depression) occurring after childbirth or at other times. This does not mean that the other conditions are not important but rather that the small number of women who do have a history of severe mental disorder have particular problems. They will require referral to psychiatric services, a proactive management plan and face a high risk of a sudden deterioration in their mental health in the days and early weeks following delivery. The proper response to those with a positive previous history of other non-psychotic or milder conditions will be different. Whilst it is undoubtedly helpful to be aware of risk, the response and the action may be different.

Early pregnancy assessment (booking clinic) screening questions
At the appropriate stage in the assessment schedule, in the section of enquiry into significant previous history, the midwife should ask 'Did you ever have...after your previous babies?' and 'Have you ever had any problems at any other time?' The term used should be that which is appropriate to the locality, culture and education of the respondent. It might include terms such as 'serious mental health problems' or 'problems with your nerves' or 'psychological problems'. Although the section on family history often follows later in assessment schedules, it is often appropriate at this time to ask of the woman 'Has anyone in your family ever had serious mental health problems?' 'Did your mother/sisters/aunts have any problems after their babies were born?' Clearly, if the answer to these questions is 'no', then the midwife can move on to other areas of enquiry. However if the answer is 'yes', the midwife then has to discover the nature and seriousness of the previous condition without placing the entire

responsibility for accurate recall and indeed knowledge of the previous diagnosis upon the woman herself.

Suggested questions would include 'What was it like?' 'How was it treated?' 'How long did it last?' An illness that requires treatment by psychiatric services and in particular an illness that resulted in an admission to a psychiatric hospital is likely to have been severe. The use of certain types of medication, particularly lithium and antipsychotic medication, should also raise concern. Another useful question is 'Are you worried that this illness might come back after you have had the baby?' Most women who have had a serious postnatal depressive illness will be considerably concerned about the risk of recurrence and this in itself is often an indicator of severity.

Asking questions in a systematic fashion (see Box 10.1) will allow the enquiry to stop if the answers are negative or if it seems that the problem was previously managed satisfactorily in primary care. It allows the midwife to only spend additional time enquiring into the precise nature of the condition if it is likely that it was serious.

Box 10.1 Booking clinic questions

- Have you ever had…after your previous babies? or at other times?
- What was it like? (seriousness)
- How was it treated?
- Are you worried it might come back?
- Has anyone in your family ever had…?
- Has anyone in your family ever had any serious problems after a baby?

Training requirements for screening

In order for these simple screening questions to be posed and answered satisfactorily, the majority of midwives and obstetricians will need some refreshment of their knowledge of psychiatric disorders in general and perinatal psychiatric disorders in particular. Training sessions such as those described in Chapter 11 and Oates (2003) will need to be conducted periodically to cover all practitioners in the field and to allow for new recruits. Apart from formal teaching sessions, practice using case vignettes has been demonstrated to be an effective way of learning.

The next step: care pathways

As in other situations, screening is only justifiable if there are systems and resources in place to appropriately manage those women who are found to be at high risk. Care pathways must be locally designed and have to take into account the local organization of maternity and psychiatric services and the presence or absence of a specialized perinatal mental health service.

The minimum requirements are that those women with current or previous serious mental illness (bipolar disorder, schizoaffective disorder, severe unipolar depression and schizophrenia) either following childbirth or at other times must be referred to specialist psychiatric services for assessment during pregnancy. To this list could also be added women with current or previous history of severe anxiety disorder, agoraphobia and panic and those with severe obsessive-compulsive disorder. The second basic requirement of a care pathway is that the level of care that follows upon detection should be appropriate to the condition and the needs of the woman and that access to the appropriate level of care should be as direct as possible.

A woman with a current or previous history of minor mental health problems, adversity and stressors, or mild anxiety and depression does not usually require referral to a specialist psychiatric team. Most of these women will benefit from extra attention from their health visitor, midwife and GP. The risk of recurrence following delivery can be managed with a watchful eye, listening visits and social support. For the more problematic and complex women in this category, primary mental health care teams may be able to offer advice and support.

For those women with moderate to severe non-psychotic psychiatric disorder either currently or previously, consideration should be given to referral to specialist psychiatric services. In some instances this may not be necessary as the GP may be competent to manage the woman him or herself. However, in others, particularly if there is comorbidity or other complicating issues such as major physical health problems, mild learning disability, epilepsy, current major stressors to name but a few, referral to psychiatric services should be considered.

All those women who have a previous history of very severe non-psychotic illness or psychotic illness should be referred in pregnancy to secondary psychiatric Services. Whilst specialist perinatal mental health services will be familiar with seeing women who are well but at risk, this is not the tradition within general adult psychiatry. In the absence of a local perinatal mental health Service, protocols need to be agreed with the mental health trust to ensure that such women receive an assessment of their future risk, whilst pregnant (see Box 10.2).

Box 10.2 Care pathways

- Minor mental health problems

  Adversity stressors

  → GP

  Watchful eye

  Listening visits

  Social support

- Moderate/severe problems

  + Complexity/+ severity/+ family history

  → Specialist assessment

- Severe/psychotic problems

  → Specialist care

- Advice service
- Check with GP

The specialist psychiatric services, (perinatal mental health services or general adult services) should be prepared to receive referrals directly from midwives (Department of Health 2003) and should be prepared to discuss with the woman and her maternity professionals a management plan in the event of a recurrence.

Midwives should be able to access advice from mental health professionals if they are in doubt as to the seriousness of a previous condition, as the relevant information may be contained within psychiatric case notes. Midwives are also strongly advised to seek further information from the woman's GP to clarify the nature of previous episodes, which may be different to the woman's recollection or account of her difficulties.

The management plan

The majority of women who are at risk of a recurrence of a serious illness following childbirth will be well during pregnancy. This offers a unique opportunity to all involved to get to know the woman's own wishes and preferences, to establish a baseline of what she is like when she is well and for all to agree a management plan.

Again, this will have to take into account local service design, resources and the presence or absence of a specialist perinatal mental health team. However, the basic minimum requirements are as follows. First, the woman, her family, GP, midwife, obstetrician and psychiatrist should all clearly understand the risk of recurrence and the likely timing and nature of the recurrence. The actions needed to be taken immediately before, during and after delivery should be clear. This will include the nature, dose and starting date of any medication thought necessary. The plan should also include whether or not the woman needs to be reviewed in the maternity hospital before she goes home, the frequency of monitoring, and by whom, once she has gone home and the names and telephone numbers of all the personnel involved. Any action to be taken in an emergency needs to be clarified.

The woman and her family, as well as the midwife, health visitor, obstetrician and GP, need to be familiar with the relapse signature of the illness and in particular the very early warning signs of a developing illness.

All women in the UK carry their own obstetric records (the 'hand held record'). This provides an ideal opportunity for a written management plan to be held by the woman herself in her own records as well as being copied to all the professionals involved. This written management plan should contain the bare minimum of essential information (see Box 10.3).

Box 10.3 Written management plan in hand-held records by 34 weeks

- Medication
- Breastfeeding
- Nature and frequency of contact
- Names and contact Nos
- Crisis plan

Midwives and obstetricians, GPs and psychiatric services often work for different trusts, at different organizations and with separate case notes. The risk management of this small group of women who are at a very high and predictable risk of recurrence rests upon frequent documented communication between all professionals involved so that relevant information can be accessed quickly and everyone, most particularly the woman and her family, know what to do should problems arise.

Conclusion

Antenatal screening for a previous history of serious psychiatric illness is now a requirement for all maternity trusts in the UK.

The identification of women at risk of a severe and life threatening recurrence of a serious psychiatric illness following delivery will, it is hoped reduce the mortality and morbidity associated with these conditions.

Midwives and obstetricians will need training to elicit a previous history. Local guidelines for the management of those at high risk will also need to be in place before screening is implemented.

Chapter 11

Screening and the Role of the Midwife

Mary Ross-Davie, Lucinda Green and Sandra Elliott

This chapter outlines how guidelines have begun to exert a similar pressure on midwives to that previously experienced by health visitors in the UK. It describes preliminary findings on midwives' knowledge, confidence and attitudes towards increasing the detection of mental health problems and the use of this information to ensure the appropriate care of their clients with mental health problems. Finally, it describes how one project has gone about implementing the recommendations.

Professional and political demands

The overall context for this chapter and the research discussed is the convergence of a number of factors raising the profile of perinatal mental health. This includes the Labour government's agenda for the health service, which has raised mental health and mental health promotion to one of five priority areas in the NHS Plan (Department of Health 2000c) and the 1999 public health agenda *Saving Lives – Our Healthier Nation* (Department of Health 1999b). The Government has also highlighted their intention to develop the public health role of the midwife in *Making a Difference – Strengthening the Nursing, Midwifery and Health Visiting Contribution to Health and Health Care* (Department of Health 1999c), emphasizing health promotion and the provision of tailored services for vulnerable women.

The historical development of maternity services and the role of the midwife have also had a part to play. It can be argued that the predominance of the medical model in maternity services throughout the second half of the twentieth century led to a fragmentation of care. This had a detrimental effect on the development of trusting relationships between women and their midwives and thus weakened the quantity and quality of psychological support given to childbearing women. Lay and midwifery groups (National Childbirth Trust, Association of Radical Midwives) worked throughout the 1980s to re-establish continuity and midwife-led woman-centred care. This pressure ensured that women's experiences of maternity services were a central focus of the Winteron Report of 1992 (Department of Health 1992) and the resulting *Changing Childbirth* (Department of Health 1993) report of 1993 with its central goals of 'choice, continuity and control' for women. Projects to improve continuity of care sprang up around the country, but such schemes have unfortunately only ever been available to the minority of women, largely due to the chronic shortage of midwives (Buchan and Seccombe 2002).

The need for change has also been emphasized by research: a growing body of research has highlighted the effects untreated postnatal depression can have on relationships, families, children and society (Boyce 1994; Coghill *et al.*1986; Holden 1991; Murray 1992; Sharp 1994; Wrate, Zajicek and Ghodsian 1980). As discussed in Chapter 10, the *Confidential Enquiries into Maternal Deaths* (CEMD, Lewis and Drife 2001) further strengthened the political and professional drive to improve and develop perinatal mental health services.

Many questions arise when considering how best to implement service changes to improve perinatal mental health. A central question discussed below is how best to screen women at risk of perinatal mental illness. If such screening is to take place antenatally, it is likely that the responsibility for carrying out screening will fall to midwives as the primary providers of antenatal care. This raises questions about how ready midwives are to screen effectively. One of the few pieces of research in this area was the 2002 study, which aimed to identify current practice in maternity units in England and Wales and to investigate the role of midwives in identifying depression and making referrals (Tully *et al.* 2002). This study found that 94% of maternity units asked women about previous or current psychological problems in the booking session, with 25% undertaking some formal screening to identify depression antenatally. While midwives were responsible for antenatal screening in 27% of units, only 16% of units provided training for midwives to undertake the screening. The study concluded that maternity units are involved in screening for antenatal and postnatal depression, but training, referral and support systems appear inadequate. The work described below aims to improve training, referral and support systems in one London maternity service.

Another study has explored the important question of whether midwives are ready and willing to take on the more developed roles in public health suggested by the government, including mental health promotion. To explore midwives' views of the recommendations outlined in the *Making a Difference* document, a regional study was conducted in seven hospitals across the north west of England by researchers at Lancaster University (Lavender *et al.* 2001). Seven hundred and thirty-five semi-structured questionnaires were distributed and 468 were returned (63.7%). *Making a Difference* proposed in particular that midwives play a bigger role in the government's public health strategy and become integrated into the primary health care team. The survey asked midwives whether they felt they could make a difference in a number of different 'public health' areas including postnatal depression, smoking cessation, dietary advice, alcohol use, contraception, domestic violence, substance misuse and exercise. The majority (71%) felt that midwives could make 'a lot' of difference in relation to postnatal depression, the highest proportion for any of the questions. The majority of midwives (72%) also felt that all midwives should have a role in the area of postnatal depression. Such findings are encouraging as they suggest a high level of acceptance of mental health promotion as a central part of the midwives' role.

The questionnaire also asked midwives to rate their level of confidence in relation to these health promotional aspects of their role. Midwives felt most confident in relation to smoking cessation, dietary advice and contraception (with a median score of 7 in a range of 1 to 10), with postnatal depression next (median score 6), with the lowest scores in relation to cervical screening (median score 1) and domestic violence (median score 3).

Although the majority of midwives in this study supported the recommendations, they perceived difficulties in several areas. The main barriers reported included lack of adequate training and insufficient resources. However, midwives did recognize that they are in a unique and optimum position to promote health. The main strength identified was the 'special' relationship midwives have with the women they care for (Lavender *et al.* 2001, p.670). In their conclusions, the researchers suggested that perhaps the biggest challenge to midwifery educators is to provide realistic training programmes for post-registration midwives. Midwives welcome the public health role. However, educators and managers need to assess the knowledge, skills and wishes of the clinical midwives before implementing any changes (Bennett *et al.* 2001, p.746).

Knowledge, confidence and attitudes of midwives

The opportunity to assess the knowledge, confidence and attitudes of midwives was presented by a requirement to train midwives as part of a project to improve the mental health aspects of maternity care. All midwives working for the trust were invited to attend a mental health training day as part of the mandatory continuing education programme for midwives. One hundred and thirty of the 180 in post participated in the first eight of these study days held during a six-month period. This section presents preliminary findings from the items relevant to screening on a questionnaire completed by these midwives prior to attending the training day. The questionnaires were anonymized to protect confidentiality and 114 replies were obtained (a response rate of 88%).

The majority of respondents had received some training relating to mental health issues in their basic pre-registration training (66%). However, for the majority of these midwives (68%) this consisted of only classroom based learning rather than practical experience, such as any practice placements in mental health settings. The large majority of midwives (82%) considered this training inadequate.

Most respondents (91%) stated that they always asked about current or previous history of psychological problems. Seventy-seven per cent reported that they asked about previous psychiatric illness and postnatal depression, 7% said they asked about family members, and 5% said that they asked if the woman had required treatment for a previous postnatal depression. When asked of whom they asked these questions, 87% replied 'all women', 6% said 'depressed mums' and 4% said 'single mums'.

In the past there has been considerable discomfort expressed and some resistance shown among some midwives to the addition of questions that are perceived as being difficult or stigmatizing and where midwives perceive that adequate services do not exist to help the women who disclose the information. This has been debated in the profession in the areas of sexual health and HIV, previous sexual abuse, eating disorders and domestic violence. In this study, the majority of midwives (63%) responded that asking about mental health is 'fine, like any other question', while 30% felt that 'I know it is needed but it is a difficult question to ask' and 6% considered it 'too personal for the first meeting'.

When asked about how they feel about a positive answer to a question on mental health history, 48% said they felt 'fine, I always have a plan for what to do if they answer "yes"', 38% felt 'concerned about how to respond to a positive answer'; and 14% felt 'worried that it may be opening a can of worms, and the woman may become distressed'. With regard to overall confidence in asking about mental health at booking: 13% felt very confident, 35% felt confident, 38% felt quite confident, 12% felt not very confident and just 1% felt unconfident.

When considering the role of the midwife, on a Likert scale on the new role, 91% agreed with the statement that 'psychological care is a central part of the midwife's role' and 76% agreed that 'midwives are well placed to provide good psychological care to women'. However, a significant gap was identified between what midwives felt they should be able to provide and what they are actually able to deliver, as 75% said that many midwives do not have the time, skills or knowledge to provide such care. This may translate into ambivalence about improving detection.

Encouragingly, 98% of respondents agreed that mental health is as important as physical health in the perinatal period. However, the majority of the midwives were unable to correctly identify the general risk of having a mental health problem in the childbearing year, the general risk of developing puerperal psychosis, or the increased risk of developing puerperal psychosis if a woman has a personal history of previous puerperal psychosis or bipolar disorder. The rationale for recommendations for improved detection of risk, such as in the CEMD, would therefore not be apparent to them.

The evidence base for mental health screening in pregnancy

The research described above shows that midwives in the UK are ready to improve their skills in mental health. However, is there any evidence that improving their performance in detection is actually of benefit? The evidence base is complex because it covers both identification of current, antenatal problems and identification of risk of later, postnatal problems for both common mental disorders and severe mental illness.

Antenatal screening for risk factors for postnatal depression

There are many factors known to be associated with postnatal depression that can be measured in pregnancy (O'Hara and Swain 1996). It seems reasonable, therefore, to develop a predictive index to identify vulnerable women for a primary prevention programme. Such measures have successfully identified vulnerable groups for research studies, but none has significant predictive power to be effective in a clinical context (Appleby et *al.* 1994; Austin and Lumley 2003; Cooper *et al.* 1996; Elliott *et al.* 2000). Furthermore, there are ethical concerns about labelling women as 'at risk' and primary prevention is difficult to achieve (Brugha *et al.* 2000; Buist, Westley and Hill 1999; Elliott *et al.* 2000; Hayes, Muller and Bradley 2001; Stamp, Willains and Crowther 1995; Zlotnick *et al.* 2001). Complex indices for antenatal assessment of background factors indicating risk of postnatal depression are therefore not currently recommended. Nevertheless, one of the best predictors is previous history of depression, particularly major depression requiring treatment by a mental health service, and this is relatively easy to include in the medical history section of the initial booking interview for maternity services.

Antenatal screening for risk of severe postnatal mental illness

In the previous chapter, Oates has outlined the literature which reveals that there are some powerful predictors of severe mental illness postnatally, notably previous severe mental illness requiring treatment by a psychiatrist. It is therefore recommended that bipolar disorder, previous puerperal psychosis and severe depression are specifically enquired about in the initial booking interview and referred to in leaflets sent prior to this contact.

Mention of specific mental disorders at the booking interview is also consistent with the enquiry about physical illnesses, which are listed separately in the medical history section. It is unlikely that any midwife would undertake this part of the interview by just asking 'Have you ever had any physical illnesses in the past?' yet many booking interviews have in the middle of the list of diabetes, asthma, etc. a tick box question enquiring about 'psychiatric illness'. How would someone who had experienced significant anxiety respond to this? How about a woman admitted to a mother and baby unit after her last child who thought of her puerperal psychosis as postnatal depression? Would women experience the rest of the list as asking 'Are you, or have you ever been, ill?' but this question as 'Are you, or have you ever have been, mad?'

To conclude, there are several questions it is essential to ask women because positive responses are background factors we must know about as they indicate a significant risk of a severe postnatal mental illness, with serious implications if left untreated. However, it is vital that booking interview schedules frame questions in an acceptable way and that midwives have the knowledge, skills and attitudes to elicit the appropriate information.

Antenatal screening for substance misuse

The CEMD also highlighted the role of substance misuse in relation to maternal death and it is already well recognized as a predictor of poor fetal outcomes. It is therefore essential that maternal alcohol, drug (prescribed and non-prescribed) misuse and smoking be enquired about at booking, bearing in mind that many women may be reluctant to disclose what they feel may lead to negative attitudes from staff and to social services involvement. Midwives must have good relationships with substance misuse services and clear referral pathways for women with problems.

Antenatal screening for antenatal depression

Many screening tools for depression are inappropriate for use during pregnancy due to the inclusion of somatic items which could be affected as a result of pregnancy rather than mood disorder. The EPDS has been shown to have acceptable sensitivity and specificity when used antenatally, but the cut-off score may need to be raised (Green and Murray 1994; Murray and Cox 1990). Even then, there is the risk of a high false positive rate due to the common worries in late pregnancy (Elliott *et al.* 1983; Ross *et al.* 2003). In the UK, the midwifery services are less likely to have the time to institute psychological interventions in pregnancy than health visitors are to institute them postnatally. Clearly any woman who seeks help with depression should be offered it whether it is antenatally, postnatally or at any other time in life. However, if resources are limited for finding and treating hidden cases it might be argued that these are focused on the most sensitive time for the family, when there is a new baby.

Antenatal questionnaires for current mood as screen for risk of postnatal depression

High scores on measures of anxiety and depression at one time point are predictive of high scores at another. The childbearing period does not differ in this respect. Factors contributing to such continuity include genetic vulnerability, early experiences, personality and ongoing life circumstances. However, as with using background factors to identify risk of postnatal depression, the predictive power is not good enough to predict the postnatal mental health of individuals. More importantly, the value of a predictive index would be for primary prevention, but women with currently raised depression scores may not be able to engage with prevention programmes (Brugha *et al.* 2000) because they are actually in need of treatment for current antenatal depression (or anxiety). The National Institute for Clinical Excellence guidelines (www.nice.org.uk) for antenatal care therefore concluded that pregnant women should not be offered screens designed for current depression in the antenatal period in order to identify risk of postnatal depression.

Summary of evidence base for antenatal screening

There is little evidence to date on antenatal screening or case finding. Nevertheless, a consensus appears to be emerging that:

- The initial booking interview for maternity services must include previous psychiatric history, with illnesses included in the medical history section in the same way as physical illnesses. In particular, bipolar affective disorder (manic depression), puerperal psychosis and depression must be included in the list. Eating disorders and substance misuse must continue to be included either in the medical history or in an alternative section if they fit better. Anxiety and depression can also be enquired about in other sections such as previous obstetric history and current general well being.

- Neither a questionnaire using a compound of background factors nor a questionnaire for current mood should be employed as predictors of postnatal depression and anxiety in clinical practice, though they continue to be useful tools in research.

- Aids for improving detection of antenatal depression and anxiety should be used where there are the resources to provide effective interventions.

Modifying the initial booking interview for maternity services

For midwives the primary current imperative derives from the Confidential Enquiry into Maternal Deaths and the conclusions regarding severe mental illness outlined by Margaret Oates in the previous chapter. Various responses to this challenge are being developed around the UK.

This section describes the process employed as part of a three-year trial by the MAPPIM (Maternity and Perinatal Partnership in Mental Health) team for maternity services at St Thomas' Hospital. The existing booking interview followed the model recommended throughout the UK with postnatal depression and 'psychiatric illness' listed in the medical history section along with various specific physical illnesses, eating disorders and substance misuse.

The following factors were considered before making changes:

- views from 50 interviews with a wide range of stakeholders
- views of the Trust steering group and consortium of wider stakeholders
- availability of mental health services
- priorities of mental health services
- literature on antenatal screening and information
- impact of illness on the individual, her family, postnatal wards and services
- time available for booking interview
- flow of booking interview
- acceptability of items to women and to midwives
- information needs of women
- training needs of midwives.

The key changes decided for the trial were:

- a leaflet to be included with the blood test leaflet in the welcome letter from maternity services to newly pregnant women
- five new questions in the booking interview with extension questions for positive answers
- referral decisions process provided on a flow chart
- referral form and referral form guidelines
- introducing study days and workshops for ongoing training in mental health practice for midwives.

Leaflet

The leaflet is effectively a brief form of informed consent. It enables women to know the basic purpose of the mental health questions and the likely consequences of positive answers. It also educates women about mental health issues during childbearing, normalizes mental health care as part of the maternity service and introduces key diagnostic terms, which may prompt further enquiry about personal and family history prior to attendance. A copy of the leaflet is available from the first author on request.

New questions in booking interview

Initially, these were provided to midwives as stickers, which fit into the relevant section of the hand-held records. The questions were subsequently printed in a new version of the hand-held notes. The computer drop-down menu and booking form to be posted back by midwives with no computer access were also changed.

Extension questions were provided for each of the five questions and practised by role-play in the study day.

Referral decisions

The flow chart developed by the MAPPIM team is shown in Figures 11.1 and 11.2. A laminated version in A5 was provided for all maternity staff.

Referral form and referral guidelines

The referral form was designed for two sides of A4 sheet, which could be faxed or posted. A laminated version in A5 for keeping in the midwife's diary, with the referral decisions flow chart, contains a list of the information required in each section. This is extremely important. A delivery rate of 5000 per year would result in approximately 1,200 women with a mental health problem at sometime during pregnancy or the postnatal period and over 2,000 with at least one antenatal indication of risk. The MAPPIM team has a capacity which varies over time but never exceeds 400 assessments or 60 therapy episodes in a year. The referral guidelines aim to ensure that referrals are appropriate and that adequate information is provided on the referral form to allow the MAPPIM team to identify those women most in need of specialist assessment and treatment.

Introductory study days and workshops

All midwives were required to attend a mental health study day. This introduced the rationale for screening for mental health problems, the new screening questions, referral decisions and process, an outline of common mental health problems and postnatal mental illnesses, and the role of midwives in promoting positive mental health for all in pregnancy. It was recommended that midwives attend workshops relevant to mental health three times per year. These provide new topics and revision of the screening and referral process.

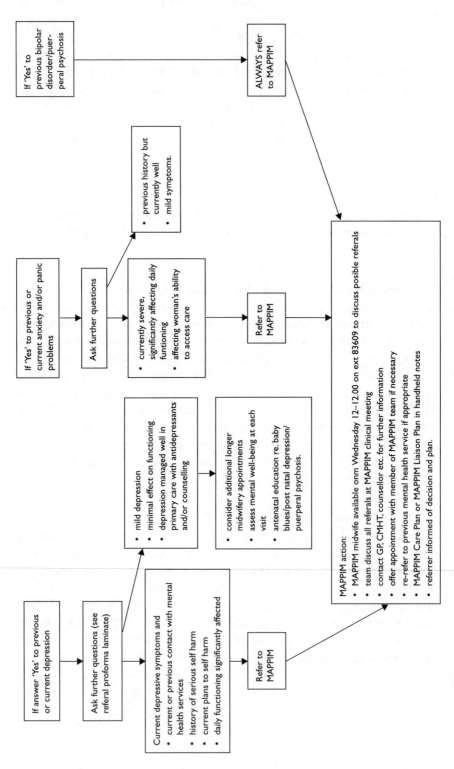

Figure 11.1 Referral flowchart for mental health questions at booking – page 1. Copyright © MAPPIM Team 2003. Reproduced with permission.

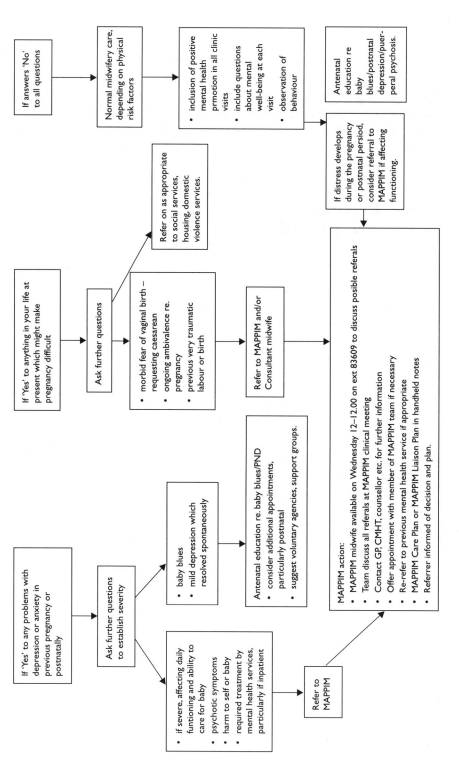

Figure 11.2 Referral flowchart for mental health problems at booking – page 2. Copyright © MAPPIM Team 2003. Reproduced with permission.

Conclusion

This section has described the process undertaken by the collaboration of a maternity service in an acute trust and a mental health trust. Materials have been described to illustrate the chosen screening and referral process. However, the authors recommend the process of collaborative reflection on local populations, services and priorities and adapting the materials to suit local needs, rather than the adoption of materials utilized in a different area.

Acknowledgements

The MAPPIM project is funded by the Guy's and St Thomas' Charitable Foundation.

Chapter 12

The Postpartum Depression Screening Scale (PDSS)

Cheryl T. Beck and Robert K. Gable

Rationale for the development of the PDSS

Depression is not necessarily the first or most important symptom of mothers suffering from postpartum depression (Dalton 1996). In Dalton's research on initial symptoms of postpartum depression, the top five first symptoms in order of frequency reported were: anxiety, insomnia, agitation, irritability, and confusion. Depression was last on the list. It came in tenth place. Dalton reported that irritability was a marked feature of postpartum depression, which is not usually present in typical depression. She termed it irrational irritability. Recently, Born and Steiner (1999) brought attention to irritability as the forgotten dimension of perinatal mood disorders. They propose that shining the spotlight on depressive symptomatology has undermined any focus on irritability.

Not all postpartum depressed mothers present with the same constellation of symptoms, which makes detecting this mood disorder even more challenging for clinicians. To provide clinicians with a second option in screening, Beck and Gable (2000) developed a new measure, the Postpartum Depression Screening Scale (PDSS). The Edinburgh Postnatal Depression Scale (EPDS) was designed purposely to focus on depressive symptoms and to be able to also be used outside of the postpartum period. Beck and Gable designed the PDSS for a different purpose. These authors wished to cast a wider net in screening for symptoms other than just the depressive symptoms. Beck's (1992, 1993, 1996a) series of qualitative studies on postpartum depression provided the rationale for including additional symptoms such as irritability, concentration difficulty, loss of self, loneliness, and unrealness. Beck and Gable also wanted to design an instrument which had items written in the context of new motherhood, such as 'Even when my baby is asleep, I have difficulty falling asleep.' The PDSS was designed specifically for use only in the postpartum period and it has an additional use beyond just screening. Each of the seven symptom content subscales that comprise the PDSS are interpreted by means of ranges of elevation. When a woman scores in the elevated range for a particular symptom subscale, it alerts the clinician that the mother is having problems and difficulties in this symptom area and interventions are needed.

Scale construction

The PDSS is a 35-item, Likert-type self-report scale with summative scoring (Beck and Gable 2000, 2001a, 2001b, 2002). Beck's qualitative research program on postpartum depression (Beck 1992, 1993, 1996b) provided the conceptual basis for the development of the PDSS and its seven dimensions of symptoms/distress. All the items on the PDSS were created using actual quotes from mothers who had participated in Beck's research.

The PDSS consists of the following seven dimensions: sleeping/ eating disturbances, anxiety/insecurity, emotional lability, mental confusion, loss of self, guilt/shame, and contemplating harming oneself. Each dimension is composed of five items that describe how a mother may be feeling after the birth of her baby. Women are asked to indicate their level of disagreement or agreement with each item on a range of strongly disagree (1) to strongly agree (5). In completing the scale a woman is asked to circle the answer that best describes how she has felt over the past two weeks. Because all items are negatively worded, agreement with an item constitutes endorsement of a psychological distress. Higher scores on the PDSS indicate higher levels of postpartum distress. Total scores on the PDSS range from 35 to 175. Based on the Flesch Reading Ease score, the scale requires a third grade or better reading ability (Flesch 1948).

Content validity

The expert judgment method (Gable and Wolf 1993) was used to ensure that the PDSS items adequately captured the symptomatology of postpartum depression (Beck and Gable 2001c). First, a panel of five content experts individually reviewed the PDSS. Four of the five panel members not only were clinical experts in postpartum depression, but also had experienced this mood disorder personally. Second, a focus group consisting of 15 graduate students in nursing, whose clinical specialties were obstetrics and psychiatry, reviewed the PDSS. Each expert and focus group member was provided with the conceptual basis for the PDSS, as well as the operational definitions of the seven dimensions. The judges were asked to rate how well each item fit the dimension to which it had been assigned (on a 5-point Likert scale, where 1 = strongly disagree; 5 = strongly agree). The mean ratings of fit for the pilot items ranged from 4.00 to 5.00 for the expert group and from 3.73 to 5.00 for the focus group. These ratings suggest that the judges found that the items adequately described the experience of postpartum depression. Next, two studies were conducted to establish the psychometric properties of the PDSS.

Psychometric studies
Study 1
In the first study the reliability and construct validity of the PDSS were assessed (Beck and Gable 2000). The sample consisted of 525 mothers in the community who completed the PDSS approximately eight weeks postpartum. Eight different sites were used to recruit women who were between two weeks and six months postpartum. These sites were located in six different states: Connecticut, Massachusetts, Rhode Island, New Jersey, Ohio, and Indiana. Clinicians in these health care agencies distributed the PDSS to women. Mothers completed the scales and mailed them back to the researcher. In addition to these sites, Postpartum Support International's (PSI) executive director distributed the PDSS to mothers who contacted PSI for help with their postpartum depression. The predominant race/ethnic group was white (79%), followed by black (11%), Hispanic (7%), and other (3%).

The PDSS demonstrated excellent internal consistency reliability coefficients of .97 for the total score and coefficients ranging from .83 to .94 for the seven symptom content scales. Confirmatory factor analysis was used to evaluate the construct validity of the PDSS. The standardized weights for the five items assigned to each of the seven symptom content scales were sufficiently high, with a minimum t value of 14.79, thus indicating all the items fit the hypothesized model. The Tucker-Lewis index of .87, the root mean square residual of .05, and the values of the modification indices all were judged supportive of a seven-factor model (Tucker and Lewis 1973).

Item response theory (IRT) techniques were used as an additional examination of the PDSS' construct validity (Beck and Gable 2001d). The one-parameter Rasch latent trait analysis was performed using the Facets program (Linacre 1993). IRT assessed the adequacy with which the attitude continuum underlying each dimension was measured by the respective items. IRT also allowed the examination of the 'model fit' data regarding how well the 5-point Likert response format worked for these items and the respondents. The differentiation of each of the seven attitude dimensions of the PDSS was illustrated by examining the spread of the item scale values across the attitude continuum. The spread of the items in each dimension was quite good for the types of items and people included in this study. Next, the response options for the Likert categories of the PDSS were examined to confirm whether there was an 'ordered attitude continuum' in which higher responses corresponded to higher levels of agreement. For each of the seven dimensions, the fit statistics (the average logit scale score) increased with each higher category, indicating that the 5-point Likert response categories operated properly for these items and the women, and that they contributed to the supportive construct validity findings.

Study 2

In the second study the sample consisted of 150 women who were on average 5 1/2 weeks postpartum (Beck and Gable 2001a, 2001b). This convenience sample was recruited from prenatal childbirth classes and also by newspaper advertisements. After the women delivered, they made an appointment to return to the hospital when they were between 2 and 12 weeks postpartum to participate in the study. The women were predominantly white (87%) and married (89%). First, each mother completed in random order three questionnaires: the PDSS, the EPDS, and the Beck Depression Inventory-II (BDI-II: Beck, Steer and Brown 1996). Immediately after completing these three questionnaires, the mother was interviewed privately by a nurse psychotherapist, blind to the instrument scores, using the Structured Clinical Interview for DSM-IV Axis I Disorders (SCID) (First *et al.* 1997). Twelve per cent (n = 18) of the mothers were diagnosed with major postpartum depression, 19% (n = 28) with minor postpartum depression and 69% (n = 104) with no depression. A total of 31% (n = 46) of the sample suffered from either minor or major depression after the delivery. For this sample of 150 mothers, the alpha coefficients for the PDSS' seven dimensions ranged from .80 to .91. The PDSS was strongly correlated with both the BDI-II (r = .81, p<.0001) and the EPDS (r = .79, p<.0001) and the SCID diagnostic status (r = .70, p<.0001). These findings offer support for the construct validity of the PDSS by showing that the measure is highly associated not only with other established self-report depression inventories, but also with depression status as ascertained by a different method (diagnostic interview).

The ability of the PDSS to explain variance in diagnostic classification of postpartum depression above that explained by the BDI-II and EPDS (i.e. incremental validity) was assessed using hierarchical regression. Incremental validity should be addressed for any screening instrument which is intended for applied, predictive use (Sechrest 1963). The independent contribution of a screening instrument should be judged on the basis of its contribution over and above the best source that is currently available (Cronbach and Gleser 1957). Entered first, the BDI-II accounted for 38% of the variance (p<.0001) in group classification. Next, the EPDS increased the variance by 3% (p = .039). After explaining variance in group classification by the other depression instruments, the PDSS explained an additional 9% (p<.0001) of the variance in the depression diagnosis. This increase in prediction of group classification provides support for the construct validity of the PDSS.

In order to assess how well the PDSS predicted membership to either the depressed or non-depressed groups, a discriminant function analysis was performed using the seven symptom dimensions of the PDSS. The depressed group consisted of the 18 mothers diagnosed with major postpartum depression plus the 28 mothers with minor depression. The non-depressed group included the 104 women who were not depressed. The discriminant function calculated was significant at the p<.0001 level ($X^2 = 106.2$). A Wilks' Lambda = 0.480 indicated this discriminant function accounted for 52% of the variability between the two groups of depressed and non-depressed women. The classification procedures revealed that 84.7% (n = 127) of the sample of 150 women were classified correctly.

The correlations between the PDSS' seven dimensions and the discriminant function suggests that all seven dimensions can be interpreted as predictors that distinguish between non-depressed and depressed mothers. Correlations of greater than .33 (explaining 10% of the variance) are considered interpretable (Tabachnick and Fidell 1996). All seven content scales qualified as interpretable predictors of classification.

Receiver Operating Characteristic (ROC) curves were constructed to help determine optimal cut-off scores for the PDSS. Based on the sensitivity, specificity, and predictive values of the PDSS, when screening for major postpartum depression a cut-off score of 80 is recommended. At a score of 80 the PDSS' sensitivity was 94%, specificity was 98%, positive and negative predictive values were 90% and 99%, respectively.

When screening for major/minor postpartum depression, 60 is the recommended cut-off point. This cut-off point yielded a sensitivity =.91 and specificity =.72. Beck and Gable (2001b) compared the sensitivity and specificity of the PDSS with those of the EPDS and the BDI-II. The following published recommended cut-off scores for major depression were used to calculate these values: PDSS 80, EPDS 12/13, and the BDI-II 20. Of the three instruments, the PDSS had the highest combination of sensitivity and specificity at .94 and .98, respectively. The EPDS sensitivity was .78 and specificity was .99 while the BDI-II's sensitivity and specificity were .56 and 100, respectively. One of the purposes of that study was to determine the level of agreement among these three self-report scales with emphasis on whether the instruments identified the same subgroup of mothers as having major postpartum depression. Using the recommended cut-off scores, all three scales identified 10 of the 18 women (56%) diagnosed with major postpartum depression. Four women (22%) were identified by only two instruments, the PDSS and the EPDS. Three mothers (17%) were identified as suffering from major depression by only one of the three instruments, the PDSS. Lastly one woman (6%) who was diagnosed with major depression was not identified by any of the three scales.

In comparing the three cases in which the PDSS was the only instrument that detected their major postpartum depression, the difference makers were items assessing sleeping disturbances, mental confusion and anxiety. Since the EPDS does not contain any items measuring mental confusion, the EPDS was not able to detect the mothers' problems with this symptom. Since the BDI-II does not include any items on anxiety, it was not able to assess this symptom.

Interpreting the PDSS

- *PDSS total score.* It is based on responses to all 35 items and has a possible range of 35–175. It provides an index of the general severity of a woman's postpartum depressive symptoms. The PDSS total score is interpreted by means of ranges. Total scores in the range 35–59 are interpreted as representing normal adjustment, or lack of significant symptoms of postpartum depression. Scores in the total score range 60–79 represent significant symptoms of postpartum depression. Many, though not all, of the women scoring in this range are in need of formal psychiatric evaluation.

  A total PDSS score in the range 80–175 constitutes a positive screen for major postpartum depression. Although this is not equivalent to a DSM-IV diagnosis of major depressive disorder, it does indicate a high probability that the woman has this disorder. Women scoring in this range are in definite need of psychiatric evaluation and should be referred as soon as possible to the mental health team for further assessment and treatment.

- *Symptom content scores.* Whenever the PDSS total score is elevated above the range of normal adjustment, it is useful to examine the scores for the seven symptom content scales in order to characterize the pattern of symptoms for an individual respondent. The content scales are interpreted by means of ranges of elevation, which are provided for each scale. The symptom content scale scores range from 5 to 25. When a woman scores in the elevated range for a particular content scale, it indicates that she is reporting substantially more problems in that symptom area than the average respondent.

- *The inconsistent responding (INC) index.* It was developed to detect response patterns that do not consistently reflect the item content of the PDSS. The INC index is a useful basic measure of a woman's consistency in completing the PDSS items. It may be especially helpful in identifying those women who, because of limited English skills or neurologically based cognitive impairment, are having difficulty following the scale instructions and/or concentrating on the scale items from start to finish.

  The INC index is derived from ten pairs of PDSS items for which ratings tend to be very similar. The INC score is a count of the number of item pairs for which the respondent's ratings differ by more than one point. When the INC score is 4, there is an 85% likelihood that the PDSS items were not completed in a way that consistently reflected the scale's content (Beck and Gable 2002). Therefore, the clinician should consider the possibility that the respondent did not complete the PDSS in an accurate manner.

PDSS Short Form

The PDSS Short Form consists of the first seven items on the full 35-item PDSS (Beck and Gable 2002). The Short Form consists of one item from each of the seven dimensions that had the highest reliability. Internal consistency reliability coefficients for the Short Form were .87 in Study 1 and

.81 in Study 2. The PDSS Short Form total score correlated significantly (p<.0001) with the full PDSS (r = .94) and the EPDS (r = .76).

The PDSS Short Form yields a short total score. The short total score has a possible range of 7–35. It is analogous to the full PDSS total score in that it provides an index of the general severity of a woman's postpartum depressive symptoms. The short total score is interpreted by means of two ranges. Short total scores in the range 7–13 are interpreted as representing normal adjustment, or a lack of significant symptoms of postpartum depression. Short total scores in the range 14–35 represent significant symptoms of postpartum depression. If a mother falls in this range, it is recommended that the full 35-item PDSS be administered. It should be kept in mind that the PDSS Short Form, unlike the full PDSS, does not include a total score range that specifies a positive screen for major postpartum depression, indicating a definite need for referral for psychiatric evaluation. The full version of the measure must be completed in order to attain this level of certainty about whether a referral is needed.

In conclusion, based on the psychometric testing of the PDSS that has been reported in this chapter, the PDSS is considered ready for use in routine screening for mothers. It is published and distributed by Western Psychological Services (www.wpspublish.com).

Acknowledgements

This research was supported by the Patrick and Catherine Weldon Donaghue Medical Research Foundation and the University of Connecticut Research Foundation.

Chapter 13

What is the EPDS Measuring and How Should We Use It in Research?

Josephine M. Green

The Edinburgh Postnatal Depression Scale (EPDS) is a simple paper and pencil questionnaire with a very specific purpose, but it has fast become one of the most widely used mood assessment instruments in the field, far exceeding the purpose for which it was designed.

Many of the concerns raised about the use of the EPDS are, rightly, concerned with its use in clinical practice. The focus of this chapter, however, is on its use in research. I want to explore two apparently different but linked questions:

1.   What is the EPDS measuring?

2.   How should we use it in research?

What is the EPDS measuring?
Two groups or a continuous distribution?

If we imagine a world in which any given individual is either 'depressed' or 'not depressed' and in which the EPDS were a direct measure of this clinical state, then all the 'depressed' people would have high scores and all the 'not depressed' people would have low scores. We would therefore see a bimodal distribution of scores: one peak for high scorers and one for low scorers. In practice, this is not the case. All studies that have reported the distribution of EPDS scores in an unselected population have shown distributions that are continuous and near normal. We do not see discontinuities at the cut-offs. The cut-offs that we use in clinical practice and in research are ones that have been chosen for convenience, there is no 'right' cut-off. Murray and Carothers'(1990) community validation paper presents sensitivity, specificity, and positive predictive value scores for a whole range of different cut-offs and there is no point at which you can say 'everyone who scores above this is depressed' or 'anyone below this is not depressed'. So whatever it is that the EPDS is measuring has a continuous distribution.

Screening versus diagnosis

An important distinction is made, for example when talking about tests of fetal well being, between *screening* tests and *diagnostic* tests. Diagnostic tests are those that can give a (fairly) definitive answer to the question 'Does the baby have...?' (a particular disorder e.g. spina bifida or Down's Syndrome). If we had diagnostic tests for common disorders that were cheap and risk free, then we could apply them to everybody. In practice this is not the case, either for Down's Syndrome or for depression, and so we use *screening* tests to categorize people as 'high risk' ('above cut-off') and 'low risk' ('below cut-off') so that specialist resources can be focused on those most likely to need them.

So this is an important thing to note: the EPDS is not *measuring* depression; it is a *screening tool* for depression. It is looking at various 'markers' – signs and symptoms that are known to be statistically associated with depression – in the same sort of way that biochemical screening tests use markers. As with biochemical tests, not all people who score 'above cut-off' will be depressed and, conversely, some who are depressed will be missed by the screening tool. When screening in clinical practice, cut-offs are generally set which will minimize the number of cases missed, but this is at the expense of specificity. In other words, there will be a lot of people who score above cut-off who are not, in fact, 'cases'. Nevertheless, EPDS scores are talked about in many research papers as if they were a direct measure of depression. We frequently see the shorthand of people with high scores being called 'depressed' and the rest 'not depressed'. This is clearly inaccurate and leads to misleading conclusions in a research setting and, potentially, inappropriate protocols and treatment decisions in a clinical setting. The extent to which this is a problem is different in different contexts. The question of what the EPDS is actually measuring – is it depression or something else? – need not be a problem to us in research depending, of course, on what our research is about and what we want to measure.

The Cambridge Prenatal Screening Study

To support some of my other arguments, I will draw on data collected as part of the Cambridge Prenatal Screening Study. Women were recruited in early pregnancy from nine hospitals in south east England. All women booking for antenatal care during the recruitment period were eligible. The study aimed to examine women's experiences of screening for fetal abnormality in the context of other sources of anxiety during pregnancy, and to measure subsequent effects. We therefore collected a large amount of data relevant to mood both during pregnancy and after. These included some measures devised especially for the study and some established measures, including the EPDS and the Spielberger State-Trait Anxiety Inventory (STAI) (Spielberger, Gorsuch and Lushene 1970). The STAI has two scales: the 'State' scale measures how you feel at that moment, the 'Trait' scale measures how anxious a person you generally are. In our study, data were collected via postal questionnaires on four occasions. The STAI Trait scale was administered pre-booking at 12 to 16 weeks of pregnancy, and the State scale and the EPDS at time three (35 weeks of pregnancy) and time four (six weeks after the expected date of birth). Over 1800 women were recruited and complete antenatal and postnatal data were available from over 1250.

EPDS and anxiety

Factor analysis carried out by Victor Pop's group (1992) has indicated that EPDS scores reflect two distinct factors which they call 'depressive feelings' and 'cognitive anxiety'. These findings have been replicated by my own group (unpublished). The questions that load on the 'cognitive anxiety' factor happen to be those same items that women are most likely to endorse (Evans *et al.* 2001): 'self-blame', 'worried and anxious' and 'things getting on top of me'. This means that those anxiety items make a disproportionate contribution to the total score. Furthermore, data from the Cambridge Prenatal Screening Study also show that total EPDS scores correlate very highly with STAI scores. Table 13.1 shows correlations between EPDS and STAI scores at various time points. These data have been discussed in more detail elsewhere (Green 1998). As the table shows, the correlations between EPDS and State Anxiety scores taken at the same time, both in late pregnancy and six weeks postnatally, are over 0.7. That is a very high correlation, particularly on that sample size. Without doubt there is a very high anxiety component in what the EPDS is measuring. This message is reinforced by the correlation between EPDS and *Trait* Anxiety scores (first column of the table). Although these correlations are lower, they are still very highly significant. Bear in mind both that Trait anxiety was measured in early pregnancy, and that it is measuring what is supposedly a relatively stable personality characteristic rather than a transient mood. This suggests the likelihood that a certain percentage of the variation that we see between individuals' EPDS scores can be accounted for by personality characteristics rather than by situational variables.

Table 13.1 Correlation between EPDS and Spielberger State-Trait Anxiety Inventory (STAI) scores

	STAI(TR)	EPDS(AN)	EPDS(PN)	STAI(AN)
EPDS(AN)	0.49			
EPDS(PN)	0.43	0.49		
STAI(AN)	0.49	0.71	0.40	
STAI(PN)	0.48	0.43	0.73	0.50

Note: EPDS and State anxiety scores measured antenatally at 35 weeks (AN) and postnatally at 6 weeks (PN). Trait Anxiety (STAI(TR)) was measured in early pregnancy (at approximately 12–16 weeks). Numbers range from 1263 to 1367. Data from the Cambridge Prenatal Screening Study.

EPDS and commonsense measures

In addition to the measures already described, the Cambridge Prenatal Screening Study also included, at each time point, a list of 21 adjectives from which women were asked to choose all the words that described how they were feeling at that time. When we look at the relationships between the words chosen and EPDS scores we can see a commonsense pattern: the higher the EPDS score the less likely that positive words are chosen, and vice versa. This is illustrated in Figure 13.1 for just two of the adjectives: 'happy' and 'depressed'. In the histograms, women are grouped according to their six week postnatal EPDS scores (0–4, 5–8, 9–12 etc.) and the height of the bar shows the percentage of women in each of those groups who circled the word 'depressed' in the top picture and 'happy' in the second. Once again, there is no obvious point of discontinuity. It is not the case that high scorers all circle the word 'depressed' and low scorers do not, it is a continuous progression both with the word 'depressed' and also with the word 'happy'. I take this as external validity for the idea that the EPDS is actually a continuous measure of dysphoria, i.e. general unhappiness.

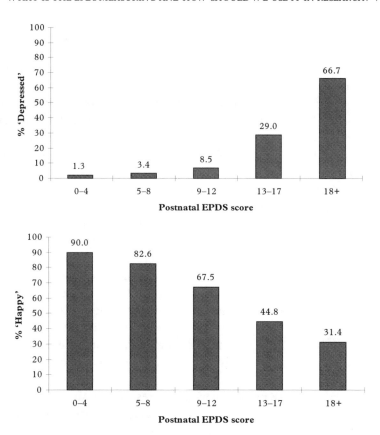

Figure 13.1 Percentage of women with different EPDS scores choosing 'depressed' and 'happy' from an adjective checklist (postnatal data, N=1327). Green, J.M. (1998). Reproduced with permission of Taylor and Francis (UK).

How should we use the EPDS in research?

My second question is 'how should we use the EPDS in research?' Clearly, the answer to this question depends on what the research is about. I am limiting my answer to the sort of research where what is wanted is a way of describing the emotional well being of a group of people at some particular point in time, and comparing them, either with others in the same study or with some norms. As I have already remarked, the EPDS is used in this way very often, as any simple literature search will reveal.

The key question is: is this a valid way to use the EPDS? As we have seen, this is far from being the purpose for which it was designed so, if it is to be used in this way, the onus is on researchers to demonstrate its validity. This is where the discussion about what it is that the EPDS is measuring becomes important. If the EPDS were indeed *measuring* depression, then using the scores to allocate people to one of two pigeon-holes – 'depressed' and 'not depressed' – and to report research findings in terms of the proportion of women who are 'depressed' in each of two groups might be appropriate.

However, as I have shown above, the EPDS is *not* a direct measure of depression, and whatever it is measuring is broader than that, having a very strong anxiety component as well. So, labelling people as depressed or not on the basis of EPDS scores is most certainly not valid. But perhaps this is just semantics: maybe we should just call our two groups something different to get around this difficulty. Would that then be a valid use of the EPDS? I would argue that it would not.

In clinical practice, EPDS scores are used with a cut-off because their function is to identify a high-risk group for further investigation. That is the only reason for creating two groups; there is nothing magic about the particular cut-offs chosen in clinical practice, they are chosen for entirely pragmatic reasons. In the type of research study that I have been describing, we do not have this particular imperative for dichotomizing our participants. Furthermore, as I have shown above, the distribution of EPDS scores is continuous, as is their relationship with commonsense indicators of mood, so there is no statistical justification for dichotomizing data either.

So, we need to ask ourselves what our research is about. Are we only interested in those extremes of mood that qualify for psychiatric labels or are we actually interested in the full range? Does it matter to us if an unhappy woman actually qualifies for a label of 'depressed' or 'anxious' or are we still interested in the fact that she is unhappy anyway? If we are interested in the full range, irrespective of psychiatric labels, then it does not make sense to use the EPDS to dichotomize samples into high and low scorers. If we do that, we are saying that somebody with a score of 13 is equivalent to someone with a score of 20 and that somebody with a score of 12 is equivalent to someone with a score of 5. Do we believe that to be true? Certainly there is no support for it from the data presented here. Dichotomizing our samples on the basis of arbitrary cut-offs simply throws away data.

The EPDS was not designed to be used as a continuous measure of emotional well being. Nevertheless, I have demonstrated both that scores are continuously distributed and that they measure something general enough to be called 'emotional well being' or, as I have argued elsewhere (Green 1998, Green and Murray 1994), 'dysphoria'. Arbitrarily dichotomizing continuous data wastes valuable information. We can and should be using the EPDS as a continuous measure in research.

Conclusion

- The distribution of EPDS scores in an unselected sample is continuous.

- An individual's EPDS score corresponds well with other indicators of emotional well being especially anxiety, i.e. it is not purely an indicator of depression.

- EPDS scores have a linear relationship with commonsense indicators of emotional well being.

- There is no clinical basis for using one cut-off rather than another in research.

- Dichotomizing wastes data.

- Therefore, for research which uses the EPDS to describe and compare emotional well being, it makes more sense to use EPDS as a continuous measure. This makes better use of the data and has external validity.

Acknowledgements

The arguments in this chapter were originally presented at the 15th Annual Conference of the Society for Reproductive and Infant Psychology, Leicester, in September 1995 and subsequently published in the *Journal of Reproductive and Infant Psychology* in 1998 (Green 1998). Reproduced here with permission.

The data presented were collected as part of a study funded by the Health Promotion Research Trust.

Chapter 14

Screening for Perinatal Depression: A Denial of Human Reality?

Walter Barker

It is generally known that there are very high social and psychological costs of false positives in screening for any important condition (Cockburn *et al.* 1995). There is also the false reassurance of a negative finding. In both cases screening obscures the far greater need for changes in people's environment, lifestyles, nutrition and other factors in order to prevent the condition arising. The problem of false positives, even when shown to be false, does not subside with that reassurance. Many people remain convinced either that they still have the condition or that they have somehow been cured of it (Le Fanu 1997).

There are many problems with screening. We have to recognize that there is huge political and popular pressure to screen for almost everything; we look for the security of reassurance that we do not have the screened condition. We seem unaware of questions about the reliability and effectiveness of the screen; it is almost impossible to close down a screening programme, however ineffective it may have been shown to be.

For those of us who have done a good deal of research, it is evident that there is great scientific value in using screening for epidemiological purposes. This is because screens can provide fairly reliable evidence on the prevalence of a condition within a population sample. The problem arises when we try to use screens for individual prediction, ignoring the questionable reliability of assessing single individuals with a screen, and the psychological consequences of pronouncing either a positive or a negative finding. Screening also encourages over-diagnosis and over-treatment.

There are reasons for thinking that screening for conditions such as depression would not have become a major focus of the community health services if there had been a greater willingness to recognize the value of intuition as a legitimate nursing and health-visiting tool. Instead, this powerful human skill has been denigrated as unscientific (Appleton 1997; King and Appleton 1997). Among the reasons for its denigration is the prejudiced view that intuition is a largely feminine trait and can therefore be viewed as 'unscientific' and 'subjective'.

The criticism of nurses and health visitors for attempting to rely on intuition contrasts sharply with the freedom given to medical doctors to diagnose and give drug treatment largely on the basis of their hunches. This brings one back to the historical ascendancy of the medical professions with their chemical potions and surgical skills, over the herbalists and counsellors who relied on gentler and more natural and intuitive remedies. The historical roots of this denigration of feminine health remedies are hinted at in Shakespeare's presentation of the witches preparing their brew – in reality these were likely to have been wise women preparing a herbal mixture for ill people.

In more modern times it is interesting to note that a leading cancer specialist warned some years ago that research into effective treatments is seriously limited by the vast and increasing cost of screening for cancer (Baum 1995). Other leading medical figures have also raised major questions about screening (Stewart-Brown and Farmer 1997). Repeat cancer screens on a population in one large area in the US showed that over a ten-year period up to 50% of the women were found positive, nearly all of them turning out to be false positives.

Moving to another area, that of hearing screens, about which the author has reviewed a fair volume of evidence, it has been shown since the early 1980s, in repeated research studies, that a high proportion of hearing-impaired children are missed by the standard hearing screens used by health visitors (Barker 1997). Despite this, health visitors have been pressured by management and other health professions to continue using those screens.

Only now, after decades of missing up to one-third of hearing-impaired children, is it slowly coming to be accepted that the only reliable method for checking on children's hearing is to use a combination of the neonatal evoked auditory response, a test given soon after birth, coupled with asking parents to make regular observations of their children's hearing and report anything unusual.

Looking at screening from a different angle, research in 1990 across an entire health district concluded that nearly all the significant findings from the pre-school examination and the health visitors' earlier developmental assessments were already known to the GPs and the local health service (Dearlove and Kearney 1990). One wonders how much of the vast national expenditure of time, energy and cost on screening children can be justified (Robinson 1998).

Regrettably, there is now a new and rapidly developing form of screening, using various vulnerability indices to assess parents' potential for abusing their children. This approach is particularly worrying, because in many of these new screens most of the elements used to derive a score for potential abuse are social variables rather than evidence of heavy-handed parenting behaviour. Thus, a family can be targeted by the services as potentially abusive largely on the strength of their level of deprivation and other social problems. What is even more worrying is that a considerable proportion of those who end up as abusers are not picked up by these screens, while a significant number are identified who do not become abusers – who are, in other words, wrongly identified (Barker 1990). In fairness, parents are not told of these suspicions, but most parents would realize that they are getting much more attention than neighbouring families, without knowing the real reason for that.

The Edinburgh Postnatal Depression Scale

There is little doubt that this scale has considerable value in its ability to confirm or question the intuitive judgement of a health visitor or other worker, where there is uncertainty as to the level of depression or where there are barriers to communication and understanding. But having observed the use of this instrument by health visitors and discussed it with many visitors over recent years, the author has to conclude that there are serious doubts as to whether the Edinburgh Postnatal Depression Scale (EPDS) can ever be justified as a *routine* screening instrument. This is in view of the problems that have been outlined above about all screening: the psychological and social costs of false positives, the postnatal depression cases that are missed because of false negatives, and the narrowing of the focus on the mother's mental state without considering the wider nutritional and other environmental contributors to the depression. In effect, a checklist becomes the dominant factor in deciding on how to respond to a vulnerable client.

There are problems with the EPDS scale itself. Eight out of the ten questions are negatively slanted, which can cause a problem of biased responses. The intrusive nature of the questions tends to influence many mothers to see themselves as depressed. The biggest ethical doubts arise over the last item concerning self-harm. Only a trained psychiatric counsellor should be entitled to ask that question. For anyone else to ask it could not only be deeply intrusive but also potentially dangerous, because the way it is used might appear to sanction or suggest self-harm as an acceptable or inevitable response by depressed people.

By comparison, the Hospital Anxiety and Depression Scale (Zigmond and Snaith 1983, 1994), used by a considerable number of GPs and hospital doctors, balances positive and negative questions to avoid biasing mothers' views of themselves, and asks friendly rather than intrusive questions about the mothers' feelings.

There are also serious doubts about the effectiveness of the treatments offered as a result of a positive finding from the EPDS. The conventional health visiting response of offering four to eight weeks of listening visits is far too unstructured; rather than empowering depressed mothers, such visits tend to focus either simply on listening sympathetically, or offering guidance and advice. It is an approach very different from the kind of empowering support and parallel concern about nutrition that we believe should be central when visiting depressed mothers, alongside a willingness to listen and empathize.

Perhaps we should be training health visitors and other professional staff in how to identify the symptoms of depression, relying mainly on their intuition and judgement, rather than on the kinds of epidemiological instrument we have discussed. In other words, instead of using a questionnaire or having professional barriers between the visitor and the mother, approach her as an equal. And, in the light of one's professional training, form a judgement as to whether one feels that there is a cause for concern and, if so, then do something about it. Only in situations of doubt should screening instruments such as the EPDS be brought in to confirm or disconfirm judgements.

In conclusion one might suggest that the *routine* use of the EPDS and other screening instruments (rather than ancillary use when in doubt) may have damaging consequences. By blocking awareness of the greater value of intuition and experience in judging someone's level of depression, it may unwittingly do more harm than achieve any limited positive effects.

Chapter 15

Acceptability of Using the EPDS as a Screening Tool for Postnatal Depression

Jan Cubison and Jane Munro

Introduction

The research described here was undertaken in Sheffield in 1998, in response to comments from a group of severely depressed women who had been referred to their local community mental health team. The women suggested that they had manipulated the answers to a postnatal question-naire, derived from the Edinburgh Postnatal Depression Scale (EPDS), to avoid professional intervention and in some cases they had lied. Over a period of several years, many women repeated these kinds of comments. These seemed important suggestions to follow up, given the recommenda-tion for widespread use of the EPDS (Cox 1994), and the considerable investment of health visitor resources in administering such questionnaires.

Sheffield had been using a screening test for postnatal depression based on the EPDS since 1987, administered by health visitors at one month postpartum. In 1995 a questionnaire containing six questions taken from the EPDS (see Appendix 1) was introduced with locally devel-oped guidance and training for its use (Sanderson 1995). Six items from the EPDS had previously been used within measures in a study of sudden infant deaths in Sheffield. Re-analysis of research data suggested that using these six of the ten items in the original EPDS were as good at predicting postnatal depression as all ten. However, no validation study has been undertaken with these six items presented on their own or in this format. This six-item questionnaire will be referred to as the 'postnatal depression questionnaire'.

The extensive literature on the EPDS has covered its development (Cox, Holden and Sagovsky 1987) and its validation (Boyce, Stubbs and Todd 1993; Murray and Carothers 1990; O'Hara 1991; Pop et al. 1992). Its acceptability was originally tested 'by interviewing over 100 women attending local health centres, and by discussing the wording of items with health visitors' (Cox and Holden 1994, p.118). With no clearer description of the methodology, it is difficult to fully understand this testing process. It appears to have considered the detail of 'which questions?' rather than the concept of the whole screening tool. Holden reports on the responses of the women being asked to complete the EPDS in her Edinburgh counselling intervention study, finding that 'Most commented that it had been a relief to be asked about their feelings' (Cox and Holden 1994, p.127). Only one woman is reported to have 'expressed frustration at being confronted with a form', though this was a skewed sample in that all the women had been depressed. Previous research has assumed acceptability based upon response rate (Murray and Carothers 1990) and lack of objections by those tested (Cullinan 1991).

This study sought an in-depth exploration of women's experience of being screened for postnatal depression and used the definition of acceptability as 'receiving favourably' (Chambers 1993). Some publications have commented on the fact that women may be afraid to answer honestly (Comport 1987; Elliott 1994; Holden 1994). There appears to have been little further research investigating the extent of this problem and its implication for the use of the EPDS. These two issues of acceptability and honesty, in relation to women's response to the postnatal depression questionnaire, developed as our key areas of research.

Method

The research was conducted by a multidisciplinary group of two social workers, a midwife and a research worker, in collaboration with a university research department. The research design was a survey using semi-structured interviews with 19 women and 120 postal questionnaires to health visitors.

The work presented here is from the qualitative study (Cubison 1998) exploring and describing women's experiences of being screened with the postnatal depression questionnaire. In an attempt to find the 'missing voices' of women, this study assumed that women's own judgements and evaluations were central rather than peripheral to an understanding of the issue (Brown *et al.* 1994, p.6).

Two sample groups of mothers with babies between 6 and 18 months were approached. The first was a convenience sample of 15 mothers attending mother and toddler groups or National Childbirth Trust groups. The mother and toddler groups were selected from a list of five different groups, chosen for the study from geographical areas of different socio-economic status, using the Townsend Deprivation Index and electoral ward profiles. The second group was a purposive sample of four severely postnatally depressed women who had been referred to their local community mental health team. Several attempts to include mothers from different ethnic minorities were unsuccessful and so all the mothers interviewed were white British. The interviews were tape recorded, transcribed in full and analysed by three members of the team, using the constant comparative method (Strauss and Corbin 1990).

Findings

Four major themes emerged:

1. concern over the administration of the postnatal depression questionnaire

2. concern over the format and content of the tool

3. concern over the ability to be honest

4. suggestions for improvements.

Concern over the administration of the postnatal depression questionnaire

The postnatal depression questionnaire was administered between four to six weeks postnatally. It was either left with women for them to complete by themselves or in discussion with the health visitor. Neither of these methods were strongly preferred over the other, but both methods were criticized.

Criticisms were:

PRESENCE OF OTHERS AT TIME OF INTERVIEW

She came and I didn't actually know that she was coming to do this, so she was here quite a long time on that visit, so it was just a little bit inconvenient at the time... Actually I'd got company as well... I'd got my brother-in-law and father-in-law had come and she said 'Do you mind doing it?' I said 'Well, while you're here, no', but it was a little bit inconvenient.

PRESSURE

It was very much 'Can you fill this in and hand it in?' So it felt very rushed and I sat in the waiting room with my two babies in the car seats, crying while I was busy trying to read questions and tick it.

LACK OF EXPLANATION

It was briefly explained every person does it, but it wasn't qualified as to what happens to it next, or what we do with this information or whatever.

LACK OF DISCUSSION ABOUT THE SCORE

She had a look at it while I was there and that's when she sort of said 'Oh, you're on the borderline' and it was sort of left at that and I just thought 'Oh what's that mean, that I'm going mad?

Concern over the format and content of the tool

Most women were critical of the use of a questionnaire with multiple choice tick boxes: they saw it as 'impersonal', 'crude', 'brutal', 'blunt' and 'clumsy'. This woman described explicitly how she thought the overall style was inappropriate:

It's rather like the old questionnaires that used to be in *Jackie* magazine, you know, when you were either devastatingly beautiful, witty and successful, or just the pits, you know…the questions are so transparent that you were always witty, devastating.

It was suggested that there should be an option for open questions where they could go into more detail. Several women commented on the overall negative nature of the questions.

It's concentrating on all the negative feelings like being miserable, being unhappy, which I suppose is what they're trying to find out, but it almost puts you off before you start answering it.

The women were asked if they wanted to comment on specific questions of the postnatal depression questionnaire.

I HAVE LOOKED FORWARD WITH ENJOYMENT TO THINGS…

In response to this question, which asks women to compare their feelings with how they used to feel, women commented on the difficulty of making comparisons with life before the baby.

Well when you've got a new baby, everything's not the same as it was before the new baby, so how do you compare?

I HAVE FELT WORRIED AND ANXIOUS FOR NO GOOD REASON...

Women commented on the value judgement in this and questioned whether a new mother, particularly a first-time new mother, could possibly define 'no good reason'. They also commented on what they thought was normal anxiety at the responsibility of parenthood and therefore challenged the relevance of this question.

> I might be worried or anxious because I've got a new baby and, you know, you get bombarded with information about cot deaths...every new mum is quite anxious about their baby – '...for no very good reason' isn't correct – it's because I've got a new child and I'm looking after it, it's not because I'm depressed.

I HAVE BEEN SO UNHAPPY THAT I HAVE DIFFICULTY SLEEPING...

Women clearly felt that they were having a lot of difficulty sleeping because they had a young baby and this question was seen as particularly inappropriate. There were many similar comments to this one:

> It's a silly one. Because with babies, you don't get a chance to sleep unless they're one of them that sleep all night, and I've never had one of them. This one here, I used to feed him every hour.

Some of the women, who admitted to having felt very depressed during the interview, said they felt that part of their illness was sleeping too much.

> I just wanted to sleep all the time, because if I was asleep I wasn't worried, and I wasn't thinking about things that were awful that I didn't want to think about, so the minute Ann was asleep I'd go to sleep, just to blank everything out, and I think that's as important as not sleeping.

I HAVE FELT SAD OR MISERABLE...

Comments about this question suggested that women thought it was so negative that to admit to it would be very difficult.

> I don't like to think of myself as feeling miserable or unhappy and I would think quite a few people are in that boat as well.

I HAVE BEEN SO UNHAPPY THAT I HAVE BEEN CRYING...

Women here seemed to find difficulty in clearly relating the crying to unhappiness. They talked about feeling very emotional and having mood swings and crying, but did not assess that as unhappiness.

I mean I cried lots. It didn't mean that I was unhappy. It meant all sorts of different things. It meant joy, exhaustion...

THE THOUGHT OF HARMING MYSELF HAS OCCURRED TO ME...

Several women were very clear that this was the one question they would not consider being honest about.

I remember thinking, you know, I'm definitely going to put 'never' there.

One woman in the sample, from the severely depressed group, said that she didn't understand this question as applying to her, even though she was spending a lot of time considering harming herself.

I didn't see what I was feeling as being that, causing yourself harm to me is someone who self-mutilates...me wanting to break my legs so I didn't have to go to work, I didn't equate as being causing yourself harm.

Concern over the ability to be honest

Five women admitted to lying when completing the EPDS, whilst most others comment on the difficulties of being honest. The reasons that the women gave for not answering honestly were:

FEAR OF BEING REMOVED AS MAD

They'd have probably come with the men in their white coats and a lot more strangers would have come into the house.

FEAR OF CHILDREN BEING REMOVED

You know, if you're not careful, there are going to be people knocking on your door and taking the children away from you...simply on the merits of answering this honestly.
I just filled it in and lied all the way through it. Because I knew what it was about and I really believed that they were going to take Laura away from me if they knew how I felt, so I just lied.

Even women who said that they themselves had had no difficulty in answering it honestly suggested that they might have had difficulty in doing so if they had felt 'bad' at the time.

CONCERNS ABOUT INVASION OF THEIR LIVES

But I just felt like, I always feel as though when you're telling health visitors and it feels as though they're prying a little bit, and you feel a bit scared to tell them anything in case they're on your backs a bit.

FEAR OF THE STIGMA OF MENTAL ILLNESS

> I'm afraid of that end of the scale, the postnatally depressed end of the scale. I'm afraid of being anywhere near it...because the stigma involved with postnatal depression is major and I think the idea of being anywhere near it is just terrifying.

In 14 out of 19 interviews, it is possible to find at least one suggestion that women might have difficulty in being honest.

One woman described how they talked very openly about lying in response to the questionnaire at her local mother and toddler group:

> Basically everybody I meet who has babies they just laugh...laugh at this questionnaire...in my group we call it the lie test, to see who can lie the easiest.

The concurrent study by the team, investigating health visitors' views, found that 51% of health visitors thought that mothers might have problems answering the postnatal depression questionnaire truthfully.

Suggestions for improvements

Most of the women's comments centred round the role of the health visitor and whether they were acting as agents of social control and whether they had any training in mental health.

> I think there's this preconceived idea about what health visitors do, and what they come to look for, and there's all kinds of things that run through your mind...and it's almost a thing that goes round new mums, or even second or third time around... 'Well, they come to inspect your house you know...'

The women welcomed a focus on themselves rather than the baby, but wanted time to talk about how they were feeling rather than a written questionnaire:

> If they wanted to know, why couldn't they just talk to me?

Only 2 out of 19 mothers made any positive comments about the value of using the postnatal depression questionnaire as a tool to detect postnatal depression. Both comments focused on its value in raising an issue that might otherwise be overlooked, where health visitors' primary focus is the development of the baby:

> I suppose that it made me realise how I did feel and I did talk to my mum about it after...so that was one positive thing.

A few women commented on the role of the health visitor as 'policing', which made it difficult for them to feel relaxed and able to talk honestly. This problem was more difficult for the women who didn't know the health visitor before this baby or who had a relationship with which they weren't happy.

> If you already think that this person is coming to check up on you and you're sort of conscious of the fact, then I don't think you are going to be honest with her.

However, women who felt they had a good relationship with their health visitor did not challenge their role in this context, but expressed concerns about the appropriateness of a questionnaire. One woman described how the experience disrupted her good relationship with the health visitor and suggested that she should simply use guidelines:

> Without a questionnaire, but with some sort of guidelines for herself obviously so she knows, so a woman isn't faced with a cardboard figure which was once a health visitor, and now she's just like this alien sat on the sofa, do you know what I mean?

Overall, women were clearly saying that they wanted some health professionals to be interested in how they were feeling postnatally and to be aware of the risk of postnatal depression. However, they were asking for a situation with time, with someone that they felt able to talk to and with no need to have any fear of the outcome.

> I think that somebody who spends time with a mother and talks to her about where she's at and how she feels would be a lot more constructive and supportive than a written questionnaire.

Discussion

The mothers in this study valued the health visitors' attempts to detect postnatal depression but were unhappy with the way in which they administered the postnatal depression questionnaire. Many were not satisfied with the rushed and cursory way in which they were expected to complete it, nor the limited discussions around the purpose of the exercise. It was this very *routine* use of the postnatal depression questionnaire, in rushed and inappropriate settings, that concerned the mothers and increased the likelihood of them answering dishonestly. Additionally, the perceived policing role of health visitors (Abbott and Sapsford 1990) increased women's uncertainties about the potential outcome.

All of the women in this study completed the postnatal depression questionnaire but most did not find the process acceptable as they experienced it. It is clear from the comments of the women in this study, that willingness to complete a questionnaire is not synonymous with its acceptability. Similar findings were recently reported from research in Oxford (Shakespeare *et al.* 2003).

Since this study was completed, there has been a wide-ranging debate on the use of the EPDS following the National Screening Committee statement, which did not recommend the introduction of screening for postnatal depression outside of research contexts (National Screening Committee 2001). Much of the debate and the National Screening Committee's subsequent modification to their statement emphasized the need for clinical judgement, health visitor training and support for their mental health role.

Screening tools such as the EPDS are likely to be used routinely and in doing so, over time, they are not always administered in the ways originally intended. Other variables that influence the process can be introduced, e.g. completion under pressure. The EPDS is not a simple pass/fail test and recent research by Murray *et al.* (2004) questions the validity of the EPDS in the context of routine care where health professionals are not appropriately trained.

Summary and recommendations

This study raises questions about the acceptability of routine administration of a postnatal depression questionnaire and identifies barriers to women responding honestly.

The changes asked for by women are:

- a clear explanation of the process
- feedback about the score and its meaning
- training for health visitors in mental health
- health visitors to have time to sit down and talk to them
- health visitors to have sensitivity about their statutory role.

Postnatal depression has significant consequences in terms of maternal health and infant development (Hall 1996; Murray and Cooper 1996), making it an important public health issue: see *National Service Framework for Children, Young People and Maternity Services* (Department of Health 2003), *A National Service Framework for Mental Health* (Department of Health 1999a), *Women's Mental Health Strategy* (Department of Health 2002).

Early identification is key, but is one of a number of tasks that health visitors have to perform and this severely constrains the amount of time and training that can be devoted to this one task. However, if health visitors are to continue to screen for postnatal depression and use a postnatal depression questionnaire, they must do so properly, otherwise one might question the benefit of them administering these questionnaires at all.

Acknowledgements

We would like to thank the women who gave their time to be interviewed and the health visitors who completed the questionnaires.

Also thanks to Professor David Hall for his comments on the research and for highlighting the importance of the issues raised.

Chapter 16

What do Black Caribbean Women Think about Screening with the EPDS?

Dawn Edge

Research has established a strong and consistent link between ethnicity and mental illness (Baker, Mead and Campbell 2002; Bhopal 2001; Lloyd 1998; Modood 1997; Nazroo 1997). However, to date, research into mental illness among Black Caribbeans in the UK has tended to focus on serious and enduring mental illness among Black men at the more coercive end of psychiatry. There has been relatively little research into more common mental illness, such as perinatal depression, among Black Caribbean women.

Although there have been many studies of perinatal depression in the UK, both social science and medical research have focused largely on White British women (Appleby *et al.* 1994; Bolton *et al.* 1998; Evans *et al.* 2001). Research into depression during pregnancy and following childbirth among women of minority ethnic status has tended to focus on qualitative research among women of South Asian origin (See for example Bostock *et al.* 1996; Fenton and Sadiq-Sangster 1996). Accordingly, there has been little published research into the prevalence, causal or predictive models, or the subjective experience of perinatal depression among women of Black Caribbean origin in the UK.

Viewed in the context of research suggesting disproportionate levels of social triggers of maternal depression among this ethnic group – such as poor or absent partner support, high levels of lone parenthood, low levels of social support, and socio-economic disadvantage (Baker et al. 2002; Baker and North 1999; Greene et al. 1991; Smith et al. 2000) – anecdotal evidence suggesting lower levels of consultation for perinatal depression among Black Caribbean women than in the general population and their absence from associated research is intriguing and worthy of investigation.

Outlining the research

Against this background, the author undertook a multi-method, longitudinal cohort study among women of Black Caribbean origin living in Manchester, UK (Edge 2002). During 12 months of data collection, 429 women in the final trimester of pregnancy were approached by the researcher at antenatal clinics – 297 described themselves as being of 'White British' and 132 of 'Black Caribbean' origin. A self-selected sample of 301 women (101 Black Caribbean and 200 White British) consented to the antenatal study: a response rate of 70.2%. Informed consent was facilitated by providing women with written information about the nature and aims of the study and affording them the opportunity to seek further information from the researcher (Edge 2002). The study received ethical approval from the Central Manchester Local Research Ethics Committee.

The quantitative element of the research sought to establish the prevalence of depressive symptoms among Black Caribbean compared with White British women living in the same geographical area. Quantitative research also focused on the relationship between generally agreed psycho-social risk factors and onset of depressive symptoms during pregnancy and following childbirth and identified the variables associated with above-threshold EPDS (≥ 12) scores for both Black Caribbean and White British women. Participants self-completed the EPDS in the last trimester of pregnancy and again when their babies were six weeks old because there is general agreement that these are the periods of peak onset of perinatal depression (O'Hara et al. 1990; Bhatia and Bhatia 1999; Eberhard-Gran et al. 2001). The EPDS was validated with a recommended cut-off of 12/13 during pregnancy (Cox, Holden and Sagovsky 1987), and 14/15 antenatally (Murray and Cox 1990). However, a threshold of (≥ 12 was used in this study because anecdotal evidence suggested that, at the time of data collection, this cut-off was being used by health visitors in routine clinical practice in the area in which the research was undertaken. Using this cut-off therefore facilitated comparison of findings from this study with prevalence data derived from clinical practice.

Qualitative research was undertaken in order to explore Black Caribbean women's beliefs about mental illness in general and perinatal depression in particular and to examine how these beliefs influenced attitudes to help-seeking. This aspect of the research also facilitated exploration of Black Caribbean women's perceptions of service response to their distress and of the appropriateness or otherwise of various interventions. Such interventions might be predicated on the outcome of screening. In this context, the EPDS, which has been used to screen for postnatal depression in Manchester since the mid-1990s, would be the instrument of choice. According to Appleby and colleagues (2003, p.262), alongside training in the use of cognitive behavioural counselling (CBC), 'all health visitors serving the city of Manchester' have been offered training in the EPDS. However, since the EPDS has not been validated among Black Caribbean women, its use in this study enabled the researcher to comment on its accessibility, acceptability and utility within this ethnic group among whom this work has not previously been undertaken.

Summary of research findings

Against a number of generally agreed psycho-social variables, Black Caribbean women in the study appeared to be at greater theoretical risk of depression during pregnancy than their White British counterparts. For example, they were more socio-economically vulnerable than White British women living in similar circumstances. Although the study sample lived in some of the most deprived wards in England (Department of Environment, Transport and the Regions 2000), Black Caribbean women were almost twice as likely as their White British peers to have lived in the most deprived areas of the city (p = .002).

In addition to material disadvantage, Black Caribbean women who reported lower levels of social support than White British women in the study, also appeared to be more emotionally vulnerable. For example, in line with previous findings (National Statistics 2002), rates of lone parenthood among Black Caribbean women were twice that found among the White British sample (p < .000) and double the national average (Walker *et al.* 2001). Black Caribbean women who had partners were also significantly more likely to report dissatisfaction with partner support during pregnancy (p = .013) and were less likely than White British women to have had confiding relationships with their partners (p = .042). Instead, they were more likely to confide in their siblings (p = .027), extended families (p = .001) and/or religious sources (p = .004) in times of adversity.

However, despite the presence of a larger number of putative risks for antenatal depression, Black Caribbean women (8.76; SD= 6.61) recorded lower mean EPDS scores than White British women (9.98; SD = 5.86). At a cut-off of EPDS ≥12, Black Caribbean women were significantly less likely than White British women to record above threshold scores during pregnancy (p = .041). Although numbers were small, Black Caribbeans were also significantly less likely than White British women to report having previously received diagnosis and treatment for depression or postnatal depression (p = .005).

Of the 301 women in the original antenatal sample, 200 (130 White British and 70 Black Caribbean) also completed postnatal questionnaires, which included the EPDS, when their babies were approximately six weeks old.

In the early postnatal period, Black Caribbean women continued to report relatively poor levels of social support. They were three times as likely as White British women to report receiving little or no support from their husbands or partners (p = .009). Black Caribbean women were also significantly less likely than White British women to have had supportive relationships with their own mothers (p = .043) or with their partners' parents (p = .004) and were significantly more likely to have had no support at all outside their spousal relationships (p = .050).

In light of the putative protection women derive from close confiding relationships with their partners or spouses (Boyce *et al.* 1998; Marks *et al.* 1996) and research implicating the aetiological role of lone parenthood (Baker and North 1999; Greene *et al.* 1991) these findings suggest that Black Caribbean women might be more vulnerable to onset of depressive symptoms in the early postnatal period. Among this cohort, however, they were no more likely than White British women to score above threshold on the EPDS six weeks following delivery.

Methodological issues

In reporting these findings, it is acknowledged that the EPDS has not yet been validated among Black Caribbean women living in the UK. This has implications not only for the generalizability of these findings, but also raises issues about the validity of adopting a 'one size fits all' approach to using the EPDS as a community screen in a multicultural society.

This is a potentially important issue since it has been previously noted that, although the EPDS has been validated in many different languages, problems have sometimes arisen when it has been used among non-Western women. For example, when validating the Chinese EPDS, Lee and colleagues (1998) lowered the cut-off to 9/10 in order to achieve a prevalence rate of 5.5% because, at the recommended cut-off (12/13), they failed to detect any Chinese women with postnatal depression. They therefore suggested that, 'when a low false negative rate is desired, a cut-off of 6/7 [lowering the threshold for "caseness" to half the recommended level] can be used' (Lee *et al.* 1998 p.434).

In their South African study among 100 'low-income, socially disadvantaged urban' postnatal women, Lawrie *et al.* (1998, pp.1340–41) altered four of the ten EPDS items (items 4, 6, 7 and 9) to improve clarity because 'it became evident that some patients had difficulty with the language used in the scale'. Alterations to the EPDS have also been made when the EPDS has been used to conduct research in the UK. In their longitudinal study, Green and Murray (1994) omitted item 10 ('the thought of harming myself has occurred to me') because pregnant women interpreted this item to include accidental self-harm and 'concern that harm might befall [them] during labour and delivery' (Green and Murray 1994, pp.183–184).

In addition, despite its reported high sensitivity, high specificity, and acceptability among women and health professionals (Murray and Carothers 1990), some commentators have expressed reservations about whether the EPDS fully explores all aspects of perinatal depression. For example, it has been noted that the EPDS does not contain items related to irritability and anger (Beck 1993; Born, Steiner and Koren 2003), which are among the 'atypical' characteristics said to distinguish perinatal depression from depression in general (Pitt 1968). Neither does the EPDS examine other themes common to women with postnatal depression such as feelings about motherhood, maternal attachment to the baby, 'unbearable loneliness, inability to concentrate, or loss of control over one's emotions' (Fowles 1998, p.91).

Aware of the potential relevance of these issues to the research reported here, the author undertook a qualitative study, which complemented the quantitative work by examining issues that could not be addressed by quantitative work alone. Specifically, using a purposive sample of 12 Black Caribbean women who were interviewed in depth between 6 and 12 months following delivery, the author explored women's perceptions of the validity, utility and acceptability of the EPDS as a screen for perinatal depression.

Black Caribbean women's perceptions of the EPDS

Women in the study were asked whether they thought that the EPDS was a valid tool for detecting depressive symptoms and whether there were items within it which they thought were especially valid indicators of probable depression. In light of the work of Lawrie *et al.* (1998), who found that they had to alter items in order to clarify their meaning for a sample of Black

African women, Black Caribbean women in this study were also asked whether they had found any items problematic. This work was undertaken because, although all of the Black women in this study spoke English as their first language, it has previously been noted that people from different cultures have their own unique language of distress (Cermele, Daniels and Anderson 2001; Pill, Prior and Wood 2001). It has also been suggested that apparently low rates of diagnosed common mental illness among this ethnic group in the UK might result from subtle linguistic differences between patients within this ethnic group and diagnosticians (Lloyd 1993). Finally, in light of previous research suggesting that the EPDS does not measure all the symptoms of perinatal depression, which might result in false negative cases (Guedeney *et al.* 2000), women were also asked whether they felt that there were any items 'missing' from the screen.

Face validity of EPDS

According to the Black Caribbean women in this study, the EPDS has good face validity. The consensus was that, taken together, the ten items were capable of identifying women who were likely to be experiencing symptoms of depression, a view typified by these women's responses:

> I think these questions are really, really good ... This is *exactly* what I was feeling at the time...all these is what I was feeling at the time. [emphasis in original] (Antenatal EPDS 2; Postnatal EPDS 22)

> I'd say that I've gone through all of these feelings at some point and probably been at the top end [of the scale]... (Antenatal EPDS 16; Postnatal EPDS 7)

> I think it's a very good measure and I think they should repeat it like six months down the line and again a year down the line and six months after that. (Antenatal 11; Postnatal EPDS 11)

Items related to experiencing difficulty sleeping, inability to cope, tearfulness and self-blame were frequently cited as being particularly good indicators of depression. However, according to these women, the symptoms most likely to signal the presence of depressive illness were those relating to anxiety (feeling scared or panicky and being anxious or worried).

> Yeah, those two 'anxious or worried', 'cos I've found that since I've had the baby, I worry about things much more than I would before, I don't know why...and that 'panicky' one... And that's a good one, 'things have been getting on top of me'. (Antenatal EPDS 2; Postnatal EPDS 22)

> I wouldn't say I blame myself for things but...'anxious or worried for no good reason', well, yeah – I think that's a good one and I get panicky over the slightest thing... (Antenatal EPDS 11; Postnatal EPDS 11)

These comments gain salience in light of findings from the quantitative study, which indicated that Black Caribbean women recorded lower scores on items related to anxiety (p =.001) and were significantly less likely than White British women to report that they had not been 'coping as well as ever' (p = .038).

Problematic items

When self-completing the EPDS, few women reported difficulties. However, around 10% of the Black Caribbean women elected to complete the EPDS in face-to-face interviews during which the interviewer read items to the women and recorded their responses (Edge 2002). Under these circumstances, in common with previous research (Lawrie *et al.* 1998), women sought clarification of items that they found problematic (most commonly items 4, 5 and 10). Problems with items 4 and 5 arose because of the suffix 'for no good reason'. It is clear from the guidance that accompanies the EPDS that, where there is a good reason for these feelings, women should record zero score. However, women wrestled with the dilemma of wanting to indicate that their feelings were atypical, unde-sirable, and warranted attention – even though (by their own definition) they had good reason to experience these feelings. In common with women in Green and Murray's (1994) research, pregnant women also experienced difficulty with item 10 because they were unsure whether it referred to accidental or deliberate self-harm. However, they suggested that this item was a particularly powerful indicator of the severity of depression as this would be a desperate course of action – which only the thought of what would happen to her children, kept this woman from following through.

> Maybe if I was on my own, I probably would think like, 'I feel like killing miself'…but when you've got children…you look at them and think, 'What would they do without me?' (Antenatal EPDS 4; Postnatal EPDS 14)

Utility and acceptability of the EPDS

Women reported that one of the major benefits of completing the EPDS was that it enabled them to recognize and understand their feelings.

> When she [health visitor] asked me these questions, it's like they helped me to understand what I was going through. It was only when I was doing the questionnaire that I realized that I must be depressed and I remember bursting into tears… I was so shocked! (Antenatal EPDS 2; Postnatal EPDS 22)

> I was answering these questions and I thought, 'This is so awful'...and it was such a shock when I got to the 5th question [scared or panicky] ... I didn't realize I felt so *bad*. You'd look [at the answers] and go, 'Gosh! Have I been like that?!' [Emphasis in the original] (Antenatal EPDS 11; Postnatal EPDS 20)

However, such 'self-diagnosis' was not always reflected in the women's recorded scores. Some women, concerned about the consequences of recording high EPDS scores, made the conscious decision to falsify their responses. Falsification became more likely the more familiar women became with the screen, which has implications for its use as a repeated measure.

> The health visitor was absolutely shocked that I scored so high – *I* was shocked! I mean, I didn't know how you scored it but once you've read it, you thought, ' If I put that she'll think...' [pause]. At first, I just sort of did it naturally...but then I started to think, 'Hang on here, these are all coming up not very good! So do I change it or not?' ...'cos you can manipulate it, can't you? And I thought, 'I will be truthful' but I have to admit I wasn't totally truthful... (Antenatal EPDS 11; Postnatal EPDS 20).

Missing items

As previously stated, women thought that the EPDS was a 'very good measure' of probable depression. When women were asked whether they thought that any key symptoms were missing from the EPDS, only two emerged: irritability/anger and ruminating (having unwelcome thoughts from which they were unable to escape).

> Not really [long pause] except like being snappy with people...irritable – angry. I sorta found myself getting wound up a lot quicker... (Antenatal EPDS 19; Postnatal EPDS 1)

> My brain wouldn't shut down...too much thinking. My brain would not stop... I couldn't seem to fall asleep, I'd try to sleep but I'd be awake after two minutes... (Antenatal EPDS 11; Postnatal EPDS 20)

Conclusions

Women in this study thought that the EPDS was a valid and acceptable indicator of probable depression. However, further work needs to be undertaken to formally test its sensitivity and specificity for Black Caribbean women in the UK. In the absence of such work, it remains unclear whether the constituent items of the EPDS carry the same meaning for this ethnic group as for other women among whom the EPDS has been validated.

Ten per cent of the Black Caribbean sample in this study chose to complete the EPDS in face-to-face interviews. Although this method has been previously employed among Black African women (Lawrie *et al.* 1998), it is unclear whether or how this affects the validity and reliability of the resultant scores. However, for women accessing services who may not be fluent in English or who may be unable to read, face-to-face interviews might provide an effective means of ensuring that they are not excluded from screening programmes. Further work is therefore needed in order to test the validity and reliability of EPDS scores when alternative methods of completion are utilized.

The work reported here was conducted for research purposes. Although these findings suggest that Black Caribbean women found the EPDS a credible and acceptable screen for perinatal depression (Edge 2002), careful consideration must be given to the worth of screening for these women. By this I mean that further studies are warranted to determine the most effective and appropriate interventions for this group of women. For example, other findings from this research indicated that whilst Black Caribbean women were willing to engage in counselling and other talking therapies, they experienced multiple barriers such as the unavailability of culture-specific counsellors, long waiting times, or not having access to counselling at all. In light of Black Caribbeans' mistrust of mental health services in general and of pharmacological management in particular (Keating *et al.* 2002; Edge 2002), there is an urgent need to address the disparity between low levels of consultation and diagnosis of common mental illness and reports suggesting higher levels of such disorders among Black Caribbean women than in the general population (Erens, Primatesta and Prior 2001; Nazroo 1997; Shaw *et al.* 1999). Until such work is undertaken, it is difficult to dispute the charge that a 'significant proportion of depression experienced by people of Caribbean origin is going untreated' (Berthoud and Nazroo 1997, p.323). This includes perinatal depression, which is regarded as a serious public health issue with potentially deleterious consequences for women, their families, and for wider society (Cox 1994; Kumar and Robson 1984; Sinclair and Murray 1998; World Health Organization 2000).

Conclusions

Sandra Elliott and Carol Henshaw

This book derives from a conference designed to help health professionals make sense of directives and guidelines that appeared to be in conflict. The primary source of confusion probably arises from the fact that the phrase 'using the EPDS' was used as a shorthand to designate health visiting services that addressed maternal mental health in addition to undertaking their core responsibilities in relation to the babies' health. Reports that point to the absence of studies on the impact of introducing the EPDS in routine practice on clinical outcomes were therefore read as meaning that services did not have to be provided or funded for postnatal mental health care.

This chapter will therefore begin within that wider area of concern. It will identify where there is apparent agreement and where agreement has not yet been reached. Finally, it will debate the issues raised by the National Screening Committee and the other chapters then suggest a process for managing the variation in interpretations of the evidence base and the guidelines in the development of local protocols.

Agreement

We have found no disagreement in the guidelines, wider literature or this book on the following:

- Mental health problems are unpleasant for the person experiencing them, have an impact on their family and on the wider society and the economy.

- Many mental health problems are treatable.

- Delay in reaching treatment can result in increased severity and secondary problems for the sufferer and their family.

- People with severe mental health problems require care.

- The children of people with severe mental health problems may require additional services.

- Mental health problems should be the concern of all health professionals.

- Mental health problems in pregnancy or after the birth of a child can be particularly poignant for the woman, particularly problematic for the mother–child relationship and present particular problems to other parts of the health care system.

- Childbearing women are having more frequent contacts with the health care system, particularly with professionals who have a remit for non-stigmatizing and holistic care, than at any other time in their adult life.

- Health visitors and midwives should provide holistic care that optimizes psychological as well as physical outcomes for women having babies.

- Health professionals in maternity and primary care services require improved mental health training both pre- and post-qualification.

- Maternity and primary care professionals should receive liaison, consultancy and facilitated peer supervision from mental health professionals if they are using systems to improve detection of mental health problems and providing brief interventions for mild mental health problems, in particular to help with the recognition of problems that are outside their boundary of competence and require referral to the GP or to secondary care.

- Care pathways should be in place so that maternity and primary care staff are confident that detecting mental health problems will not leave them trying to contain problems outside of their remit.

- Specialist perinatal mental health services should be available to provide assessments, care, treatment, training and supervision.

- Specialist perinatal mental health services should include an inpatient mother and baby unit, community mother and infant mental health service and a specialist perinatal liaison mental health service to the maternity unit.

- Midwives should ask about history of illnesses such as bipolar disorder, puerperal psychosis and depression as well as illnesses such as diabetes and heart conditions.

- Women with a history of severe mental illness should be referred to a perinatal psychiatrist to enable plans to be made during pregnancy and labour and for the mother and baby after the birth.

- Midwives should not be using questionnaires or risk factor lists in pregnancy to predict postnatal depression.

- Systems should be in place to educate women and their partners about perinatal mental health problems and when and where to self-refer for appropriate help.

- Screening questionnaires have been developed that have demonstrated predictive validity for current depression.

- The EPDS has extensive evidence of predictive validity for current clinical depression in research contexts.

- There have been no studies of the predictive validity of the EPDS for current clinical depression in routine clinical use.

- Questionnaires should not be used to make a diagnosis.

- Statements should not be made which imply a diagnosis has been made from questionnaires, such as 'Your score is low. You are fine.' Or 'This questionnaire confirms what I thought. You have postnatal depression.'

- The principles of informed consent apply to the use of questionnaires in clinical contexts as well as in research contexts.

- Questionnaires or other information pertaining to the woman should not be kept in the records for the child.

- Systems introduced to improve the mental health of perinatal populations have the potential to be implemented in ways that are harmful rather than helpful.

- Systems may be presented in a way that makes them unacceptable so are avoided or subverted.

- Systems introduced to improve the mental health of perinatal populations should be evaluated against their objectives for outcomes and/or process.

- Randomized controlled trials should be developed to compare systems of detection and intervention for postnatal depression both with respect to the predictive validity of detection procedures and with respect to mental health outcomes for women.

- Copyright procedures should be observed with questionnaires used in a clinical context, e.g. the reference should be given on every copy of the EPDS (Cox and Holden 2003, p.67).

- Questionnaires adopted because of the existence of validation data on their relationship to a diagnosis should not have their format, layout or content altered because the impact on predictive validity is unknown. It may also influence acceptability.

- Introducing screening questionnaires such as the EPDS increases rates of identified depression (Cox and Holden 2003).

Disputed

Issues that have been disputed include:

- Whether care by maternity and primary care staff is better when they are aware that an antenatal or postnatal woman is depressed than when they are unaware.

- Whether maternity and primary care staff should improve their ability to determine whether antenatal and postnatal women they are caring for are depressed or anxious.

- Whether brief interventions provided by maternity or primary care staff for antenatal or postnatal depression improve outcomes regardless of approach, training and supervision.

- Whether training maternity and primary care staff in brief interventions for depression results in improved outcomes.

- Who can be trained to provide brief interventions for depression in maternity and primary care services.

- Whether outcomes are better when maternity or primary care staff identify depression early rather than when they wait for women to feel sufficiently depressed that they seek medical or other advice.

- Who can make the decision to treat and how.

- Whether the use of self-report questionnaires, including widely used and extensively researched questionnaires such as the EPDS, GHQ (General Health Questionnaire), BDI (Beck Depression Inventory) and HADS (Hospital Anxiety and Depression Scale), improves detection regardless of the systems or training used to introduce them.

- Whether increased detection results in improved outcomes without associated changes in intervention provision or regardless of the type of intervention provision.

- Whether self-report questionnaires can be used as an initial screen in under-resourced areas to exclude a group less likely to require emotional support from the health system so that only high-scoring women receive a mood assessment by interview.

- Whether self-report questionnaires can be given without any explanation of their purpose or of the way in which records will be kept.

- Whether information about the system of detection and intervention, record keeping, the purpose of the questionnaire and outcomes for high or low scores should be given at the time of administration, at least 24 hours before, in pregnancy and the new birth visit for postnatal administration or all of these.

- Whether information should be provided verbally or in writing or both.

- Whether questionnaires should be given out by the same person who provided the prior information and who undertakes the interview to determine the need for additional care.

- Whether questionnaires should be given out in clinics, in the woman's home or by post.

- Whether questionnaires should be completed in the clinic or in the woman's home.

- Whether questionnaires should be used as checklists rather than screening tools.

- Whether questionnaires can provide an index of level of distress or dysphoria as well as probability of diagnosable depression or other disorder.

- What the distress or dysphoria is best called when measures designed as screening tools are used as continuum measures.

- What terms can be used to refer to high scores on questionnaires such as the EPDS. The research community has agreed not to use the term 'postnatal depression' because of the differences apparent when groups are defined this way rather than by diagnostic interview (O'Hara and Swain 1996) and the tendency of readers to assume that it refers to the diagnosis rather than the mood. Should they be referred to as 'probable depression' if the measure has been designed and validated as a screening tool for a diagnosis rather than as a continuum measure of a defined construct? If a continuum term is used, is 'postnatal depressive symptomatology' most appropriate to ensure that clinical relevance is clear to mental health care providers or should broader terms such as 'dysphoria' or 'well being' be used so the measures are not confused with comprehensive checklists of depressive symptomatology?

- If used as a checklist, what measures such as the EPDS would be a checklist of.

- Whether questionnaires devised to describe the experience of perinatal depression would prove better at representing the continuum of experience than those devised as screening tools.

- Whether questionnaires devised as screening tools work better in routine practice to detect depression than those devised to describe the experience of perinatal depression.

- Whether a screening questionnaire could be devised which is more practical or acceptable or has better predictive validity in the perinatal period than the EPDS.

- Whether the decision to provide brief interventions in primary care, such as four person-centred 'listening visits', can be made on the basis of interviews (with or without questionnaires) that identify the presence of distress or dysphoria without a diagnostic interview taking place.

- Whether a diagnostic interview should be undertaken with everyone scoring above a threshold on a questionnaire or just those who present a cause for concern at the initial interview, during or after the brief intervention.

- Whether all maternity and primary care staff can, or should, be trained to undertake a diagnostic interview or whether the diagnostic interview should only be undertaken by GPs or mental health staff.

- Whether all women whose problems are above the severity threshold for diagnosable disorder should be referred to the GP.

- Whether all women whose problems are above the severity threshold for diagnosable disorder should be referred to secondary mental health services.

- Whether women should be referred to secondary mental health services only where primary care treatment has not been successful or where there is a concern of risk of suicide or of harm to the baby.

- Whether questionnaires should be kept, whether or where scores are recorded, and whether the content of listening visits should be recorded in health records accessed by other staff or just the fact that they are taking place.

- Whether the routine provision of questionnaires results in universal, non-stigmatizing person centred expression of interest in maternal well being or 'big brother' depersonalizing intrusion and stigmatizing drives to label. For example, a recent article in *The Observer* by Hill and Revill (2004), quotes Ellie Lee as stating 'What is happening now is that mothers are being misdiagnosed with postnatal depression by a medical industry intent on pathologising childbirth.' Similar arguments have been made for at least 25 years (see, for example, Oakley 1980; Welburn 1980). Responsibility for the overuse of the medical model in responding to maternal distress was attributed in the article to screening questionnaires such as the EPDS, as if the one necessarily follows from the other. This is despite the fact that the procedure it implied 'automatically takes place' nationally is one neither author has ever heard of, namely 'a score of 14 or more...necessitates a referral to a GP'.

- Whether stopping the routine provision of questionnaires in areas already using them will result in better or worse mental health outcomes for women.

- Whether or when medicalizing maternal distress results in better outcomes for mothers or babies.

- Whether or when medicalizing maternal distress is experienced as helpful by women.

- Whether the increased rate of detection of depression following the introduction of questionnaires such as the EPDS is due to the EPDS *per se*.

National Screening Committee (NSC) recommendation

This recommendation is the one that appeared to differ most from the others so warrants some further attention here.

> Until more research is conducted into its potential for routine use in screening for postnatal depression, the National Screening Committee recommends that the Edinburgh Postnatal Depression Scale (EPDS) should not be used as a screening tool. It may, however, serve as a check-list as part of a mood assessment for postnatal mothers, when it should only be used alongside professional judgement and a clinical interview.
> The professional administering it should have training in its appropriate use and should not use it as a pass/fail-screening tool. Practitioners using it should also be mindful that, although it has been translated into many different languages, it can pose cultural difficulties for the interpretation, particularly when used with non English speaking mothers and those from non-western cultures. (National Screening Committee 2001)

We are not aware of any disputes relating to the second paragraph. It is also clear from Judy Shakespeare's chapter that the recommendation against screening is not derived from a perception that postnatal depression is not an important clinical problem or that available treatments are not effective. They note that we do not know which would be the most effective. The National Institute of Clinical Excellence guidelines for depression are helpful in consideration of treatment decisions. The disagreements seem to follow from the lack of validation studies for questionnaires such as the EPDS in the clinical context as well as the weakness of evidence on the impact of introducing screening.

Lack of validation studies in the clinical context

It is the case that all the validation studies on the EPDS have been in a research context and that women's inclination to lie will be determined by their beliefs about the consequences of revealing their emotions on paper in the clinical context. Questions that occur to us are:

1. If we already know that validity in the clinical context will differ from that in the research context when women chose to lie because of their perception of the consequences, why do we need to wait for validation studies?

2. If we do not know what influences validity, how can we construct studies of validity in an appropriate range of clinical uses and how can we generalize from the clinical context of the researched area to our own clinical context?

3. If questionnaires are perfect predictors, that is they have a 100% record of predicting current diagnosis, then they are diagnostic tools not screening tools. We already know that a questionnaire can never be devised to be diagnostic but can only be an index of probability of the presence of diagnosable disorder. If we know that a questionnaire provides some indication of level of distress, but cannot tell us whether the individual in front of us has problems above a diagnostic threshold, does it make any difference whether the predictive validity in studies in similar contexts is 60% or 80%? Why do we need validity studies? Do we not need instead guidelines relating to the fact that screening measures are by definition approximations and systems that minimize women's perceived need to lie whilst recognizing their absolute right to do so?

4. If screening questionnaires are used by non-medical health professionals to detect distress that they can ameliorate with a person centred approach, which is not treatment for a defined diagnosis, in a group of women who do not need or may even have an aversion to being given a diagnosis, why would further validation studies be required? In other words, is the relationship of level of self-reported distress to diagnosis relevant for explaining to funders and providers why the service is required, but not important in determining the decision to interview, or the decision to offer listening visits as the first stage in stepped care, for the individual woman?

5. Why did the NSC not mention that there should be validation studies of the EPDS used as 'a check list as part of a mood assessment for postnatal mothers'? We are aware of no such studies. We are aware that the Community Practitioners' and Health Visitors' Association (CPHVA) contested the use of the

term 'checklist'. We share their concerns because a checklist is defined as a list for reference and verification (Oxford Dictionary) and implies a comprehensive or inclusive list that can be used to check. The EPDS was not designed as a checklist and so, not surprisingly, is not one. The ten items that were retained are those that best predict the diagnosis of depression at interview. There are no validations of its use as a checklist so it is not clear what research was used to underpin the new statement. The most likely interpretations of the statement are that it could be used as a mood checklist or as a checklist for depression. A mood checklist should represent all moods. The EPDS clearly does not. Nor, however, is it a checklist for depressed mood since some of the items are for anxiety. To be a checklist for depression, it would need to include all the symptoms for the diagnosis of depression. The EPDS deliberately does not since somatic items that could be influenced by the biological or lifestyle aspects of the puerperium have been omitted. Furthermore, even if it were a comprehensive list, for example of the symptoms listed in DSM-IV for depression, it should not be used as a checklist for depression because to do so would be seen to imply that a diagnosis of depression has been made/confirmed. Clearly, that is misleading and possibly dangerous since a diagnosis should only be offered after a differential diagnosis has been arrived at by a person trained in diagnostic interviewing.

6. Is the purpose of so-called screening questionnaires for depression to provide the health professional with percentage estimates of the probability of diagnosable disorder in the person in front of them? Is the purpose of screening questionnaires to make the decision to treat in the manner the original developers of diagnostic manuals in psychiatry hoped diagnoses would dictate the treatment? Or is the purpose of screening questionnaires in mental health to provide a medium for people to report their distress and for health professionals to improve their detection?

In summary, would studies in clinical contexts aimed at validation *per se* provide any more information than we already have as a result of validation studies in the research setting combined with a commonsense understanding of human behaviour?

Lack of studies on the impact of introducing screening

It is clear that the definitive evidence for the best system to reduce the prevalence of postnatal depression, or other perinatal mental health problems, and their associated problems for the woman, the baby and the rest of the family has not yet been produced. Most studies of the impact of introducing a screening measure have focused on increases in the level of depression detected. The only study we are aware of that attempted to measure the impact of introducing screening and intervention on the prevalence of depression did not assess depression by diagnostic interview but only estimates of the prevalence of diagnosis by the use of the EPDS. It was also unable to provide information on non respondents so could not rule out a change in the systematic bias in responders before and after health visitors were trained in and introduced the system (Elliott *et al.* 2001).

The implication of the first NSC report in 2001 was that service providers should wait until research has demonstrated that service systems utilizing questionnaires such as the EPDS improve outcomes for postnatal women:

> the evidence being weak in many areas, in particular, the lack of evidence about the validity of the EPDS as a screening tool, uncertainty about the most effective treatment when treating women with, or at risk of postnatal depression and uncertainty about the magnitude of the effects, both beneficial and harmful, of screening for postnatal depression.
>
> At present the NSC does not recommend that screening for postnatal depression is introduced except in a research context with the research protocol having been reviewed externally and internally and with the protocol having been approved by an ethics committee. Where screening programmes are being offered they must be backed up by high quality specialist psychiatric services. (National Screening Committe 2001)

The problem is how can the research into the validity of the EPDS in a research context be extended into its validity and value when used as a screening tool in the clinical context? In theory a range of different systems can be devised. Indeed, as the NSC points out, a variety of systems are already in use. In theory, areas that have not yet introduced detection and treatment systems could be randomly allocated to detection systems to provide the research base the NSC require. However, the number of variables these systems can vary on is so high that the number of permutations potentially exceeds the number of adequate size areas in the UK, and the number of variables would increase with the number of countries in the study. Relevant variables include:

- type of information antenatally
- type of information at the new birth visit

- written information provided with the EPDS
- postal, clinic or home administration
- administered by receptionist, health care assistant, health visitor etc.
- whether two stages (EPDS then interview) of detection and decision to treat occur in two sessions or same session (for example, EPDS as initial screen and only interview those with high scores or for whom EPDS is not appropriate versus EPDS as part of assessment interview provided for all women)
- manner of presenting/explaining the EPDS
- perception of scoring
- perception of what will happen to low scorers and high scorers
- perception by health visitors of detection systems
- level of health visitor training on detection
- level of health visitor training on mental health
- level of health visitor training on interventions
- level of health visitor clinical supervision in health visiting
- frequency of consultancy from a mental health professional
- accessibility of primary mental health services
- type of referral pathways to secondary mental health services
- literacy levels of the population
- main languages in the population
- predominant cultural attitudes to health care
- predominant cultural attitudes to mental health
- predominant cultural attitudes to detection and intervention
- range of alternative cultural attitudes to health care in minority ethnic or other groups
- range of alternative cultural attitudes to mental health in minority ethnic or other groups
- range of alternative cultural attitudes to detection and intervention in minority ethnic or other groups.

Issues raised in preceding chapters

Questionnaire content, format and layout

The desire to change validated questionnaires to suit local idioms and languages or to change the layout to suit personal preference is understandable. However, changes will compromise the validity so any version with new content or layout should be revalidated. Furthermore, as we have seen with the postnatal depression questionnaire that was presented to women in Sheffield under the title *Edinburgh Postnatal Depression Scale*, change can also seriously compromise acceptability and the perception of the measure.

The six-item extract used in Sheffield had no instructions at the top nor an example. It had nothing to set the philosophy of the enquiry such as the 'How are you feeling?' question. It was also reorganized and administered with tick boxes rather than underlining. All these may have led to it appearing 'impersonal', 'crude', 'brutal', 'blunt' and 'clumsy'. A comparative study is required to determine whether these reactions occur equally often with the validated EPDS.

User comments in chapters 15 and 16 remind us not to interpret the meaning of individual items. The EPDS should be completed quickly with the first response that occurs to the woman as representing herself over the past week. There is no 'gold standard' meaning for the items. The comments are criticizing the items as not being good representations of a meaning that has not been claimed for them. The difficult thing to grasp is that a questionnaire devised as a screening instrument does not need to function well as a descriptor. It only has to be predictive. It really does not matter how good women think the items are at reflecting what they want them to reflect or believe that they are designed to reflect. For example, in the EPDS the ten items that were retained were those that best predicted the diagnosis of depression at interview. It could have contained items such as 'I enjoy standing on my head in the corner of a room', provided that women who were not depressed consistently answered it differently to those who were. What does matter is that health professionals appear to have developed beliefs about what they should mean. This could lead to them misguiding women completing the questionnaire or misinterpreting their responses. If a health professional chooses to discuss responses to individual items they should ask the woman what she was indicating, not guess.

The Black Caribbean women in Dawn Edge's study suggest that irritability and anger and rumination items would improve the sensitivity of the EPDS. If these were added, would the number scoring above cut-off be similar in the Black and White pregnant populations? Would Black women score higher than White postnatally?

Administration of questionnaires

Aids to detection, such as questionnaires, can be used in ways that are experienced as unpleasant and possibly in ways that can be harmful. The fundamental concern of the NSC relates to the administration of screening measures rather than the measures themselves. This sets the context of completion that will affect the validity, acceptability and ethics. This is why validity in various clinical settings will differ from validity in research settings (which will all share the fact that they have informed consent procedures set by ethics committees). The anecdotal reports that Walter Barker has described over the years are now being added to by systematic qualitative studies of user views such as Shakespeare, et al. (2003), chapters 15 and 16.

Tessa Leverton was confronted with the different perspective that comes from the type of stakeholder group you belong to. She moved from the position of researcher and service provider to that of service user. This brought sharply into focus the first three locally determined administrative components that influence the value of screening procedures.

1. The context for screening.

2. The patient's understanding of the context for screening.

3. The patient's interpretation of non-verbal communication.

In particular, she was struck by the absence of information that would help her decide whether to consent to answer the questions or to answer them truthfully. The way the EPDS was administered in Sheffield (Chapter 15) came in for criticism, with poor provision of information both before and after administration.

Honesty will be affected not only by the questionnaire layout and lack of instructions but also by the lack of information about the meaning of the measure. It is clearly totally unacceptable, and unethical, for women to be asked to undertake tests when they are left to guess the interpretations and consequences. Completing a questionnaire in such circumstances would constitute consent but it clearly does not constitute informed consent. This is exactly the type of maladministration that led to the NSC warning of the potential for harm in the use of postnatal depression screens and why they recommend their introduction be approved by a research ethics committee. It is not clear whether the reported Sheffield practice of administering the EPDS without explanation or instructions was a fault in the guidelines, the training or the practice of individual health visitors. It is no surprise that 'Most of the women's comments centred round the role of the health visitor and whether they were acting as agents of social control and whether they had any training in mental health.' (Chapter 15, p.158)

Another quote describes exactly the problems that concern Walter Barker: 'Without a questionnaire, but with some sort of guidelines for herself obviously so she knows, so a woman isn't faced with a cardboard figure which was once a health visitor, and now she's just like this alien sat on the sofa, do you know what I mean?' (Chapter 15, p.159).

Jan Cubison and Jane Munro attribute the problems in how women experienced the piece of paper to the health visitor coming to treat it as a routine administrative duty rather than to the questionnaire *per se*. Either way, the research question is 'can training in the use of measures within a person centred approach prevent this maladministration?'

Finally, Tessa Leverton makes a valuable suggestion. Once the purpose of the detection aids had been explained, why do we not let the woman decide whether a questionnaire or a discussion or both should be used to determine her need for additional support?

Decision to treat

Several chapters reminded us of a common mistake, that of using the EPDS as if it were a diagnostic instrument rather than a first screen or case finding measure. There are, in fact, two aspects to this error:

1. labelling the high-scoring woman's problems as postnatal depression

2. making the 'decision to treat' based on the EPDS score.

Frequently, measures such as the EPDS are criticized for their poor performance in these functions. This is inappropriate because such questionnaires are not designed to do this. It is a misuse to tell a high-scoring woman that she has postnatal depression. It is also a misuse use to tell a low-scoring woman that 'she is fine, she does not have postnatal depression'. Protocols set up so that different treatments or referrals follow directly from a defined score range *per se* are also misuses. The score indicates current levels of distress but only the possibility or probability of clinical levels of disorder. It also tells nothing else of the contextual and historical issues for this woman that determine the choice of approach. All perinatal mental health specialists and health professionals with an interest in this area are in agreement that a high score must be followed by an interview. It is the information gleaned in the interview that determines the decision to treat.

If you do use a questionnaire to increase detection of depression in postnatal women, how are you going to decide what the nature of their problem is and who should receive additional care or what they should receive? Do non-medical maternity and primary care health professionals

continue to make decisions in the same way they did before they introduced a questionnaire to improve detection? If they use questionnaires
that were originally designed to screen for a named psychiatric disorder
should they require all women confirming distress at interview to undertake a psychiatric diagnostic process before the decision on further help is
taken? To take the most frequent example, should the interview health visitors undertake with women who score high on questionnaires use a diagnostic framework to make the decision to treat?

Does this all come down to a philosophical position on whether health
visitors should be operating within the medical model? Should they
become diagnosticians who utilize diagnostic criteria to inform their own
decision to treat or should they operate as person centred practitioners
who hear a woman's story and consult the GP and mental health professional trainer when they have concerns? This issue of how to make the
decision to treat when screening questionnaires have been used as part of
the process was addressed in chapters 4 to 8. There are many ways to do
this.

In the context of frequent routine health visiting contacts

With a health visiting schedule that requires an antenatal home visit and a
series of postnatal visits, the health visitor knows the woman well (such as
the Cambridge service pre-1997). When she undertakes the interview
with a high scorer she soon knows whether the depression represents a
change from her normal state, how long it has lasted, what factors were
associated with its onset and what is affected by it. Sheelah Seeley's three
questions for high scorers helped to clarify this.

This is the context within which the EPDS was introduced following
the original Edinburgh study (Holden *et al.* 1989). The frequent visits,
with a relationship with the mother, is no more scientific than other aspects
of health visiting or indeed, general practice, but it is human. Unfortunately, it is also expensive for a service supplied to all women regardless of
need, so in some areas it has led to the cutbacks Sheelah Seeley and Ann
Girling described.

Second screen by psychiatric interview

The Edinburgh study employed the EPDS distributed in the clinic by
health visitors then placed in a postbox in a sealed envelope. It was scored
by the researcher and high scorers were interviewed by a psychiatrist
within four weeks. The psychiatrist undertook a diagnostic interview producing a differential diagnosis, permitting the exclusion of women whose

primary diagnosis was not depression as well as those who were no longer depressed.

Some health visitors have expressed concern about administering questionnaires in the clinic without ensuring the facilities to complete it, such as a table, a place for the baby, a screen from others overseeing their writing or any visible distress. There is also a risk that questionnaires distributed in a clinic will be inadequately described. If the health visitor is not handing it out herself, she would have to ensure adequate descriptions have been given in antenatal classes and her new birth visit and that the instructions attached to the questionnaire explain the whole system it forms a part of. In particular, it should be very clear how long it may be before the questionnaire is looked at and how to seek urgent help if completing the questionnaire clarifies their need for such help.

To replicate the original trial the high-scoring women will require a diagnostic interview, with a differential diagnosis of depression determining the decision to treat, using health visitor 'listening visits'. This would mean either the GP spends considerable time diagnosing women who do not have a disorder (false positives and spontaneous recoveries) or the health visitors would need to be fully trained in psychiatric diagnostic interviewing. This would not only be expensive but also raises the question of diagnoses being made by someone without the full medical training necessary to recognize medical conditions that include depressive symptomatology such as thyroid disorders.

Second screen by health visitor interview with DSM criteria for depression

Sheelah Seeley and Ann Girling administer the EPDS in a home visit so all women receive the clinical interview immediately following the EPDS, not on a separate occasion. For high scorers they suggest that diagnostic criteria for depression should be used in the interview to inform the decision to treat. Those with symptom severity above the diagnostic threshold for clinical depression should be treated. However, this will only determine whether the person has depressive symptomatology and whether these are at clinical levels of severity i.e. whether a psychiatrist would recognize them as a 'case', not whether a psychiatrist would consider them a 'case' of depression. The health visitor must take care not to imply that they have made a diagnosis of depression. If the woman or health visitor want to know the diagnosis before making a decision on treatment, the GP would still need to undertake a differential diagnosis. Whilst this is most likely to be depression, clinical levels of depression could be secondary to other diagnoses, particularly anxiety disorders, given the high levels of comorbidity in primary care. The advantage of including the DSM-IV criteria in the health visitor interview would be to reduce the times that the GP spent diagnosing women with no disorder. If the GP does not see her, this type of interview would enable the health visitor to let the woman know that her depressive symptomatology is sufficient to meet criteria for clinical levels of depression, so may facilitate the woman reaching the decision to accept help. It may also be used to limit referrals to secondary care to those above threshold on the DSM-IV criteria for depression or indeed in areas with cutbacks in the health visiting provision, to limit postnatal depression 'listening visits' to those with levels of symptomatology above thresholds traditionally used by psychiatric services. This may be particularly important in those areas where financial resources for mental health have led to raising the threshold for secondary care to those with severe and enduring mental health problems.

However, does the use of a diagnostic threshold approach, i.e. the use of a cut-off for the interview as well as for the questionnaire, reintroduce the pass/fail mentality?

Single screen with two measures

Lee et al. (2000) have demonstrated that specificity can be increased by using two questionnaires in a first screen such as the EPDS and GHQ. This could reduce the time spent by GPs on false positives. It also reduces the risk of missing those with psychomotor retardation. However, unless two questionnaires can reach 100% specificity, in other words function as diagnostic, all the previous problems with the diagnosis and decision to treat remain. They are just less common.

Double universal screen with one questionnaire

When Jeni Holden and colleagues first attempted to extend the original trial into the community the use of a psychiatric interview was dropped as expensive, impractical and unnecessary. The two-screen process was retained with the idea that requiring a raised score at both six weeks and at ten weeks would rule out transient depressions from unnecessarily consuming health visitor time in home visits for clinical interviews to make the decision to treat. However, when the health visitors were scoring the EPDS themselves, they were understandably reluctant to hold on to high scores and wait four weeks (Gerrard et al. 1993).

Second screen for antenatal or early postnatal high scorers only

Philip Boyce and Caroline Bell examine the possibility of a quite different two-stage model. In response to the finding that a screening policy was not being consistently pursued, they suggest identifying women at risk in the antenatal or early postnatal period who health professionals should make sure to see for a second screen process postnatally. They state: 'Such targeted screening programmes, where women identified (either antenatally or early postnatally) as high risk are then more assertively followed up, may be a more cost-effective strategy.' This clearly lends itself to a research study. In the first instance, a quasi-experimental design comparing two areas may be viable to compare their new strategy with an area operating by their old protocol of a single universal screen at six to eight weeks. Is this type of 'two bites of the cherry' cheaper than the more common single bite in cash-strapped areas? This may depend on whether cheaper strategies such as the educational package containing a self-completion EPDS are acceptable, given the views of the CPHVA that have been incorporated into the NSC guidelines.

Pattern of scores in women with a previous diagnosed depression

The strategy proposed by Kathleen Peindl relates specifically to women with a previous history of depression in the postnatal period, which had been confirmed by a diagnosis at the time. The strategy suggested is similar to that in the previous chapter. It identifies women at higher risk to focus further screening resources on this group.

Stepped care

The original Edinburgh data was scrutinized to determine which scores above the 9/10 threshold at six weeks were likely to remain high at ten weeks. It emerged that scores of 10 and 11 were likely to reduce below threshold whereas those of 12 or more were more likely to remain elevated. In a three-centre trial of training health visitors in this approach, it was therefore decided that the health visitor would respond to a score or 12 or more within two weeks. She would institute a second screen by interview allowing the woman to explain her problems in her own words. Consistent with the philosophy of person centred, non directive counselling on which the health visitor 'listening visit' approach was based, the 'decision to treat' would be made collaboratively based on the severity and duration of distress and perceived benefit of the visits or referral to GP or referral to mental health services. Only four listening visits were offered in the first instance so that progress could be reviewed and the decision to refer to the GP or mental health services revisited as an alternative to offering a further four sessions (Elliott et al. 2001; Gerrard et al. 1993). This model of trying a brief treatment in primary care and making referrals to a 'higher' level of care based on non-response is now generally referred to as a 'stepped care' model. It can operate without a diagnosis or with a diagnosis made after a basic intervention for maternal distress has already been tried. Either way, it requires ongoing supervision or consultancy from a mental health professional who can advise when the problems presented are mental health problems outside the boundaries for health visitors.

The tensions between philosophical models, which led to differing 'decision to treat' processes, were in fact already represented in the original Edinburgh study (Cox *et al.* 1987; Holden *et al.* 1989). The EPDS was developed from a medical model that perceived depression to be under-diagnosed, and consequently left untreated, prolonging the suffering of the woman and placing the baby and other family members at risk of developing problems secondary to her depression. The validity of the EPDS was measured by determining how well it predicted the diagnosis made in a psychiatric interview within the same visit. The value was therefore presented as determined by how accurate it was in separating those who had diagnosable depression and those without. Mismatches between EPDS score and diagnosis were referred to as 'false' positives and 'false' negatives. Consequently, improving on the EPDS was perceived in terms of improving the health visitor's ability to determine whether the diagnosis of postnatal depression would fit the maternal distress presented to them. Could they reduce the false positives and false negatives thus defined by interview techniques, such as those using DSM-IV criteria for depression?

The health visitor intervention in the same study was founded on the Rogerian approach to person centred, non directive counselling. This presupposes that people have within them the ability to discover the solutions to their own problems once they are provided with a safe therapeutic space within which to hear themselves tell their story. Medicalizing distress is typically anathema to a Rogerian counsellor who would view a diagnosis as pathologizing without providing any information relevant to the treatment process.

The issues to consider when deciding local resolution of these dilemmas and system choices therefore include the following.

- Pros and cons of using a second questionnaire or one questionnaire twice. These will vary with the questionnaires chosen and the time interval.

- The relative cost, as well as relative effectiveness and acceptability, of different systems, in particular the cost of clinical interviews with low-scoring women if the home visits are undertaken purely for the purpose of mood assessment.

- Pros and cons of diagnoses (Pilgrim 2005). This is extensively debated in the psychiatry versus antipsychiatry literature, which will not be reproduced here. Basically, diagnoses carry the risk of stigmatizing and pathologizing without themselves providing definitive treatment decisions. Not diagnosing carries the risk of providing an ineffective treatment contrary to the evidence base for the problem or a treatment which exacerbates the undiagnosed primary problem (though the latter is not likely with non invasive interventions such as 'active listening'). Problems that could be picked up by high scores on a depression questionnaire for which non directive counselling would not be the treatment of choice include severe depression (antidepressants), panic and phobias (cognitive behaviour therapy) and possibly traumatic stress reactions to the birth. Health visitors utilizing a diagnostic approach may be more attuned to assessing risk such as suicidal thoughts or thoughts of harm to the baby, and severity of depressive symptomatology.

- Pros and cons of diagnoses at the initial decision to treat or at the point of decision to refer. Delaying a referral for a diagnostic interview until a simple health visitor intervention has been tried reduces the risk of stigmatizing mild reactive problems but runs the risk of choosing a first-line treatment that is unlikely to be effective with the primary problem (as above), thereby delaying treatment suggested by the evidence base, which may involve risks if the severity of the depression is missed. However, we are aware of no study comparing a structured diagnostic interview with an interview encouraging the woman to describe her problems and issues in her own words followed by the health visitor discussing this with a mental health professional supervisor.

- Pros and cons of using one part of diagnostic process. Including an extract from the DSM-IV to determine the extent and severity of depressive symptoms provides more information for making the decision to treat and may reduce the risk of missing severity or other information relevant to risk. The information will be presented to the mental health supervisor or GP in a more systematic fashion. However, it may lead the health visitor or the woman to act as if a diagnosis had been made.

Finally, Philip Boyce and Caroline Bell contend that effective co-ordination of services across the potential care pathway is essential to the success of programmes that aim to increase detection and early intervention. This aspect is explicit in and central to systems that utilize training of multidisciplinary trainer groups as the medium for system change and is implied by the NSC statement regarding the importance of perinatal mental health services to the success of screening in primary care. However, the research base on these systems aspects of the introduction of detection aids is even weaker than that on the validity of measures and effectiveness of treatment (Elliott *et al.* 2003). A study may be viable if the system recommendation is held constant by choosing one of the many described in this book then comparing a number of areas in their adherence to the advocated systems of process change. In practice this will be difficult, since one of the key aspects advocated in the system change is stakeholder consultation on system choice, thus rendering it highly unlikely that areas could adhere to both the process recommendation on stakeholder consensus and the recommendation to adhere to the screening system nominated for evaluation. An alternative research study on this theme would be a comparison of implementation in areas with a local multidisciplinary team of trained trainers, areas where system change is driven by individual health visitors who have attended training courses and areas where implementation was driven by purchasers who view the use of the EPDS as demonstration of the implementation of evidence based practice.

False positives and false negatives: implications for the women

What does false positive and false negative really mean when the screening measure gives you a score on a relevant continuum and the cut-off between positive and negative is placed at different points according to the purpose? A false positive in a cancer test will cause unnecessary anxiety in a person who does not have cancer at all. Depression, on the other hand, lies on a continuum so a high score on a depression questionnaire will convey information. A false positive means that the duration or level of depressive symptomatology does not meet the psychiatric criteria for a primary diagnosis of depression. It does not mean that they are not feeling depressed. If scoring above the chosen cut-off means receiving an interview to determine whether more help is required because a self-report of dysphoria has been made, then false positives are not a real problem. It is only where inappropriate actions or labels follow from a high score in women whose depression is not above diagnostic threshold that a 'false positive' is a problem.

False negatives will consist of two main groups. The first will have symptoms not included in the scale, such as psychomotor symptoms. The ethical question would be should you not use a measure because it misses some, resulting in missing more? The second group will be those who choose not to represent their feelings accurately on the measure. This could be viewed as addressing the ethical issue of patient choice rather than an unethical fault in the measure. The authors have heard several anecdotal reports of deliberate concealment on the EPDS response to the health visitor, which is followed by help-seeking from a therapist or other professional prompted by the self-recognition resulting from reading the EPDS. The ethical problem does not arise from women choosing to produce false negatives. It arises from them feeling the need to do so, rather than feeling free to decline to complete the questionnaire offered.

False positives and false negatives: implications for health professionals

Walter Barker refers to 'the psychological consequences of pronouncing either a positive or a negative finding'. Clearly, this is a training issue rather than a necessary result of the use of a screening questionnaire. Local service users should be consulted on whether or how scores *per se* should be communicated to women. Similarly, denigration of 'intuition' is not inherent in the use of screening questionnaires but may, indeed, follow on from protocols for their use. It is far easier to write protocols that indicate clear pathways dependent on scores rather than incorporate a messy stage on interview and 'clinical judgement' to determine the decision to treat. Health professionals who introduce screening because of such protocols, rather than through training, will feel obliged to prefer the scale score. Actually, the little evidence that is available suggests that it is a screening questionnaire and health visitor judgement together that are the most predictive of diagnosable disorder (Leverton and Elliott 2000).

Managing risk

Barker articulates the concern that many people have with question 10, 'the thought of harming myself has occurred to me'. Many people have strong views about whether this question should be included, what it means, who can ask it, how they should ask it and what, in fact, they are really asking. The problem is that answers to the question have not been analysed for their relationship to fear of accidental injury, obsessional thoughts, suicidal thoughts, suicidal intent or deliberate self-harm such as arm cutting that is unrelated to suicidal ideation. Some of the women interviewed by Dawn Edge in Chapter 16 reported interpreting this question as reflecting not suicidal thoughts but self-harm (deliberate or accidental).

As with the other items, question 10 is there because depressed women scored on it more often than non-depressed women. It is not at all clear that there is any value to interpreting this item separately from the total score. It is understandable that, despite this, interviews would be offered to those who score on this item, regardless of whether their total score is also above the threshold for interview. Indeed Cox and Holden (2003) recommend this in their recent guide to the EPDS. However, great care must be taken not to over-interpret this item. It should not be assumed that those not scoring on question 10 have no suicidal ideation. Nor should a score on it lead to the panic, which some health professionals experience and which leads them to want to automatically call emergency services or a psychiatrist, which in turn could induce fear and panic in the woman and her family.

Tessa Leverton (Chapter 2) also stressed the importance of asking about thoughts of harming the baby. This is yet another area where research evidence is lacking. Does asking provide the information that prevents harm to children or does it alienate parents so that they decline treatment and thereby increase risk to the children? Is the answer to this different in depressed women who have had thoughts of harming their children to non-depressed women who have had such thoughts? Does it depend on when and how the question is asked? If so, what are the training needs?

Antenatal screening

Margaret Oates drew on the findings of the *Confidential Enquiry into Maternal Deaths* (CEMD) and made the case for screening at antenatal booking for risk of severe mental illness including puerperal psychosis which may be present in women who are well and socially advantaged.

Mary Ross-Davie and colleagues were less optimistic than Philip Boyce about the prospect of clinically meaningful antenatal identification of risk of postnatal depression and the cost-effectiveness of primary prevention, given the existing evidence base. Austin and Lumley (2003) argue that predictive indices can be improved by adding factors such as personality, a past history of abuse and postnatal events. Unfortunately these carry practical and ethical problems. Personality measures take time, language and reading skills. Abuse questions may prove unacceptable in this context. Waiting to add postnatal events to the predictive index removes the advantage of time to intervene.

Mary Ross-Davie and colleagues endorsed the recommendations of the CEMD and implemented changes in the screening questions for mental health at booking despite the lack of evidence for effectiveness. Whilst it is possible to monitor change in the information obtained at screening, there are no plans for an RCT or even the availability of data prior to the new service to provide a naturalistic comparison of outcomes. It remains merely an article of faith that sensitive screening questions about previous mental illness to enable referral to non-stigmatizing mental health services provided within a maternity unit will prevent deaths.

Detection in different contexts

Postnatal depression screening was first tried in Edinburgh in the mid-1980s. Even if we accept that validity of measures in the clinical context would not differ from the research context within Edinburgh, different cultural contexts to that in Edinburgh may mean not only that the validity of the measure is different, but that all aspects of the whole system must be revisited. The difference in cultural context may be due to different health care cultures such as in the US and Australia, or difference in the ethnic or religious beliefs and traditions in the majority and minority groups.

Bryanne Barnett and her colleagues put the context within which detection aids are introduced to centre stage from the outset. Their system starts from the presupposition that all families need support at the time of transition and that the task is to match the level of support to need. Framed in this way, they suggest that the term 'screening' is a misnomer and therefore that the criteria employed by medical screening committees are not applicable. They refer to using a clinical assessment of all the things that research and clinical practice suggest might make life difficult rather than of 'screening for risk'. They are fortunate to have a range of services available to match the answers given and avoid any sense of pass/fail administrations or labelling. Context is also addressed at the level of the individual woman and at the level of the individual staff member's support needs.

They have included evaluations of the views of both users: the pregnant woman and the interviewing midwife. The authors are clearly in favour of the process of improved detection but were open about the negatives, which speak for themselves. What they do not have is a validation of the EPDS *per se* as used in this context. Would a trial of their system with and without the EPDS be essential or a waste of resources? Is the whole system too expensive for most health care systems? If so, which aspects would be most valuable to copy?

Lisa Segre and Mike O'Hara describe the background to the development of screening within a very different health system to that in the UK and Australia. For example, they raise one risk of screening being the creation of a mental health file that would increase the price of their health insurance in the future. This is a classic example of the stigma that can arise from telling someone about your unhappiness. Should the insurer be encouraged not to set up a file until a health professional has established that a label of clinical depression is accurate and helpful? What should be stated in the letter asking women to complete and return the EPDS?

The system within the Healthy Start public sector programme also labels the women as having mental health problems, since a score of 12 or more results in referral into the mental health system. Research has shown that detection can be increased by introducing questionnaires such as the EPDS. However, in the US as elsewhere, the overall impact of the use of screening questionnaires on outcomes has yet to be determined.

Abi Sobowale and Cheryll Adams began by considering the problems of the lack of validated screening questionnaires for many cultural groups in the UK including long-lasting depressions due to missed opportunities for earlier detection. Extensive user consultation led them in directions that they had not anticipated. The result was systems to encourage self-referral, avoiding the ethical issue for screening raised by Judy Shakespeare and culturally appropriate materials that facilitate discussion of psychological issues. Unlike all the existing screening measures in mental health, the development of these materials demonstrates a model of good practice in user consultation. Also, unlike existing screening measures, the relationship of responses to these materials to diagnoses of mental illness, whether within the majority culture or their own minority culture, is untested and unknown. As the authors themselves say, however, the big worry is how families will react to health professionals raising questions about the mental health of a family member.

Reporting research findings

Jo Green provides data to back up her argument that the EPDS scores lie on a continuum. Research reports will benefit from providing analyses utilizing the full range of scores. This will usually be as well as, not instead of, analyses using a cut-off to indicate numbers in the range indicative of probable or possible diagnosable depression. The problem arises when determining what it is a continuum of. When used as a continuum, the probability of a diagnosis increases with increasing scores but this relationship is not a perfect linear relationship and, besides, referring to scores as level of probability of diagnosis of depression is clumsy. Many papers refer to high EPDS scores as reflecting postnatal depressive symptomatology, which is preferable to referring to high scorers as having postnatal depression, since casual readers of a paper may believe that the diagnosis has been made. However, this new terminology seems to have led to the assumption that the EPDS represents a checklist of all the symptoms of depression and that items can be analysed to produce symptom profiles. Perhaps Jo Green is right to suggest that emotional well being, or levels of dysphoria are more fitting, less misleading descriptors. The downside of those terms, however, is that they lose sight of the important implications for mental health needs in the high score ranges.

Ideas for further research

Walter Barker's preference for the style of empowering support and nutritional advice in his programme over the listening visits based on non directive counselling (Holden *et al.* 1989) could easily be submitted to an RCT.

Similarly, the idea of using the EPDS to 'confirm or disconfirm judgements' that there is ' a cause for concern' could be tested by an RCT. This could then be compared with systems where the EPDS is used as the first screen and the health visitors' judgement is used to confirm or disconfirm only in high scorers, and those such as recommended by the CPHVA to use both together with everyone.

The research in Chapter 15 by Jan Cubison and Jane Munro was undertaken because severely ill women referred to secondary care reported not completing the EPDS as instructed, resulting in deliberately inaccurate scores. For these women the important issue is whether that experience caused them to delay help-seeking or whether it clarified their problems for them and prompted them to seek help from someone other than the health visitor, or whether it made no difference. If an RCT is ever devised to compare systems in different areas, a key comparison will be of how quickly severely ill women reach secondary care or are prescribed antidepressants by their GP.

The administration section raised the question of whether the use of questionnaires like the EPDS damages, rather than enhances, the performance of health visitors. Jan Cubison and Jane Munro attribute the problems in how women experienced the piece of paper to the health visitor coming to treat it as a routine administrative duty, rather than to the EPDS *per se*. Either way, the research question is 'Can training in the use of measures within a person centred approach prevent this reaction of health visitors to a piece of paper?'

Finding a way forward

It is clear that so far research has left us with more unanswered questions than answers. Fortunately, or unfortunately, the guidelines for evidence based practice in mental health do not typically rely on the production of a definitive study (Geddes *et al.* 1998). The best available research evidence is combined with consensus from clinical experts and the views of users.

Where consensus has not been or cannot be achieved nationally, then consultation should be undertaken locally. Besides, decisions about screening cannot be made without a review of local resources and mapping of care pathways across services and agencies. Once these are clear, consultation can take place with a variety of maternity service users to determine whether they want the service to wait for women to self-report depression or other difficulties or whether they want services to make systematic inquiry about their psychological well being and need for emotional support.

Ethical issues will automatically be covered in these consultation processes so that they have been addressed well before the point of application for ethical committee approval of research or audit evaluations. The process for ensuring evidence based practice in detection and treatment of perinatal mental health problems therefore requires multidisciplinary, multiagency steering group and wider stakeholder consultation. This will produce agreed processes for identifying mental health problems to or by the health service, and widely agreed care pathways for those thus identified.

Nevertheless, we have to end this book with an ethical dilemma that the research has not, and may never, answer. Is the ethical position for mental health different to that for medicine? Judy Shakespeare quotes Cochrane and Holland (1971, p.30):

> We believe there is an ethical difference between everyday medical practice and screening. If a patient asks a medical practitioner for help, the doctor does the best he can. He is not responsible for defects in medical knowledge. If, however, the practitioner initiates the screening procedures he is in a very different position. He should, in our view, have conclusive evidence that screening can alter the natural history of disease in a significant proportion of those screened.

The difference is that, unlike GPs, midwives and health visitors are explicitly charged with providing holistic care and with health promotion. They are already viewed as carrying responsibility for the psychological well being of mothers and families. However, they are no longer resourced to undertake extensive interviews at regular intervals. If there is evidence that knowing a woman they care for is depressed results in worse care and worse outcomes, then clearly systems should be in place to ensure that they do not know. This is not a flippant remark. Mental health problems still carry a stigma in most societies and even health professionals could alter their care in detrimental ways when given this information. We know that is not the case in studies such as Holden *et al.* (1989), but we do not know what happens outside of that supportive research context. Managers and purchasers may like to think about that quote in terms of their ethical duty to ensure that anyone who is asked to improve their detection of mental health problems has the appropriate skills, attitudes and back-up services to ensure care is better not worse when they obtain that information. A reasonable ethical position might be, if we cannot be sure that increased detection improves care we should not increase detection: if, for example, you suspect health visitors in your area are misusing the EPDS to stigmatize rather than help.

However, is it ethical to stop at that position and justify doing nothing? Is it ethical to say this is not permanent, we are waiting for the studies the NSC is looking for, when there are no such studies currently in place and no prospect that studies will ever be viable to fully meet their criteria? Is it ethical to do nothing when the evidence that *does* exist suggests that treatment 'works' and untreated depression at this sensitive life point is particularly distressing for women and their families? Do we really not have enough collective knowledge to know how to help depressed women and their families?

We do not know the answer to this. We can, however, state why we continue to look for the answers in this very complex area. This is encapsulated in the title of a recent book of accounts from sufferers of perinatal mental health problems. The book by Cara Aiken, *Surviving Post-Natal Depression*, carries the subtitle *At Home, No One Hears You Scream*.

The Edinburgh Postnatal Depression Scale

The scale was developed and validated in 1987. The copyright is held by the Royal College of Psychiatrists and it appears here with their permission. Cox and Holdon (2003) emphasise the copyright issues, including that the scale should be reproduced in full and must include the full reference such as in the example which follows.

The Edinburgh Postnatal Depression Scale

Name...

Address..

Baby's age................................

As you have recently had a baby, we would like to know how you are feeling. Please UNDERLINE the answer which comes closest to how you have felt IN THE PAST 7 DAYS, not just how you feel today.

Here is an example already completed:

I have felt happy:

<u>Yes, most of the time</u>
Yes, some of the time
No, not very often
No, not at all

This would mean: 'I have felt happy most of the time' during the past week. Please complete the other questions the same way.

In the past 7 days:

1. I have been able to laugh and see the funny side of things:
   As much as I always could
   Not quite so much now
   Definitely not so much now
   Not at all

2. I have looked forward with enjoyment to things:
   As much as I ever did
   Rather less than I used to
   Definitely less than I used to
   Hardly at all

3. I have blamed myself unnecessarily when things went wrong:
    Yes, most of the time
    Yes, some of the time
    Not very often
    No, never

4. I have been anxious or worried for no good reason:
    No, not at all
    Hardly ever
    Yes, sometimes
    Yes, very often

5. I have felt scared or panicky for no very good reason:
    Yes, quite a lot
    Yes, sometimes
    No, not much
    No, not at all

6. Things have been getting on top of me:
    Yes, most of the time I haven't been able to cope at all
    Yes, sometimes I haven't been coping as well as usual
    No, most of the time I have coped quite well
    No, I have been coping as well as ever

7. I have been so unhappy that I have had difficulty sleeping:
    Yes, most of the time
    Yes, sometimes
    No, not very often
    No, not at all

8. I have felt sad or miserable:
    Yes, most of the time
    Yes, sometimes
    No, not very often
    No, not at all

9. I have been so unhappy that I have been crying:
    Yes, most of the time
    Yes, quite often
    Only occasionally
    No, not at all

10. The thought of harming myself has occurred to me:
    Yes, quite often
    Sometimes
    Hardly ever
    Never

(Cox, J. Holden, J.M. and Sagovsky, R. (1987) 'Detection of postnatal depression. Development of the 10-item Edinburgh Postnatal Depression Scale. *British Journal of Psychiatry* 150, 782–786.

The following version was used in the multicentre trial of health visitor training (Elliott *et al.*, 2001). The title is abbreviated, 'How are you feeling?' has been added and item 4 reads '...for no *very* good reason'. This was added in an attempt to increase the sensitivity of the scale and this version appeared in Cox and Holden (1994), *Perinatal Psychiatry: Use and Misuse of the Edinburgh Postnatal Depression Scale*. Reproduced with permission of the Royal College of Psychiatrists.

The EPDS

Health visitor...Number..............................

Today's date..Baby's age............................

Baby's date of birth.................................Birth weight.....................

Triplets/twins/single................................Male/female......................

How Are You Feeling?

As you have recently had a baby, we would like to know how you are feeling now. Please *underline* the answer which comes closest to how you have felt in the past 7 days, not just how you feel today. Here is an example already completed:

I have felt happy:
> Yes, most of the time
> Yes, some of the time
> No, not very often
> No, not at all.

This would mean: 'I have felt happy some of the time' during the past week. Please complete the other questions in the same way.

In the past 7 days

1. I have been able to laugh and see the funny side of things:
   As much as I always could
   Not quite so much now
   Definitely not so much now
   Not at all

2. I have looked forward with enjoyment to things:
   As much as I ever did
   Rather less than I used to
   Definitely less than I used to
   Hardly at all

3. I have blamed myself unnecessarily when things went wrong:
    Yes, most of the time
    Yes, some of the time
    Not very often
    No never

4. I have felt worried and anxious for no very good reason:
    No, not at all
    Hardly ever
    Yes, sometimes
    Yes, very often

5. I have felt scared or panicky for no very good reason:
    Yes, quite a lot
    Yes, sometimes
    No, not much
    No, not at all

6. Things have been getting on top of me:
    Yes, most of the time I haven't been able to cope at all
    Yes, sometimes I haven't been coping as well as usual
    No, most of the time I have coped quite well
    No, I have been coping as well as ever

7. I have been so unhappy that I have had difficulty sleeping:
    Yes, most of the time
    Yes, sometimes
    Not very often
    No, not at all

8. I have felt sad or miserable:
    Yes, most of the time
    Yes, quite often
    Not very often
    No, not at all

9. I have been so unhappy that I have been crying:
    Yes, most of the time
    Yes, quite often
    Only occasionally
    No, never

10. The thought of harming myself has occurred to me:
    Yes, quite often
    Sometimes
    Hardly ever
    Never

Several other versions, including those used in the studies described by Edge (Chapter 16), Shakespeare (Chapter 1) and Cubison and Munro (Chapter 15), replaced underlining the correct answer with tick boxes, for example:

1. I have been able to laugh and see the funny side of things:

As much as I always could	☐
Not quite so much now	☐
Definitely not so much now	☐
Not at all	☐

A six-item 'postnatal depression questionnaire' (adapted and abridged from the original EPDS) was used by Cubison and Munro (Chapter 15), containing only items 2, 4, 7, 8, 9 and 10. This must not be reproduced under the heading of or be referred to as the Edinburgh Postnatal Depression Scale or EPDS. In this text, therefore, it is referred to as the 'postnatal depression questionnaire', with the derivation from the EPDS described in Chapter 15.

In the past 7 days:

I have looked forward with enjoyment to things:

		I have felt sad or miserable:	
As much as I ever did	☐	Yes, most of the time	☐
Rather less than I used to	☐	Yes, sometimes	☐
Definitely less than I used to	☐	Not very often	☐
Hardly at all	☐	No, not at all	☐

I have felt worried and anxious for no good reason

		I have been so unhappy that I have been crying:	
No, not at all	☐	Yes, most of the time	☐
Hardly ever	☐	Yes, quite often	☐
Yes, sometimes	☐	Only occasionally	☐
Yes, very often	☐	No, never	☐

I have been so unhappy that I have difficulty sleeping

		The thought of harming myself has occurred to me:	
Yes, most of the time	☐	Yes, quite often	☐
Yes, sometimes	☐	Sometimes	☐
Not very often	☐	Hardly ever	☐
No, not at all	☐	Never	☐

Thank you for taking the time to fill in this form. It will help us to help you and your baby and other families in Sheffield.

Bibliography of translations and validation studies

These articles include translations and validations of the Edinburgh Postnatal Depression Scale, the Postpartum Depression Screening Scale, predictive indices, psychometric studies of other instruments used during pregnancy or the postpartum period and comparisons between measures.

An asterisk (*) denotes validation against a standardized diagnostic interview or recognized diagnostic criteria.

Postnatal

*Areias, M.E., Kumar, R., Barros, H. and Figueiredo, E. (1996) 'Comparative incidence of depression in women and men, during pregnancy and after childbirth. Validation of the Edinburgh Postnatal Depression Scale in Portuguese mothers.' *British Journal of Psychiatry 169*, 1, 30–35.

Ascaso Terrén, C., Garcia Esteve, L., Navarro, P., Aguado, J., Ojuel, J. and Tarragona, M.J. (2003) 'Prevalencia de la depressión posparto en las madres españolas: Comparacíon de la estimacíon mediante la entrevista clínica estructurada y la escala de depressión posparto de Edimburgo.' *Medicina Clinica 120*, 9, 326–329.

Aydin, N., Inandi, T., Yigit, A. and Hogougil, N.N.S. (2004) 'Validation of the Turkish version of the Edinburgh Postnatal Depression Scale among women in their first postpartum year.' *Social Psychiatry and Psychiatric Epidemilogy, 39*, 483–486.

*Bagedahl-Strindlund, M. and Monson Borjesson, K. (1998) 'Postnatal depression: a hidden illness.' *Acta Psychiatrica Scandinavica 98*, 4, 272–275. Swedish

Banerjee, N., Banerjee, A., Kriplani, A. and Saxena, S. (1999) 'Evaluation of the Edinburgh Postnatal Depression Scale in evaluation of postpartum depression in a rural community in India.' *International Journal of Social Psychiatry 46*, 1, 74–75. Hindi

*Barnett, B., Matthey, S. and Gyaneshwar, R. (1999). 'Screening for postnatal depression in women of non-English speaking background.' *Archives of Women's Mental Health 2*, 67–74. Arabic and Vietnamese

*Benvenuti, P., Ferrara, M., Niccolai, C., Valoriani, V. and Cox, J.L. (1999) 'The Edinburgh Postnatal Depression Scale: Validation for an Italian sample.' *Journal of Affective Disorders 53*, 2, 137–141.

*Bergant, A.M., Nguyen, T., Heim, K., Ulmer, H. and Dapunt, O. (1998) 'German language version and validation of the Edinburgh postnatal depression scale.' *Deutsche Medizinische Wochenschrift 123*, 3, 35–40.

*Berle, J.Ø., Aarre, T.F., Mykletun, A., Dahl, A.A. and Holsten, F. (2003) 'Screening for postnatal depression: Validation of the Norwegian version of the Edinburgh Postnatal Depression Scale, and assessment of risk factors for postnatal depression.' *Journal of Affective Disorders 76*, 151–156.

*Boyce, P., Stubbs, J. and Todd, A. (1993) 'The Edinburgh Postnatal Depression Scale: Validation for an Australian sample.' *Australian and New Zealand Journal of Psychiatry 27*, 472–476.

*Carpiniello, B., Pariante, C.M., Serri, F., Costa, G. and Carta, M.G. (1997) 'Validation of the Edinburgh Postnatal Depression Scale in Italy.' *Journal of Psychosomatic Obstetrics and Gynecology 18*, 4, 280–285.

Clifford, C., Day, A. and Cox, J. (1997) 'Developing the use of the EPDS in a Punjabi-speaking community.' *British Journal of Midwifery 5*, 10, 616–619.

Clifford, C., Day, A., Cox, J. and Werrett, J. (1999) 'A cross-cultural analysis of the use of the Edinburgh Postnatal Depression Scale (EPDS) in health visiting practice.' *Journal of Advanced Nursing 30*, 3, 655–664. Punjabi

*Cox, J.L, Holden, J.M. and Sagovsky, R. (1987) 'Detection of postnatal depression: The development of the 10-item Edinburgh Postnatal Depression Scale.' *British Journal of Psychiatry 150*, 782–786.

Da-Silva, V.A., Moraes-Santos, A.R., Carvalho, M.S., Martins, M.L.P. and Teixeira, N.A. (1998) 'Prenatal and postnatal depression among low income Brazilian women.' *Brazilian Journal of Medical and Biological Research 31*, 799–804. Portuguese

Des Rivières-Pigeon, C., Sèguin, L., Brodeur, J.M., Perreault, M., Boyer, G., Colin, C. and Goulet, L. (2000) 'L'échelle de dépression postnatale d'Édimbourg: Validité au Québec auprès de femmes de statut socio-économic faible.' *Revue Canadienne de Santé Mentale Communitaire 19*, 1, 201–214.

*Eberhard-Gran, M., Eskild, A., Tambs, K., Schei, B. and Opjordsmoen, S. (2001) 'The Edinburgh Postnatal Depression Scale: Validation in a Norwegian community sample.' *Nordic Journal of Psychiatry 55*, 2, 113–117.

*Felice, E. (1999) 'The emotional disorders during pregnancy and the postpartum period.' Unpublished MPhil thesis. Keele University. Maltese

Fisch, R.Z., Tadmor, O.P., Dankar, R. and Diamant, Y.Z. (1997) 'Postnatal depression: A prospective study of its prevalence, incidence and psychosocial determinants in an Israeli sample.' *Journal of Obstetric and Gynaecological Research 23*, 6, 547–554. Hebrew

Fuggle, P., Glover, L., Khan, F. and Haydon, K. (2002) 'Screening for postnatal depression in Bengali women: Preliminary observations from using a translated version of the Edinburgh Postnatal Depression Scale (EPDS).' *Journal of Reproductive and Infant Psychology 20*, 2, 71–82.

*Garcia-Esteve, L., Ascaso, C., Ojuel, J. and Navarro, P. (2003) 'Validation of the Edinburgh Postnatal Depression Scale (EPDS) in Spanish mothers.' *Journal of Affective Disorders 75*, 1, 71–76.

*Ghubash, R., Abou-Saleh, M. and Daradkeh, T. (1997) 'The validity of the Arabic Edinburgh Postnatal Depression Scale.' *Social Psychiatry and Psychiatric Epidemiology 32*, 8, 474–476.

Glasser, S. and Barell, V. (1999) 'Depression scale for research in and identification of postpartum depression.' *Harefuah 136*, 10, 764–768, 843–844. Hebrew

Glasser, S., Barell, V., Shoham, A., Ziv, V., Lusky, A. and Hart, S. (1998) 'Prospective study of postpartum depression in an Israeli cohort: Prevalence, incidence and demographic risk factors.' *Journal of Psychosomatic Obstetrics and Gynaecology 19*, 3, 155–164. Hebrew and Russian

Glaze, R. and Cox, J.L. (1991) 'Validation of a computerised version of the 10-item (self-rating) Edinburgh Postnatal Depression Scale.' *Journal of Affective Disorders 22*, 1–2, 73–77.

*Guedeney, N. and Fermanian, J. (1998) 'Validation study of the French version of the Edinburgh Postnatal Depression Scale (EPDS): New results about use and psychometric properties.' *European Psychiatry 13*, 83–89.

Heh, S. (2001) 'Validation of the Chinese version of the Edinburgh Postnatal Depression Scale: Detecting postnatal depression in Taiwanese women.' *Journal of Nursing Research 9*, 2, 105–112.

Herz, E., Thoma, M., Umek, W., Gruber, K., Linzmayer, L., Walcher, W., Philipp, T. and Putz, M. (1997) 'Nicht-psychotische postpartale depression: Pilotstudie zur epidemiologie und risikofaktoren.' *Geburtshilfe und Frauenheilkd 57*, 282–288.

*Jadresic, E., Araya, R. and Jara, C. (1995). 'Validation of the Edinburgh Postnatal Depression Scale (EPDS) in Chilean postpartum women.' *Journal of Psychosomatic Obstetrics and Gynecology 16*, 4, 187–191.

Kit, K.L., Grace, J. and Jegasothy, R. (1997) 'Incidence of postnatal depression in Malaysian women.' *Journal of Obstetric and Gynaecological Research 23*, 1, 85–89. Malay

*Lawrie, T., Hofmeyr, G., de Jager, M. and Berk, M. (1998) 'Validation of the Edinburgh Postnatal Depression Scale on a cohort of South African women.' *South African Medical Journal 88*, 10, 1340–44.

*Lee, D.T.S., Yip, S.K., Chiu, H.F.K., Leung, T.Y.S., Chan, K.P.M., Chau, I.O.L., Leung, H.C.M. and Leung, T.K.H. (1998) 'Detecting postnatal depression in Chinese women: Validation of the Chinese version of the Edinburgh Postnatal Depression Scale.' *British Journal of Psychiatry 172*, 433–437.

Lundh, W. and Gyllang, C. (1993) 'Use of the Edinburgh Postnatal Depression Scale in some Swedish Child Health Centres.' *Scandinavian Journal of Caring Sciences 7*, 149–154.

*Matthey, S. and Barnett, B. (1997) 'Translation and validation of the Edinburgh Postnatal Depression Scale into Vietnamese and Arabic.' In B. Ferguson and D. Barnes (eds) *Perspective on Transcultural Mental Health*. Sydney: Transcultural Mental Health Centre.

*Murray, L. and Carothers, A.D. (1990) 'The validation of the EPDS on a community sample.' *British Journal of Psychiatry 157*, 288–290.

Nielsen Forman, D., Videbech, P., Hedegaard, M., Dalby Salvig, J. and Secher, N.J. (2000) 'Postpartum depression: Identification of women at risk.' *British Journal of Obstetrics and Gynaecology 107*, 1210–17. Danish

Okano, T., Murata, M., Masuji, F., Tamaki, R., Nomura, J., Miyaoka, H. and Kitamura, T. (1996) 'Validation and reliability of Japanese version of EPDS (Edinburgh Postnatal Depression Scale).' *Archives of Clinical and Diagnostic Evaluation (Seishinka Shindago) 7*, 525–533.

*Patel, V., Rodrigues, M. and De Souza, N. (2002). 'Gender, poverty and postnatal depression: A study of mothers in Goa, India.' *American Journal of Psychiatry 159*, 43–47. Konkani

Pen, T., Wang, L., Jin, Y. and Fan, X. (1994) 'The evaluation and application of the Edinburgh Postnatal Depression Scale.' *Chinese Mental Health 8*, 1, 18–19.

Pop, V.J., Komproe, I.H. and van-Son, M.J. (1992) 'Characteristics of the Edinburgh Postnatal Depression Scale in the Netherlands.' *Journal of Affective Disorders 26*, 105–110.

Regmi, S., Sligl, W., Carter, D., Grut, W., Seear, M. (2002) 'A controlled study of postpartum depression among Nepalese women: Validation of the Edinburgh Postpartum Depression Scale in Kathmandu.' *Tropical Medicine and International Health 7*, 4, 378–382.

Small, R., Lumley, J., Yelland, J., Rice, P.L., Cotronei, V. and Warren, R. (1999) 'Cross-cultural research: Trying to do it better. 2. Enhancing data quality.' *Australian and New Zealand Journal of Public Health 23*, 390–395. Vietnamese, Turkish and Tagalog

Teissedre, F. and Chabrol, H. (2004) 'Detecting women at risk for postnatal depression using the Edinburgh Postnatal Depression Scale at 2 to 3 days postpartum.' *Canadian Journal of Psychiatry – Revue Canadienne de Psychiatrie 49*, 1, 51–54.

Thome, M. (1996) 'Distress in mothers with difficult infants in the community: An intervention study.' Unpublished PhD thesis. Queen Margaret College Edinburgh and the Open University. Icelandic

Thorpe, K.J., Dragonas, T. and Golding, J. (1992) 'The effects of psychosocial factors on the mother's emotional well-being during early parenthood: A cross-cultural study of Britain and Greece.' *Journal of Reproductive and Infant Psychology 10*, 205–217.

*Uwakwe, R. (2003) 'Affective (depressive) morbidity in puerperal Nigerian women: Validation of the Edinburgh Postnatal Depression Scale.' *Acta Psychiatrica Scandinavica 107*, 4, 251–259.

*Vega-Dienstmaier, J.M., Suarez, G.M. and Sanchez, M.C. (2002) 'Validation of a Spanish version of the Edinburgh Postnatal Depression Scale.' *Actas Espanolas de Psiquiatria 30*, 2, 106–111.

*Wickberg, B. and Hwang, C.P. (1996) 'The Edinburgh Postnatal Depression Scale: Validation on a Swedish community sample.' *Acta Psychiatrica Scandinavica 94*, 3, 181–184.

*Zelkowitz, P. and Milet, T.H. (1995) 'Screening for postpartum depression in a community sample.' *Canadian Journal of Psychiatry 40*, 2, 80–86. Telephone screening

There is a detailed review of many of the above studies in:

Eberhard-Gran, M., Eskild, A., Tambs, K., Opjordsmoen, S. and Samuelson, S.O. (2001) 'Review of validation studies of the Edinburgh Postnatal Depression Scale.' *Acta Psychiatrica Scandinavica 104*, 243–249.

Pregnancy

Brouwers, E.P.M., van Baar, A.L. and Pop, V.J. (2001) 'Does the Edinburgh Postnatal Depression Scale measure anxiety?' *Journal of Psychosomatic Research 51*, 5, 659–663.

Jomeen, J. and Martin, C.R. (2004) 'Confirmation of an occluded anxiety component within the Edinburgh Postnatal Depression Scale (EPDS) during early pregnancy.' *Journal of Reproductive and Infant Psychology* (in press).

*Murray, D. and Cox, J. (1990) 'Screening for depression during pregnancy with the Edinburgh Postnatal Depression Scale (EPDS).' *Journal of Reproductive and Infant Psychology 8*, 99–107.

Other populations

*Becht, M.C., Van Erp, C.F., Teeuwisse, M.T., Van Heck, G.L., Van Son, M.J. and Pop, V.J. (2001) 'Measuring depression in women around menopausal age: Towards a validation of the Edinburgh Depression Scale.' *Journal of Affective Disorders 63*, 209–213.

*Cox, J.L., Chapman, G., Murray, D. and Jones, P. (1996). 'Validation of the Edinburgh Postnatal Depression Scale (EPDS) in non-postnatal women.' *Journal of Affective Disorders 39*, 3, 185–189.

*Lee, D.T., Wong, C.K., Ungvari, G.S., Cheung, L.P., Haines, C.J. and Chung, T.K. (1997) 'Screening psychiatric morbidity after miscarriage: Application of the 30-item General Health Questionnaire and the Edinburgh Postnatal Depression Scale.' *Psychosomatic Medicine 59*, 2, 207–210.

*Lloyd-Williams, M., Friedman, T. and Rudd, N. (2000) 'Criterion validation of the Edinburgh postnatal depression scale as a screening tool for depression in patients with advanced metastatic cancer.' *Journal of Pain and Symptom Management 20*, 4, 259–265.

*Matthey, S., Barnett, B., Kavanagh, D.J. and Howie, P. (2001) 'Validation of the Edinburgh Postnatal Depression Scale for men, and comparison of item endorsement with their partners.' *Journal of Affective Disorders 64*, 2–3, 175–184.

Moran, T. and O'Hara, M. (2004) 'Taking the partner's perspective: The Edinburgh Postnatal Depression Scale–Partner (EPDS-P).' Paper presented at the 2nd World Congress on Women's Mental Health 17–20 March, Washington DC.

*Thorpe, K. (1993) 'A study of the use of the Edinburgh Postnatal Depression Scale with parent groups outside the postpartum period.' *Journal of Reproductive and Infant Psychology 11*, 2, 119–125.

Postpartum Depression Screening Scale

Beck, C.T., Bernal, H. and Froman, R.D. (2003) 'Methods to document semantic equivalence of a translated scale.' *Research in Nursing and Health 26*, 1, 64–73.

Beck, C.T. and Gable, R.K. (2000) 'Postpartum Depression Screening Scale: Development and psychometric testing.' *Nursing Research 49*, 5, 272–282.

*Beck, C.T. and Gable, R.K. (2001) 'Further validation of the Postpartum Depression Screening Scale.' *Nursing Research 50*, 3, 155–164.

Beck, C.T. and Gable, R.K. (2001) 'Ensuring content validity: An illustration of the process.' *Journal of Nursing Measurement 9*, 2, 201–215.

Beck, C.T. and Gable, R.K. (2003) 'Postpartum depression screening scale: Spanish version.' *Nursing Research 52*, 5, 296–306.

*Clemmens, D., Driscoll, J.W. and Beck, C.T. (2004) 'Postpartum depression as profiled through the Postpartum Depression Screening Scale.' *American Journal of Maternal Child Nursing 29*, 3, 180–185.

Antenatal questionnaires to predict postnatal depression

Appleby, L., Gregoire, A., Platz, C., Prince, M. and Kumar, R. (1994) 'Screening women for high risk of postnatal depression.' *Journal of Psychosomatic Research 38*, 6, 539–545.

Beck, C.T. (1998) 'A checklist to identify women at risk for developing postpartum depression.' *Journal of Obstetric, Gynecologic and Neonatal Nursing 27*, 1, 39–46.

Beck, C.T. (2002) 'Revision of the Postpartum Depression Predictors Inventory.' *Journal of Obstetric, Gynecologic and Neonatal Nursing 31*, 4, 394–402.

*Brugha.T., Wheatley, S., Taub, N.A., Culverwell, S., Friedman, T., Kirwan, P.H., Jones, D.R. and Shapiro, D.A. (2000) 'Pragmatic randomized trial of antenatal intervention to prevent postnatal depression by reducing psychosocial risk factors.' *Psychological Medicine 30*, 1273–81.

Buist, A., Westley, D. and Hill, C. (1998) 'Antenatal prevention of postnatal depression.' *Archives of Women's Mental Health 1*, 4, 167–173.

*Cooper, P.J., Murray, L., Hooper, R. and West, A. (1996) 'The development and validation of a predictive index for postpartum depression.' *Psychological Medicine 26*, 627–634.

Hanna, B., Jarman, H., Savage, S. and Layton, K. (2004) 'The early detection of postpartum depression: Midwives and nurses trial a checklist.' *Journal of Obstetric, Gynecological and Neonatal Nursing 33*, 2, 191–197.

Honey, K.L., Bennett, P. and Morgan, M. (2003) 'Predicting postnatal depression.' *Journal of Affective Disorders 76*, 201–210.

Johanson, R., Chapman, G., Murray, D., Johnson, I. and Cox, J. (2000) 'The North Staffordshire Maternity Hospital prospective study of pregnancy-associated depression.' *Journal of Psychosomatic Obstetrics and Gynaecology 21*, 93–99.

Leverton, T.J. and Elliott, S.A. (1989) 'Transition to parenthood groups: A preventive intervention for perinatal depression?' In E.V. van Hall and W. Everard (eds) *The Free Woman: Women's Health in the 1990s. Invited papers of the 9th International Conference of Psychosomatic Obstetrics and Gynaecology.* Lancaster: Parthenon.

Nielsen Forman, D., Videbech, P., Hedegaard, M., Dalby Salvig, J. and Secher, N.J. (2000) 'Postpartum depression: Identification of women at risk.' *British Journal of Obstetrics and Gynaecology 107*, 1210–17.

*Posner, N.A., Unterman, R.R., Williams, K.N. and Williams, G.H. (1997) 'Screening for postpartum depression: An antepartum questionnaire.' *Journal of Reproductive Medicine 42*, 4, 207–215.

Stamp, G.E., Sved Williams, A. and Crowther, C.A. (1996) 'Predicting postnatal depression among pregnant women.' *Birth 23*, 4, 218–223.

*Verkerk, G.J.M., Pop, V.J.M, van Son, M.J.M. and van Heck, G.L. (2003) 'Prediction of depression in the postpartum period: A longitudinal follow-up study in high-risk and low-risk women.' *Journal of Affective Disorders 77*, 159–166.

Webster, J., Linnane, W.J., Dibley, L.M. and Pritchard, M. (2000) 'Improving antenatal recognition of women at risk for postnatal depression.' *Australian and New Zealand Journal of Obstetrics and Gynaecology 40*, 4, 409–412.

Webster, J., Pritchard, M.A., Creedy, D. and East, C. (2003) 'A simplified predictive index for the detection of women at risk for postnatal depression.' *Birth 30*, 2, 101–108.

Most of these studies have been appraised in detail in:

Austin, M.P. and Lumley, J. (2003) 'Antenatal screening for postnatal depression: A systematic review.' *Acta Psychiatrica Scandinavica 107*, 1, 10–17.

Other instruments

Campagne, D.M. (2003) 'Screening depressive patients in pregnancy with the pregnancy mood profile.' *Journal of Reproductive Medicine 48*, 10, 813–817.

Campagne, D.M. (2004) 'Dectectar la depression antes, durante y después de la gestación con el perfil anímico del embarazo.' *Progresos de Obstetricia y Ginecologia 47*, 1, 27–35. Spanish translation of Pregnancy Mood Profile

Holcomb, W.L., Stone, L.S., Lustman, P.J., Gavard, J.A. and Mostello, D.J. (1996) 'Screening for depression in pregnancy: Characteristics of the Beck Depression Inventory.' *Obstetrics and Gynecology 88*, 1021–25.

Jomeen, J. and Martin, C.R. (2004) 'Is the Hospital Anxiety and Depression Scale (HADS) a reliable screening tool in early pregnancy?' *Psychology and Health 19*, 6, 787–800.

Karimova, G. and Martin, C.R. (2003) 'A psychometric evaluation of the Hospital Anxiety and Depression Scale during pregnancy.' *Psychology, Health and Medicine 8*, 89–103.

*Kitamura, T., Sugawara, M., Shima, S. and Toda, M.A. (1999) 'Temporal validity of self-rating questionnaires: Improved validity of Zung's Self-Rating Depression Scale among women during the perinatal period.' *Journal of Psychosomatic Obstetric and Gynaecology 20*, 2, 112–117.

Mantle, F. (2003) 'Developing a culture-specific tool to assess postnatal depression in the Indian community.' *British Journal of Community Nursing 8*, 4, 176–180.

Martin, C.R. and Jomeen, J. (2003) 'Is the 12-item General Health Questionnaire (GHQ-12) confounded by scoring method during pregnancy and following birth?' *Journal of Reproductive and Infant Psychology 21*, 4, 267–278.

Ross, L.E., Evans, S.E.G., Sellers, E.M. and Romach, M.K. (2003). 'Measurement issues in postpartum depression. Part 2: Assessment of somatic symptoms using the Hamilton Rating Scale for Depression.' *Archives of Women's Mental Health 6*, 1, 59–64.

Salermo, M., Marcos, T., Gutierrez, F. and Rebull, E. (1994) 'Factorial study of the BDI in pregnant women.' *Psychological Medicine 24*, 4, 1031–35.

*Stein, G. and van den Akker, O. (1992) 'The retrospective diagnosis of postnatal depression by questionnaire.' *Journal of Psychosomatic Research 36*, 1, 67–75.

Comparisons between scales

Ayers, S. (2001) 'Assessing psychopathology in pregnancy and postpartum.' *Journal of Psychosomatic Obstetrics and Gynecology 22*, 2, 91–102. Compares HADS and GHQ

*Beck, C.T. and Gable, R.K. (2001) 'Comparative analysis of the performance of the Postpartum Depression Screening Scale with two other depression instruments.' *Nursing Research 50*, 4, 242–250. Compares PDSS, EPDS and BDI-II

Condon, J.T. and Corkindale, C.J. (1997) 'The assessment of depression in the postnatal period: A comparison of four self-report questionnaires.' *Australian and New Zealand Journal of Psychiatry 31*, 3, 353–359. Compares EPDS, HADS, Zung Self Rating Scale and depression subscale of POMS

*Guedeney, N., Fermanian, J., Guelfi, J.D. and Kumar, R. (2000) 'The Edinburgh Postnatal Depression Scale (EPDS) and the detection of major depressive disorders in early postpartum: Some concerns about false negatives.' *Journal of Affective Disorders 61*, 1–2, 107–12. Compares EPDS with GHQ-28 and CES-D

Hanna, B., Jarman, H. and Savage, S. (2004) 'The clinical application of three screening tools for recognizing post-partum depression.' *International Journal of Nursing Practice 10*, 72–79. Compares PDPI, PDSS and EPDS

Harris, B., Huckle, P., Thomas, R., Johns, S. and Fung, H. (1989) 'The use of rating scales to identify post-natal depression.' *British Journal of Psychiatry 154*, 813–817. Compares EPDS and BDI

*Lee, D.T.S., Yip, A.S.K., Chan, S.M., Tsui, M.H.Y., Wong, W.S. and Chung, T.K.H. (2003) 'Postdelivery screening for postpartum depression.' *Psychosomatic Medicine 65*, 357–361. Compares EPDS, BDI and GHQ

Lukasik, A., Blaszcyk, K., Wojcieszyn, M. and Belwoska, A. (2003) 'Characteristics of affective disorders of the first week of the puerperium.' *Ginekologia Polska 74*, 10, 1149–94. Polish

Lussier, V., David, H., Saucier, J.F. and Borgeat, F. (1997) 'Self-rating assessment of postnatal depression: A comparison of the Beck Depression Inventory and the Edinburgh Postnatal Depression Scale.' *Journal of Prenatal and Perinatal Psychology and Health 11*, 2, 81–89.

*Muzik, M., Klier, C.M., Rosenblum, K.L., Holzinger, A., Umek, W. and Katschnig, H. (2000) 'Are commonly used self-report inventories suitable for screening postpartum depression and anxiety disorders?' *Acta Psychiatrica Scandinavica 102*, 71–73. Compares EPDS, SCL-90-R and Zung SDS

Sagrestano, L.M., Rodriguez, A.C., Carroll, D., Bieniariz, A., Greenberg, A., Castro, L. and Nuwayhid, B. (2002) 'A comparison of standardized measures of psychosocial variables with single-item screening measures used in an urban obstetric clinic.' *Journal of Obstetric,*

Gynecologic and Neonatal Nursing 31, 2, 147–155. The Perinatal Self-Administered Inventory compared with CES-D (includes Spanish translation)

Thompson, W.M., Harris, B., Lazarus, J. and Richards, C. (1998) 'A comparison of the performance of rating scales used in the diagnosis of postnatal depression.' *Acta Psychiatrica Scandinavica 98*, 3, 224–227. Compares EPDS, HADS and HRS-D

Ugarriza, D.N. (2000) 'Screening for postpartum depression.' *Journal of Psychosocial Nursing 38*, 12, 44–51. Compares BDI and ADDS

A version of the EPDS for indigenous and Torres Strait islander women is being developed in Australia, and in the US the validation of the partner-rated version of the EPDS is underway. The University of Iceland is planning the validation of the Icelandic EPDS with a standardized assessment. The PDSS is being validated in New Zealand among English-speaking, Maori and other ethnic minority communities. Chinese, German, Hebrew and Portuguese translations are currently in progress and it has been validated in Spanish. Icelandic and Spanish translations of the PDPI are underway. These studies had not been published at the time of going to press.

The editors are very appreciative of the help they received in compiling this list from John Cox, Cheryl Beck and all authors who responded so rapidly to our queries.

The Edinburgh Postnatal Depression Scale: guidelines for its use as part of a maternal mood assessment

Briege Coyle and Cheryll Adams

Background

Postnatal depression (PND) affects 10 to 15% of women following childbirth, accounting for about 70,000 women in the UK annually (O'Hara and Swain 1996). It is of particular concern as a public health issue for health professionals because it occurs at a critical time for families. Numerous research studies over recent years have demonstrated the deleterious effects on the cognitive, social and behavioural development of children whose mothers have suffered from postnatal depression (Murray et al. 1999; Hay et al. 2001).

In England, the National Service Framework (NSF) for Mental Health (Department of Health 1999a) identified health visitors as having an important role in identifying and preventing PND and managing its milder forms. There was also a recommendation that protocols for its management should be implemented within health trusts. This has led to a number of local initiatives being set up to detect and manage postnatal depression to comply with this recommendation. Scotland has recently published an evidence based guideline for postnatal depression and puerperal psychosis (SIGN 2002). This also emphasizes the important role of health visitors, as part of the multidisciplinary team, in ensuring effective detection and management of postnatal depression.

National Screening Committee (NSC)

The NSC, which has a UK-wide focus, recognized that there was no national screening policy for postnatal depression, and in the light of the many screening initiatives being set up, agreed to review the evidence for universal screening. They reviewed the Edinburgh Postnatal Depression Scale (EPDS), the tool most frequently used by health professionals in the community, setting it against the NSC criteria. The outcome was that the EPDS did not match the NSC criteria as a national screening tool for postnatal depression on a number of counts. Subsequently, the following recommendation about screening for postnatal depression was issued by the NSC: 'it is not recommended that individual services introduce screening for postnatal depression except in the context of a research study...' (National Screening Committee 2004)

Following lobbying by the CPHVA and others, the NSC has now amended this statement as follows:

> The National Screening Committee recognises that its statement on the use of the Edinburgh Postnatal Depression Score (EPDS) has caused concern to some health professionals. The following is issued as clarification:
>
> 'Until more research is conducted into its potential for routine use in screening for PND the NSC recommends that the EPDS should not be used as a screening tool. It may, however, serve as a checklist as part of a mood assessment for postnatal mothers, when it should only be used alongside professional judgement and a clinical interview. The professional administering it should have training in its appropriate use and should not use it as a pass/fail screening tool. Practitioners using it should also be mindful that, although it has been translated into many different languages, it can pose cultural difficulties for the interpretation, particularly when used with non English speaking mothers and those from non-western cultures.' (National Screening Committee 2004)

The original NSC statement created a great deal of anxiety for health visitors committed to the value of using the EPDS as part of their assessment procedure in the identification of postnatal depression. Therefore in an earlier briefing (Adams 2002) the CPHVA discussed the NSC review examining the EPDS for its potential to become a national screening tool, its original statement and its implication for practice.

> We acknowledge that the EPDS does not meet the NSC criteria to become a national screening... On the other hand, it provides a useful framework for assessing the common symptoms affecting depressed mothers. As such it remains a useful tool for health visitors to support the detection of PND in their clients.

On a positive note, the NSC review did open up the debate around the effectiveness of the EPDS as a universal screening tool for health visiting practice. It is essential for the practitioner to be aware of the limitations of this tool, which have become clear from this debate. Health visitors now better understand the reasons why it does not qualify as a universal screening tool according to the NSC criteria.

Misuses/limitations

It should be evident from the above discussion that health professionals need to be aware of the limitations and potential for misuse prior to administration of the EPDS. We consider the key issues are:

1.   The sensitivity, specificity and predictive value of the EPDS are dependent on the cut-off scores chosen for its administration. If, for example, the cut-off score chosen is greater than 12 as suggested for 'probable depression' by the authors (Cox, Holden and Sagovsky 1987), some cases of postnatal depression will be missed whereas if the lower score of 9 or above is used, few will be missed but there will be a high false positive rate

(Appleby *et al.* 1994; Beck and Gable 2000, 2001a). This disparity in the cut-off score gives rise to a marked variation in the positive predictive value of the EPDS from 44% to 73% (SIGN 2002).

2.   There are also more practical issues to take into account when administering the EPDS. If a mother doesn't want to have a positive diagnosis of postnatal depression she can quite easily tick the options on the form to give her a low score. If the form is not explained properly, is sent in the post or issued by someone not trained in its use the subsequent score might reflect the mood at that particular moment in time rather than an average of the previous weeks' mood.

3.   It is frequently suggested that using the EPDS in a routine way medicalizes what could be regarded as a natural transition to motherhood. However, many health professionals assert that routine use of the EPDS reduces the stigma of postnatal depression.

4.   The EPDS is not useful in identifying puerperal psychosis. This condition is best managed by antenatal assessment of risk factors and close monitoring in the perinatal period (SIGN 2002).

5.   If the EPDS is not used by a trained professional when there is sufficient time and privacy to explain its purpose, it will have little professional value and could have negative consequences for the mother.

6.   The EPDS should not be used when there is any risk of it not being understood due to language, culture or literacy

CPHVA recommendations for use of the EPDS

What is now clear, following the NSC review and the subsequent debate, is the limitations of the EPDS. Nevertheless, the CPHVA supports the view of its members that it remains a very useful aid to professional judgement and a clinical interview for the detection of postnatal depression. Indeed, we are supported by SIGN (2002) who state 'the EPDS should be offered to women in the postnatal period as *part* of a screening programme for postnatal depression'. It further recommends that 'health professionals administering any aspect of a screening programme are adequately trained to do so' (emphasis in original). Following extensive consultation, the CPHVA would like to make the following recommendations for use of the EPDS:

1.   The EPDS should never be used in isolation; it should form part of a full and systematic mood assessment of the mother supporting professional judgement and a clinical interview.

2.   The EPDS should only be used by professionals who have been trained in the detection and management of postnatal depression, use of the EPDS and conducting a clinical interview.

3.   Formal mood assessments should only be carried out in a place where the mother is ensured privacy and when the professional has time to discuss the outcome and suitable interventions with the mother should they be necessary.

4.   The EPDS should never be used in an open clinic or posted to mothers. If the clinic is not busy and there are facilities to ensure privacy for the mother it may be the preferred option for some health professionals who are unable to do a home visit.

5.   Before using it, the professional must consider possible factors that could influence the mother's comprehension of the purpose of the EPDS and her ability to complete the questions accurately, e.g. literacy level, cultural background, language difficulties.

6.   Having asked the mother to complete the scale, the professional should discuss her individual responses one by one, being alert to a mismatch with her clinical impression, e.g. mothers with puerperal psychosis may score low on the EPDS.

7.   Use of the EPDS should be followed by a clinical interview that utilizes the nine symptoms from DSM-IV to ascertain persistent and pervasive depressive symptoms. Such an interview should also explore possible physical, emotional or social causes for the symptoms so that appropriate interventions can be discussed with the mother.

Scoring the EPDS

As we have seen, a specific score on the EPDS does not definitely confirm or repute the presence of postnatal depression. What it does offer is an indicator as to its possible presence, absence or severity. It is reasonable then to consider whether much attention should be given to the score. The CPHVA believe that the score does have a quantitative value to the service provider, as when recorded it can support a needs assessment for service provision. It also provides a benchmark for change in the mother's mood or in response to a change in service. We believe that from the individual mother's viewpoint, whilst noting the score, the health visitor should rely on her fuller mood assessment to determine the severity of any depression. This is a qualitative approach and as such is client centred.

Clinical interview

It is not expected that a health visitor or midwife should undertake a full mental health state assessment. However, when postnatal depression is suspected they need to be aware of the pervasiveness and duration of symptoms, which will be indicative of the degree of severity of postnatal depression. Seeley (2001) recommends a holistic clinical interview being conducted alongside the routine feedback from the EPDS when depression appears likely. Indeed, this type of assessment will be routine practice for many health visitors but needs to become the norm. Consequently, health visitors need to have training to enable them to feel confident in conducting such an assessment.

The nine symptoms in the DSM-IV clinical interview can be used to explore the degree of depression present. These are:

- depressed mood
- diminished interest or pleasure

- appetite
- sleep
- restlessness/slowing down
- fatigue/loss of energy
- feelings about self
- concentration/decision making
- recurrent thoughts of death.

They can be remembered using an acronym or even by working from the head down attaching each mentally to a body part, e.g. mouth for appetite, legs for sleep! They can be woven into a conversation that systematically discusses the EPDS outcome as well as physical, emotional and social pressures on the mother.

The combination of the EPDS score, clinical assessment and professional judgement should be adequate to then decide on any subsequent intervention.

Conclusion

There has been much welcome development in the management of postnatal depression over the last two decades. However, we have a long way to go before we can be sure that mothers throughout the UK can expect to receive equitable, effective screening and intervention for postnatal depression.

There is clearly a need for a more strategic approach at a local level to tackling this important public health issue. National guidelines similar to the SIGN guidelines in Scotland should be implemented throughout the UK. In this era of raised client expectation, human rights legislation and clinical governance current ambivalence to the plight of women suffering from postnatal depression, displayed in some quarters, is clearly not an option.

In the absence of a fail-safe screening tool the EPDS, despite its imperfections, has considerable value if properly used with its weaknesses acknowledged.

Acknowledgement

This paper was originally published as Coyle, B. and Adams, C. 'The Edinburgh Postnatal Depression Scale: Guidelines for its use as part of a maternal mood assessment.' *Community Practitioner*, October 2002, 394–395. Reproduced here by kind permission of the editor.

References

Abbott, P. and Sapsford, R. (1990) 'Health visiting: Policing the family?' In P. Abbott and C. Wallace (eds) *The Sociology of the Caring Professions*. London: Falmer Press.

Adams, C. (2002) 'Use of the Edinburgh Postnatal Depression Screening Scale.' *Community Practitioner 75*, 4, April, 142 –143.

Adams, C. (2003) 'Understanding our emotional health needs: What helps?' In *Postnatal Depression and Maternal Mental Health in a Multi-Cultural Society: Challenges and Solutions*. London: Community Practitioners' and Health Visitors' Association.

Adams, C. and Sobowale, A. (2003) 'Perinatal mental health: Promoting the mental health of non-English speaking women.' *Community Practitioner 76*, 6, 208–210.

Aiken, C. (2000) *Surviving Post-Natal Depression: At Home, No One Hears You Scream*. London: Jessica Kingsley Publishers.

Aitken, P. and Jacobsen, R. (1997) 'Knowledge of the Edinburgh Postnatal Depression Scale among psychiatrists and general practitioners.' *Psychiatric Bulletin 21*, 550–552.

American Psychiatric Association (1994) *Diagnostic and Statistical Manual of Mental Disorders* (4th edn). Washington DC: American Psychiatric Association.

Appleby, L., Gregoire, A., Platz, C., Prince, M. and Kumar, R. (1994) 'Screening women for high risk of postnatal depression.' *Journal of Psychosomatic Research 38*, 6, 539–545.

Appleby, L., Hirst, E., Marshall, S., Keeling, F., Brind, J., Butterworth, T. and Lole, J. (2003) 'The treatment of postnatal depression by health visitors: Impact of brief training on skills and clinical practice.' *Journal of Affective Disorders 77*, 261–266.

Appleby, L., Warner, R., Whitton, A. and Faragher, B. (1997) 'A controlled study of fluoxetine and cognitive-behavioural counselling in the treatment of postnatal depression.' *British Medical Journal 314*, 932–936.

Appleton, J.V. (1997) 'Establishing the validity and reliability of clinical practice guidelines used to identify families requiring increased health visitor support.' *Public Health 111*, 107–113.

Arroll, B., Khin, N. and Kerse, N. (2003) 'Screening for depression in primary care with two verbally asked questions: Cross sectional study.' *British Medical Journal 327*, 1144–46.

Austin, M.P. and Lumley, J. (2003) 'Antenatal screening for postnatal depression: A systematic review.' *Acta Psychiatrica Scandinavica 107*, 10–17.

Baker, D., Mead, N. and Campbell, S. (2002) 'Inequalities in morbidity and consulting behaviour for socially vulnerable groups.' *British Journal of General Practice 52*, 124–130.

Baker, D. and North, K. (1999) 'Does employment improve the health of lone mothers?' *Social Science and Medicine 49*, 121–131.

Barker, W.E. (1990) 'Practical and ethical doubts about screening for child abuse.' *Health Visitor 63*, 14–17.

Barker, W.E. (1997) 'Hearing screening: 1983 shortcomings still persist today.' A review paper. Bristol: Early Childhood Development Centre.

Barnett, B. (1995) 'Preventive intervention: Pregnancy and early parenting.' In B. Raphael and G.D. Burrows (eds) *Handbook of Studies on Preventive Psychiatry*. Amsterdam: Elsevier.

Barnett, B., Blignault, I., Holmes, S., Payne, A. and Parker, G. (1987) 'Quality of attachment in a sample of 1-year-old Australian children.' *Journal of the American Academy of Child and Adolescent Psychiatry 26*, 303–307.

Barnett, B., Lockhart, K., Bernard, D., Manicavasagar, V. and Dudley, M. (1993) 'Mood disorders among mothers of infants admitted to a mothercraft hospital.' *Journal of Paediatric and Child Health 29*, 270–275.

Barnett, B. and Parker, G. (1986) 'Possible determinants, correlates and consequences of high levels of anxiety in primiparous mothers.' *Psychological Medicine 16*, 177–185.

Barnett, B., Schaafsma, M.F., Guzman, A-M. and Parker, G.B. (1991) 'Maternal anxiety: A five-year review of an intervention study.' *Journal of Child Psychology and Psychiatry 32*, 423–438.

Baum, M. (1995) 'Screening for breast cancer, time to think – and stop?' *The Lancet 346*, 436–437.

Beck, A. (1978) *Depression Inventory*. Philadelphia: Center for Cognitive Therapy.

Beck, A.T., Steer, R.A. and Brown, G.K. (1996) *BDI-II Manual*. San Antonio: Psychological Corporation.

Beck, C.T. (1992) 'The lived experience of postpartum depression: A phenomenological study.' *Nursing Research 41*, 166–170.

Beck, C.T. (1993) 'Teetering on the edge: A substantive theory of postpartum depression.' *Nursing Research 42*, 42–48.

Beck, C.T. (1996a) 'Postpartum depressed mothers' experiences interacting with their children.' *Nursing Research 45*, 98–104.

Beck, C.T. (1996b) 'A meta-analysis of predictors of postpartum depression.' *Nursing Research 45*, 297–303.

Beck, C.T. (1999) *Postpartum Depression: Case Studies, Research and Nursing Care*. Washington DC: Association of Women's Health, Obstetric and Neonatal Nurses Lifelines.

Beck, C.T. and Gable, R.K. (2000) 'Postpartum depression screening scale: Development and psychometric testing.' *Nursing Research 49*, 272–282.

Beck, C.T. and Gable, R.K. (2001a) 'Further validation of the postpartum depression screening scale.' *Nursing Research 50*, 155–164.

Beck, C.T. and Gable, R.K. (2001b) 'Comparative analysis of the performance of the Postpartum Depression Screening Scale with two other depression instruments.' *Nursing Research 50*, 242–250.

Beck, C.T. and Gable, R.K. (2001c) 'Ensuring content validity: An illustration of the Process.' *Journal of Nursing Measurement 9*, 201–215.

Beck, C.T. and Gable, R.K. (2001d) 'Item response theory in affective instrument development: An illustration.' *Journal of Nursing Measurement 9*, 5–22.

Beck, C.T. and Gable, R.K. (2002) *Postpartum Depression Screening Scale Manual*. Los Angeles: Western Psychological Services.

Bell, A.J., Land, N.M., Milne, S. and Hassanych, F. (1994) 'Long-term outcome of post-partum psychiatric illness requiring admission.' *Journal of Affective Disorders 31*, 67–70.

Bennett, N., Blundell, J., Malpass, L. and Lavender, T. (2001) 'Midwives' views on redefining midwifery. 2: Public health.' *British Journal of Midwifery 9*, 12, 743–747.

Bennett, H.A., Einarson, A., Taddio, A., Koren, G. and Einarson, T.R. (2004) 'Prevalence of depression during pregnancy: Systematic review.' *Obstetrics and Gynecology 103*, 4, 698–709.

Berthoud, R. and Nazroo, J. (1997) 'The mental health of ethnic minorities.' *New Community 23*, 3, 309–324.

BeyondBlue Postnatal Depression Program (2003) www.beyondblue.org.au/postnataldepression/about_POSTNATALdepression_program.htm

Bhatia, S.C. and Bhatia, S.K. (1999) 'Depression in Women: Diagnostic and Treatment Considerations.' *American Family Physician 60*, 1, 225–234.

Bhopal, R. (2001) 'Ethnicity and race as epidemiological variables: Centrality of purpose and context.' In H. Macbeth and P. Shetty (eds) *Health and Ethnicity*. London: Taylor and Francis.

Bifulco, A., Brown, G.W., Moran, P., Ball, C. and Campbell, C. (1998) 'Predicting depression in women: The role of past and present vulnerability.' *Psychological Medicine 28*, 39–50.

Bifulco, A. and Moran, P. (1998) *Wednesday's Child. Research into Women's Experiences of Neglect and Abuse in Childhood, and Adult Depression*. London: Routledge.

Birleson, D. (1980) 'The validity of depressive disorder in childhood and the development of a self rating scale: A research report.' *Journal of Child Psychology and Psychiatry 22*, 73–88.

Boath, E. and Henshaw, C. (2001) 'The treatment of postnatal depression: A comprehensive review.' *Journal of Reproductive and Infant Psychology 19*, 3, 215–248.

Bolton, H.L., Hughes, P.M., Turton, P. and Sedgwick, P. (1998) 'Incidence and demographic correlates of depressive symptoms during pregnancy in an inner London population.' *Journal of Psychosomatics and Obstetric Gynecology 19*, 202–209.

Born, L. and Steiner, M. (1999) 'Irritability: The forgotten dimension of female-specific mood disorders.' *Archives of Women's Mental Health 2*, 153–167.

Born, L., Steiner, M. and Koren, G. (2003) 'Female-specific irritability: A new measure.' *Archives of Women's Mental Health 6*, 2, 87.

Bostock, J., Marsen, M., Sarwar, Z. and Stoltz, S. (1996) 'Postnatal depression in Asian women.' *Community Nurse November/December*, 34–36.

Boyce, P. (1994) 'Personality dysfunction, marital problems and postnatal depression.' In J. Cox and J. Holden (eds) *Perinatal Psychiatry. Use and Misuse of the Edinburgh Postnatal Depression Scale*. London: Gaskell.

Boyce, P.M. (2003) 'Risk factors for postnatal depression: A review and risk factors in Australian populations.' *Archives of Women's Mental Health 6*, 2, 43–50.

Boyce, P., Harris, M., Silove, D., Morgan, A., Wilhelm, K. and Hadzl-Pavlovic, D. (1998) 'Psychosocial factors associated with depression: A study of socially disadvantaged women with young children.' *The Journal of Nervous and Mental Disease 186*, 2, 3–11.

Boyce, P., Stubbs, J. and Todd, A. (1991) *The Use and Validation of the Edinburgh Postnatal Depression Scale in Australia.* Paper presented at the conference on Prevention of Depression After Childbirth, University of Keele, UK.

Boyce, P.M. and Todd, A. (1992) 'Increased risk to postnatal depression following caesarean section.' *Medical Journal of Australia 157*, 172–174.

Boyer, D.B. (1990) 'Prediction of postpartum depression.' *Clinical Issues in Perinatal Women's Health Nursing 1*, 359–368.

Bradley, E., Boath, E. and Henshaw, C. (2004) 'The prevention of postnatal depression: A narrative systematic review.' Paper presented at the Second World Congress on Women's Mental Health, Washington DC, 17–20 March.

Brown, G.W. and Moran, P.M. (1997) 'Single mothers, poverty and depression.' *Psychological Medicine 27*, 21–33.

Brown, G.W., Bifulco, A., Veiel, H. and Andrews, B. (1990) 'Self-esteem and depression, 2: Social correlates of self-esteem. *Social Psychiatry and Psychiatric Epidemiology 25*, 225–234.

Brown, S., Darcy, M.A. and Bruinsma, F. (2001) *Victorian Survey of Recent Mothers, 2000.* Melbourne: Centre for Mothers and Babies, Latrobe University.

Brown, S., Lumley, J., Small, R. and Astbury, J. (1994) *Missing Voices: The Experience of Motherhood.* Melbourne: Oxford University Press.

Browvers, E.P., van Baar, A.L. and Pop, V.J. (2001) 'Does the Edinburgh Postnatal Depression Scale measure anxiety?' *Journal of Psychosomatic Research 51*, 659–663.

Brugha, T.S., Wheatley, S., Taub, N.A., Culverwell, A., Friedman, T., Kirwan, P., Jones, D.R. and Shapiro, D.A. (2000) 'Pragmatic randomized trial of antenatal intervention to prevent post-natal depression by reducing psychological risk factors.' *Psychological Medicine 30*, 1273–1231.

Buchan, J. and Seccombe, I. (2002) *Behind the Headlines: A Review of the UK Nursing Market in 2001.* London: Royal College of Nursing.

Buist, A. (1998) 'Childhood abuse, parenting and postpartum depression.' *Australian and New Zealand Journal of Psychiatry 32*, 479–487.

Buist, A.E., Barnett, B.E., Milgrom, J., Pope, S., Condon, J.T., Ellwood, D.A., Boyce, P.M., Austin, M.P. and Hayes, B.A. (2002) 'To screen or not to screen – that is the question in perinatal depression.' *Medical Journal of Australia 177*, 101–105.

Buist, A.E., Westley, D. and Hill, C. (1999) 'Antenatal prevention of postnatal depression.' *Archives of Women's Mental Health 1*, 167–173.

Byran, T.L., Georgiopoulos, A.M., Harms, R.W., Huxsahl, J.E., Larson, D.R. and Yawn, B.P. (1999) 'Incidence of postpartum depression in Olmsted, Minnesota. A population-based, retrospective study.' *Journal of Reproductive Medicine 44*, 351–358.

Campbell, H., Hotchkiss, R., Bradshaw, N. and Porteous, M. (1998) 'Integrated care pathways.' *British Medical Journal 316*, 133–137.

Cermele, J.A., Daniels, S. and Anderson, K.L. (2001) 'Defining normal: Constructions of race and gender in the DSM-IV Casebook.' *Feminism and Psychology 11*, 2, 229–247.

Chambers (1993) *The Chambers Dictionary.* Edinburgh: Chambers Harrap.

Chandran, M., Tharyan, P., Muliyil, J. and Abraham, S. (2002) 'Post-partum depression in a cohort of women from a rural area of Tamil Nadu, India. Incidence and risk factors.' *British Journal of Psychiatry 181*, 499–504.

Chilvers, C., Dewey, M., Fielding, K., Gretton, V., Miller, P., Palmer, B., Weller, D., Churchill, R., Williams, I., Bedi, N., Duggan, C., Lee, A. and Harrison, G. (2001) 'Antidepressant drugs and generic counselling for treatment of major depression in primary care: Randomised trial with patient preference arms.' *British Medical Journal 322*, 772–775.

Churchill, R., Khaira, M., Gretton, V., Chilvers, C., Dewey, M., Duggan, C. and Lee, A. (2000) 'Treating depression in general practice: Factors affecting patients' treatment preferences.' *British Journal of General Practice 50*, 905–906.

Cleaver, H. and Walker, S. (2004) *Assessing Children's Needs and Circumstances.* London: Jessica Kingsley Publishers.

Clinical Negligence Scheme for Trusts (2002) *Clinical Risk Management Standards for Maternity Services.* London: NHS Litigation Authority.

Cochrane, A. and Holland, W.W. (1971) 'Validation of screening procedures.' *British Medical Bulletin 27*, 30.

Cockburn, J., Redman, S., Hill, D. and Henry, E. (1995) 'Public understanding of medical screening.' *Journal of Medical Screening 2*, 224–227.

Coghill, S., Caplan, H., Alexandra, H., Mordecai Robson, K. and Kumar, R. (1986) 'Impact of maternal postnatal depression on cognitive development of young children.' *British Medical Journal 292*, 1165–67.

Commonwealth Department of Health and Aged Care (2000) *National Action Plan and Monograph for Promotion, Prevention and Early Intervention for Mental Health*. Canberra: Mental Health and Special Programs Branch.

Community Practitioners' and Health Visitors' Association (2003) *How Are You Feeling?* London: CPHVA.

Comport, M. (1987) *Towards Happy Motherhood: Understanding Postnatal Depression*. London: Corgi.

Conrad, H. (1950) 'Information which should be provided by test publishers and testing agencies on the validity and use of their tests.' In *Proceedings. 1949 Invitational Conference on Testing Problems*. Princeton, NJ: Educational Testing Service.

Cooper, P.J. and Murray, L. (1997) 'The impact of psychological treatments of postpartum depression on maternal mood and infant development.' In L. Murray and P.J. Cooper (eds) *Postpartum Depression and Child Development*. New York: Guilford Press.

Cooper, P.J. and Murray, L. (2003) 'Intergenerational transmission of affective and cognitive processes associated with depression: Infancy and the preschool years.' In I. Goodyer (ed) *Unipolar Depression: A Lifespan Perspective*. Oxford: Oxford University Press.

Cooper, P.J., Murray, L., Hooper, R. and West, A. (1996) 'The development and validation of a predictive index for postpartum depression.' *Psychological Medicine 26*, 627–634.

Cooper, P.J., Murray, L., Wilson, A. and Romaniuk, H. (2003) 'Controlled trial of the short- and long-term effect of psychological treatment of post-partum depression. I. Impact on maternal mood.' *British Journal of Psychiatry 182*, 412–419.

Cox, A. and Walker, S. (2000) *The Family Pack of Questionnaires and Scales Training Pack*. London: Association for Child Psychology and Psychiatry.

Cox, J.L. (1983) 'Postnatal depression: A comparison of African and Scottish women.' *Social Psychiatry 18*, 25–28.

Cox, J. (1986) *Postnatal Depression: A Guide for Health Professionals*. Edinburgh: Churchill Livingstone.

Cox, J. (1994) 'Origins and development of the 10-item Edinburgh Postnatal Depression Scale.' In J. Cox and J. Holden (eds) *Perinatal Psychiatry: Use and Misuse of the Edinburgh Postnatal Depression Scale*. London: Gaskell.

Cox, J. and Holden, J. (eds) (1994) *Perinatal Psychiatry: Use and Misuse of the Edinburgh Postnatal Depression Scale*. London: Gaskell (Royal College of Psychiatrists).

Cox, J. and Holden, J. (2003) *Perinatal Mental Health: A Guide to the Edinburgh Postnatal Depression Scale*. London: Gaskell (Royal College of Psychiatrists).

Cox, J.L., Holden, J.M. and Sagovsky, R. (1987) 'Detection of postnatal depression. Development of the 10-item Edinburgh Postnatal Depression Scale.' *British Journal of Psychiatry 150*, 782–786.

Cox, J.L., Murray, D. and Chapman, G. (1993) 'A controlled study of the onset, duration, and prevalence of postnatal depression.' *British Journal of Psychiatry 163*, 27–31.

Coyle, B. and Adams, C. (2002) 'The Edinburgh Postnatal Depression Scale: Guidelines for its use as part of a maternal mood assessment.' *Community Practitioner 75*, 10, 394–395.

Cronbach, L.J. and Gleser, G.C. (1957) *Psychological Tests and Personnel Decisions*. Urbana: University of Illinois Press.

Cubison, J. (1998) *A 'Lie Test' or 'Just One More Form'? An Exploratory Study into the Acceptability of Using the Edinburgh Postnatal Depression Scale*. (Unpublished) MA thesis, University of Sheffield.

Cullinan, R. (1991) 'Health visitor intervention in postnatal depression.' *Health Visitor 64*, 12, 412–414.

Dalton, K. (1996) *Depression After Delivery* (3rd edn). Oxford: Oxford University Press.

Davidson, J. and Robertson, E. (1985) 'A follow-up study of postpartum illness, 1946–1978.' *Acta Psychiatrica Scandinavica 71*, 451–457.

Day, A. (2001) 'The challenges of detecting and managing postnatal depression in a multicultural society.' In Community Practitioners' and Health Visitors' Association (ed) *Postnatal Depression and Maternal Mental Health: A Public Health Priority*. London: Community Practitioners' and Health Visitors' Association.

Dean, C. and Kendell, R.E. (1981) 'The symptomatology of puerperal illness.' *British Journal of Psychiatry 139*, 128–133.

Dearlove, J. and Kearney, D. (1990) 'How good is general practice developmental screening?' *British Medical Journal 300*, 1177–80.

Dennis, C.L. (2003) 'The effect of peer support on postpartum depression: A pilot randomized controlled trial.' *Canadian Journal of Psychiatry 48*, 115–124.

Dennis, C.L. (2004a) 'Can we identify mothers at risk for postpartum depression in the immediate postpartum period using the Edinburgh Postnatal Depression Scale?' *Journal of Affective Disorders 78*, 163–169.

Dennis, C.L. (2004b) 'Preventing postpartum depression Part I: A review of biological interventions.' *Canadian Journal of Psychiatry 49*, 7, 467–475.

Dennis, C.L. (2004c) 'Preventing postpartum depression Part II: A review of non-biological interventions.' *Canadian Journal of Psychiatry 49*, 8, 526–538.

Department for Education and Skills (2002) *Making a Difference for Children and Families*. London: Stationery Office.

Department for Education and Skills (2003) *Every Child Matters – Children's Green Paper*. London: Stationery Office.

Department of Environment, Transport and the Regions (2000) *Indices of Deprivation 2000: Regeneration Research Summary*. Report 31. London: Department of Environment, Transport and the Regions.

Department of Health (1992) *Maternity Services. Health Committee Second Report Session 1991–92 (Winterton Report)*. HMSO: London.

Department of Health (1993) *Changing Childbirth: Report of the Expert Maternity Group. (Cumberledge Report)*. HMSO: London.

Department of Health (1999a) *A National Service Framework for Mental Health*. London: Stationery Office.

Department of Health (1999b) *Saving Lives – Our Healthier Nation*. London: Stationery Office.

Department of Health (1999c) *Making a Difference – Strengthening the Nursing, Midwifery and Health Visiting Contribution to Health and Health Care*. London: Stationery Office.

Department of Health (2000a) *Framework for the Assessment of Children in Need and their Families*. London: Stationery Office.

Department of Health (2000b) *Framework for the Assessment of Children in Need and their Families – The Family Pack of Questionnaires and Scales*. London: Stationery Office.

Department of Health (2000c) *The NHS Plan – A Plan for Investment, a Plan for Reform*. London: Stationary Office.

Department of Health (2002) *Women's Mental Health: Into the Mainstream: Strategic Development of Mental Health Care for Women*. London: Stationery Office.

Department of Health (2003) *Getting the Right Start; National Service Framework for Children, Young People and Maternity Services; Emerging Findings*. London: Stationery Office.

Department of Health (2004) *Why Mothers Die 2000–2002. The Confidential Enquiries into Maternal Death in the United Kingdom*. London: Stationery Office.

Durdle Davis and Cowley, S. (1999) *The Cambridge Experiment – One Year On*. London: Community Practitioners' and Health Visitors' Association.

Eberhard-Gran, M., Eskild, A., Tumbs, K., Objordsmoem, S. and Samuelson, S.O. (2001) 'Review of validation studies of the Edinburgh Postnatal Depression Scale.' *Acta Psychiatrica Scandinavica 104*, 243–249.

Edge, D.E. (2002) *Perinatal Depression among Women of Black Caribbean Origin: A Longitudinal Cohort Study of Prevalence, Beliefs, and Attitudes to Help-seeking*. Unpublished PhD thesis. University of Manchester, UK.

Elliot, S.A. (1994) 'Uses and misuses of the Edinburgh Postnatal Depression Scale in primary care: A comparison of models developed in health visiting.' In J. Cox and J. Holden (eds) *Perinatal Psychiatry: Use and Misuse of the Edinburgh Postnatal Depression Scale*. London: Gaskell.

Elliott, S.A., Ashton, C., Gerrard, J. and Cox, J. (2003) 'Is trainer training an effective method for disseminating evidence based practice for postnatal depression?' *Journal of Reproductive and Infant Psychology 21*, 3, 210–228.

Elliott, S.A., Gerrard, J., Ashton, C. and Cox, J. (2001) 'Training health visitors to reduce levels of depression after childbirth: An evaluation.' *Journal of Mental Health 10*, 613–625.

Elliott, S.A. and Leverton, T.J. (2000) 'Is the EPDS a magic wand? 2. '"Myths" and the evidence base.' *Journal of Reproductive and Infant Psychology 18*, 4, 297–307.

Elliott, S.A., Leverton, T.J., Sanjack, M., Turner, H., Cowmeadow, P., Hopkins, J. and Bushnell, D. (2000) 'Promoting mental health after childbirth: A controlled trial of primary prevention of postnatal depression.' *British Journal of Clinical Psychology 39*, 223–241.

Elliott, S.A., Rugg, A.J., Watson, J.P. and Brough, D.I. (1983) 'Mood changes during pregnancy and after the birth of a child.' *British Journal of Clinical Psychology 22*, 295–308.

Erens, B., Primatesta, P. and Prior, G. (2001) *Health Survey of England 1999: The Health of Ethnic Minority Groups*. London: Stationery Office.

Evans, J., Heron, J., Francomb, H., Oke, S. and Golding, J. (2001) 'Cohort study of depressed mood during pregnancy and after childbirth.' *British Medical Journal 323*, 257–260.

Evins, G.G., Theofrastous, J.P. and Galvin, S.L. (2000) 'Postpartum depression: A comparison of screening and routine clinical evaluation.' *American Journal of Obstetrics and Gynaecology 182*, 1080–82.

Fenton, S. and Sadiq-Sangster, A. (1996) 'Culture, relativism and the expression of mental distress: South Asian women in Britain.' *Sociology of Health and Illness 18*, 66–85.

Fergerson, S.S., Jamieson, D.J. and Lindsay, M. (2002) 'Diagnosing postpartum depression: Can we do better?' *American Journal of Obstetrics and Gynecology 186*, 899–902.

Ferro, T., Verdeli, H., Pierre, F. and Weissman, M.M. (2000) 'Screening for depression in mothers bringing their offspring for evaluation or treatment of depression.' *American Journal of Psychiatry 157*, 375–379.

Finch, J., Hill, P. and Clegg, C. (2000) *Standards for Child and Adolescent Mental Health Services – Health Advisory Service*. Brighton: Pavilion.

First, M.B., Spitzer, R.L., Gibbon, M. and Williams, J.B.W. (1996) *Structured Clinical Interview for DSM IV Axis 1 Disorders*. New York: New York State Psychiatric Institute.

First, M.B., Spitzer, R.L., Gibbon, M., and Williams, J.B. (1997) *Structured Clinical Interview for DSM-IV Axis 1 Disorders (SC1D-I), Clinical version, users guide*. Washington, DC: American Psychiatric Press.

Flesch, R. (1948) 'A new readability yardstick.' *Journal of Applied Psychology 32*, 221–233.

Fowles, E.R. (1998) 'Maternal role attainment and postpartum depression.' *Health Care for Women International 19*, 83–94.

Fuggle, P., Glover, V., Khan, F. and Haydon, K. (2002) 'Screening for postnatal depression in Bengali women; Preliminary observations from using a translated version of the Edinburgh Postnatal Depression Scale (EPDS) 2.' *Journal of Reproductive and Infant Psychology 20*, 2, 71–82.

Gable, R.K. and Wolf, M. (1993) *Instrument Development in the Affective Domain* (2nd edn) Norwell, MA: Kluwer.

Geddes, J., Reynolds, S., Streiner, D., Szatmari, P. and Haynes, B. (1998) 'Evidence based practice in mental health (EBMH notebook).' *Evidence Based Mental Health 1*, 4–5.

Gemignani, J. (2001) 'Can your health plan handle depression?' *Business and Health*, June.

Georgiopoulos, A.M., Bryan, T.L., Wollan, P. and Yawn, B.P. (2001) 'Routine screening for postpartum depression.' *Journal of Family Practice 50*, 117–122.

Georgiopoulos, A.M., Bryan, T.L., Yawn, B.P., Houston, M.S., Rummans, T.A. and Therneau, T.M. (1999) 'Population-based screening for postpartum depression.' *Obstetrics and Gynecology 93*, 5, 1, 653–657.

Gerrard, J., Holden, J.M., Elliott, S.A., McKenzie, J. and Cox, J.L. (1993) 'A trainer's perspective of an innovative training programme to teach health visitors about the detection, treatment and prevention of postnatal depression.' *Journal of Advanced Nursing 18*, 1825–32.

Gilbody, S.M., House, A.O. and Sheldon, T.A. (2001) 'Routinely administered questionnaires for depression and anxiety: Systematic review.' *British Medical Journal 322*, 406–409.

Goldberg, D. (1972) *The Detection of Psychiatric Illness by Questionnaire*. London: Oxford University Press.

Goodman, R. (1997) 'The Strengths and Difficulties Questionnaire. A research note.' *Journal of Child Psychology and Psychiatry 38*, 581–586.

Green, J.M. (1998) 'Postnatal depression or perinatal dysphoria? Findings from a longitudinal community-based study using the Edinburgh Postnatal Depression Scale.' *Journal of Reproductive and Infant Psychology 16*, 143–155.

Green, J.M. and Murray, D. (1994) 'The use of the EPDS in research to explore the relationship between antenatal and postnatal dysphoria.' In J.L. Cox and J. Holden (eds) *Perinatal Psychiatry: Use and Misuse of the Edinburgh Postnatal Depression Scale*. London: Gaskell.

Greene, S.M., Nugent, J.K., Wieczorek-Deering, D., O'Mahony, P. and Graham, R. (1991) 'The patterning of depressive symptoms in a sample of first-time mothers.' *The Irish Journal of Psychology* *12*, 2, 263–275.

Gregoire, A.J., Kumar, R., Everitt, B., Henderson, A.F. and Studd, J.W. (1996) 'Transdermal oestrogen for treatment of severe postnatal depression.' *Lancet 347*, 930–933.

Grimes, D.A. and Schultz, K.F. (2002) 'Uses and abuses of screening tests.' *Lancet 359*, 881–884.

Guedeney, N., Fermanian, J., Guelfi, J. and Kumar, R.C. (2000) 'The EPDS and the detection of major depressive disorders in early postpartum; Some concerns about false negatives.' *Journal of Affective Disorders 61*, 107–112.

Hall, D. (1996) *Health for All Children* (3rd edn). Oxford: Oxford University Press.

Halligan, S.L., Herbert, J., Goodyer, I.M. and Murray, L. (2004) 'Exposure to postnatal depression predicts elevated cortisol in adolescent offspring.' *Biological Psychiatry 55*, 376–381.

Harris, B., Huckle, P., Thomas, R., Johns, S. and Fung, H. (1989) 'The use of rating scales to identify post-natal depression.' *British Journal of Psychiatry 154*, 813–817.

Harris, R.P., Helfand, M., Woolf, S.H., Lohr, K.N., Mulrow, C.D., Teutsch, S.M. and Atkins, D. (2001) 'Current methods of the U.S. Preventive Services Task Force: A review of the process.' *American Journal of Preventive Medicine 20*, 3, 21–35.

Hay, D., Pawlby, S., Sharp, D., Asten, P., Mills, A. and Kumar, R. (2001) 'Intellectual problems shown by 11 year old children whose mothers had postnatal depression.' *Journal of Child Psychology and Psychiatry and Allied Disciplines 42*, 7871–89.

Hayes, B.A., Muller, R., Bradley, B.S. (2001) 'Perinatal depression: A randomised controlled trial of an antenatal education intervention for primiparas.' *Birth 8*, 28–35.

Hearn, G., Iliff, A., Jones, I., Kirby, A., Ormiston, P., Parr, P., Rout, J. and Wardman, L. (1998) 'Postnatal depression in the community.' *British Journal of General Practice 48*, 1064–66.

Helman, C. (2003) 'Health beliefs and behaviour: How cultural are they?' In C. Adams (ed) *Postnatal Depression and Maternal Mental Health in a Multicultural Society: Challenges and Solutions.* London: Community Practitioners' and Health Visitors' Association.

Heneghan, A.M., Silver, E.J., Bauman, L.J. and Stein, R.E.K. (2000). 'Do pediatricians recognize mothers with depressive symptoms?' *Pediatrics 106*, 1367–73.

Hickey, A., Boyce, P.M., Ellwood, D. and Morris-Yates, A. (1997) 'Early discharge and risk for postnatal depression.' *Medical Journal of Australia 167*, 5, 244–247.

Hill, A. and Revill, J. (2004) 'New mums reject depression tag.' *The Observer*, 14 March.

Hiscock, H. and Wake, M. (2002) 'Randomised controlled trial of behavioural infant sleep intervention to improve infant sleep and maternal mood.' *British Medical Journal 324*, 1062–65.

Hoffbrand, S., Howard, L. and Crawley, H. (2001) 'Antidepressant treatment for post-natal depression (Cochrane Review).' In *The Cochrane Library 4*, 2003. Chichester: John Wiley.

Holden, J. (1991) 'Postnatal depression: Its nature, effects and identification using the Edinburgh Postnatal Depression Scale.' *Birth 18*, 211–221.

Holden, J. (1994) 'Using the Edinburgh Postnatal Depression Scale in clinical practice.' In J. Cox and J. Holden (eds) *Perinatal Psychiatry: The Use and Misuse of the Edinburgh Postnatal Depression Scale.* London: Gaskell (Royal College of Psychiatrists).

Holden, J.M. (1996) 'The role of health visitors in postnatal depression.' *International Review of Psychiatry 8*, 79–86.

Holden, J.M., Sagovsky, R. and Cox, J.L. (1989) 'Counselling in a general practice setting: Controlled study of heath visitor intervention in treatment of postnatal depression.' *British Medical Journal 298*, 223–226.

Honey, K.L., Bennett, P. and Morgan, M. (2002) 'A brief psycho-educational group intervention for postnatal depression.' *British Journal of Clinical Psychology 41*, 405–409.

Houston, A.M. and Cowley, S. (2002) 'An empowerment approach to needs assessment in health visiting practice.' *Journal of Clinical Nursing 11*, 640–650.

Hughes, P.M., Turton, P. and Evans, C.D.H. (1999) 'Stillbirth as a risk factor for depression and anxiety in the subsequent pregnancy.' *British Medical Journal 318*, 1721–24.

Jebali, C. (1991) 'Working together to support women with postnatal depression.' *Health Visitor 64*, 12, 412–414.

Jennings, K.D., Ross, S., Popper, S. and Elmore, M. (1999) 'Thoughts of harming infants in depressed and non depressed mothers.' *Journal of Affective Disorders 54*, 21–28.

Jiang, H.J., Elixhauser, A., Nicholas, J., Steiner, C., Reyes, C. and Bierman, A.S. (2002) *Care of Women in U.S. Hospitals, 2000.* Rockville, MD: Agency for Healthcare Research and Quality.

Jones, I. and Craddock, N. (2001) 'Familiality of the puerperal trigger in bipolar disorder: Results of a family study.' *American Journal of Psychiatry 158*, 6, 913–917.

Keating, F., Robertson, D., McCulloch, A. and Francis, E. (2002) *Breaking the Circles of Fear: A Review of the Relationship Between Mental Health Services and African and Caribbean Communities.* London: The Sainsbury Centre for Mental Health.

Kendell, R.E., Chalmers, J.C. and Platz, C. (1987) 'Epidemiology of puerperal psychoses.' *British Journal of Psychiatry 150*, 662–673.

Kendell, R.E, Rennie, D., Clarke, J.A. and Dean, C. (1981) 'The social and obstetric correlates of psychiatric admission in the puerperium.' *Psychological Medicine 11*, 341–350.

King, L. and Appleton, J.V. (1997) 'Intuition: A critical review of the research and rhetoric.' *Journal of Advanced Nursing 26*, 194–202.

Klier, C.M., Schafer, M.R., Schmid-Siegel, B., Lenz, G. and Mannel, M. (2002) 'St. John's Wort (Hypericum perforatum) – is it safe during breastfeeding?' *Pharmacopsychiatry 35*, 29–30.

Kumar, R. (1994) 'Postnatal mental illness: A transcultural perspective.' *Social Psychiatry and Psychiatric Epidemiology 29*, 250–264.

Kumar, R. and Robson, K.M. (1984) 'A prospective study of emotional disorders in childbearing women.' *British Journal of Psychiatry 144*, 35–47.

Kumar, R.C., Hipwell, A.E. and Lawson, C. (1994) 'Prevention of adverse effects of perinatal maternal mental illness on the developing child.' In J. Cox and J. Holden (eds) *Use and Misuse of the Edinburgh Postnatal Depression Scale.* London: Gaskell.

Laungani, P. (2000) 'Postnatal depression across cultures: Conceptual and methodological considerations.' *International Journal of Health Promotion and Education 38*, 3, 86–94.

Lavender, T., Bennett, N., Blundell, J. and Malpass, L. (2001) 'Midwives' views on redefining midwifery. 1: Health promotion.' *British Journal of Midwifery 9*, 11, 666–670.

Lawrie, T.A., Herxheimer, A. and Dalton, K. (2001) 'Oestrogens and progestogens for preventing and treating postnatal depression.' In *The Cochrane Library 4*, 2003. Chichester: John Wiley.

Lawrie, T.A., Hofmeyr, G.J., de Jager, M. and Berk, M. (1998) 'Validation of the Edinburgh Postnatal Depression Scale on a cohort of South African women.' *South African Medical Journal 88*, 1340–44.

Lee, D.T., Yip, A.S., Chan, S.S., Tsui, M.H., Wong, W.S. and Chung, T.K. (2003) 'Post delivery screening for postpartum depression.' *Psychosomatic Medicine 65*, 357–361.

Lee, D.T.S., Yip, S.K., Chiu, H.F.K., Leung, T.Y.S., Chan, K.P.M., Chau, I.O.L., Leung, H.C.M. and Chung, T.K.H. (1998) 'Detecting postnatal depression in Chinese women: Validation of the Chinese version of the Edinburgh Postnatal Depression Scale.' *British Journal of Psychiatry 172*, 432–437.

Lee, D.T.S., Yip, S.K., Chiu, H.F.K. and Chung, T.K. (2000) 'Screening for postnatal depression using the double-test strategy.' *Psychosomatic Medicine 62*, 2, 258–63.

Lee, D.T.S., Yip, S.K., Chiu, H.F.K., Leung, T. and Chung, T.K.H. (2001) 'A psychiatric epidemiological study of postpartum Chinese women.' *American Journal of Psychiatry 158*, 220–226.

Le Fanu, J. (1997) 'Rise of the non-disease.' *RX Magazine*, 7 December.

Leverton, T. (2003) 'Parental psychiatric illness: The implications for children.' *Current Opinion in Psychiatry 16*, 395–402.

Leverton, T.J. and Elliott, S.A. (2000) 'Is the EPDS a magic wand? 1. A comparison of the EPDS and health visitor report as predictors of diagnosis on the Present State Examination.' *Journal of Reproductive and Infant Psychology 18*, 279–95.

Lewis, G. and Drife, J. (eds) (2001) *Why Mothers Die 1997–1999: The Confidential Enquiries into Maternal Death in the United Kingdom.* London: Royal College of Obstetricians and Gynaecologists.

Linacre, J.M. (1993) *A Users' Guide to Facets.* Chicago, IL: Mesa Press.

Lloyd, K. (1993) 'Depression and anxiety among Afro-Caribbean general practice attenders in Britain.' *The International Journal of Social Psychiatry 39*, 1–9.

Lloyd, K. (1998) 'Ethnicity, social inequality, and mental illness.' *British Medical Journal 316*, 1763–70.

Lundy, B.L., Jones, N.A., Field, T., Nearing, G., Davalos, M., Pietro, P.A., Scanberg, S. and Kuhn, C. (1999) 'Prenatal depression effects on neonates.' *Infant Behavior and Development 22*, 119–129.

Luoma, I., Tamminen, T., Kaukonen, P., Laippala, P., Puura, K., Salmelin, R. and Almqvist, F. (2001) 'Longitudinal study of maternal depressive symptoms and child well-being.' *Journal of the American Academy of Child and Adolescent Psychiatry 40*, 1367–74.

McCain, M.N. and Mustard, J.F. (1999) *Reversing the Real Brain Drain. Early Years Study Final Report.* Ontario: Canadian Institute for Advanced Research.

McIntosh, J. (1993) 'Postpartum depression: Women's help seeking behaviour and perceptions of cause.' *Journal of Advanced Nursing 18*, 178–184.

Manson, S. (1995) 'Culture and major depression: Current challenges in the diagnosis of mood disorders.' *Psychiatric Clinics of North America 18*, 487–501.

Marcus, S.M., Flynn, H.A., Blow, F.C. and Barry, K.L. (2003) 'Depressive symptoms among pregnant women screened in obstetrics setting.' *Journal of Women's Health 12*, 4, 373–380.

Marks, M., Wieck, A., Checkley, S. and Kumar, C. (1996) 'How does marriage protect women with histories of affective disorder from post-partum relapse?' *British Journal of Medical Psychology 69*, 329–342.

Marteau, T. (1989) 'Psychological costs of screening.' *British Medical Journal 299*, 527.

Martinez, R., Johnson-Robledo, I., Ulsh, M. and Chrisler, J. (2000) 'Singing "the baby blues". A content analysis of popular press articles about postpartum affective disturbances.' *Women and Health 31*, 2/3, 37–57.

Matthey, S. (2004) 'Calculating clinically significant change in postnatal depression studies using the Edinburgh Postnatal Depression Scale.' *Journal of Affective Disorders 78*, 269–272.

Matthey, S., Phillips, J., White, T., Glossop, P., Hopper, U., Panasetis, P., Petridis, A., Larkin, M. and Barnett, B. (2004) 'Routine psychosocial assessment of women in the antenatal period: Frequency of risk factors and implications for clinical services.' *Archives of Women's Mental Health 7*, 4, 223–229.

Matthey, S., White, T., Panasetis, P., Hopper, U., Larkin, M., Glossop, P. and Barnett, B. (2002) *Evaluation of the Routine Psychosocial Assessment at Liverpool Hospital Antenatal Clinic: June 2002.* Infant, Child and Adolescent Mental Health Service, South Western Sydney Area Health Service.

Meager, I. and Milgrom, J. (1996) 'Group treatment for postpartum depression: A pilot study.' *Australian and New Zealand Journal of Psychiatry 30*, 852–860.

Mental Health Foundation (1999) *Bright Futures: Promoting Children and Young People's Mental Health.* London: Mental Health Foundation.

Misri, S., Kostaras, X., Fox, D. and Kostaras, D. (2000) 'The impact of partner support in the treatment of postpartum depression.' *Canadian Journal of Psychiatry 45*, 554–558.

Modood, T. (1997) 'Conclusion: Ethnic diversity and disadvantage.' In T. Modood, R. Berthoud, J. Lakey, J.Y. Nazroo, P. Smith, S. Virdee and S. Beishon (eds) *Ethnic Minorities in Britain: Diversity and Disadvantage.* London: Policy Studies Institute.

Morrell, C.J., Spiby, H., Stewart, P., Walters, S. and Morgan, A. (2000) 'Costs and benefits of community postnatal support workers: A randomised controlled trial.' *Health Technology Assessment 4*, 1–77.

Morrell, J. (2003). 'Psychological interventions for postnatal depression: Randomised controlled trial.' *Journal of Reproductive and Infant Psychology 21*, 255.

Morris-Rush, J.K., Freda, M.C. and Bernstein, P.S. (2003) 'Screening for postpartum depression in an inner-city population.' *American Journal of Obstetrics and Gynecology 188*, 1217–19.

Murray, D. and Cox, J.L. (1990) 'Screening for depression during pregnancy with the Edinburgh Postnatal Depression Scale (EPDS).' *Journal of Reproductive and Infant Psychology 8*, 99–107.

Murray, L. (1992) 'The impact of postnatal depression on infant development.' *Journal of Child Psychology and Psychiatry 33*, 3, 543–561.

Murray, L. and Carothers, A.D. (1990) 'The validation of the Edinburgh Postnatal Depression Scale on a community sample'. *British Journal of Psychiatry 157*, 288–290.

Murray, L. and Cooper, P. (1996) 'The impact of postpartum depression on child development.' *International Review of Psychiatry 8*, 1, 55–63.

Murray, L. and Cooper, P.J. (1997) *Postpartum Depression and Child Development.* London: Guilford.

Murray, L., Cooper, P.J., Wilson, A. and Romaniuk, H. (2003) 'Controlled trial of the short- and long-term effect of psychological treatment of post-partum depression: 2. Impact on the mother–child relationship and child outcome.' *British Journal of Psychiatry 182*, 420–427.

Murray, L., Sinclair, D., Cooper, P., Ducournau, P., Turner, P. and Stein, A. (1999). 'The socioemotional development of 5-year-old children of postnatally depressed mothers.' *Journal of Child Psychology and Psychiatry and Allied Disciplines 40*, 8, 1259–71.

Murray, L., Woolgar, M. and Cooper, P.J. (2004) 'Detection and treatment of postnatal depression.' *Community Practitioner 77*, 1.

National Screening Committee (2000) *Second Report of the National Screening Committee.* London: Department of Health.

National Screening Committee (2001) www.nelh.nhs.uk/screening

National Screening Committee (2003) www.nelh.nhs.uk/screening

National Screening Committee (2004) www.nelh.nhs.uk/screening

National Statistics (2002) *Social Trends 2002*. Report 32. London: Stationery Office.

Nazroo, J.Y. (1997) *Ethnicity and Mental Health: Findings from a National Community Survey*. London: Policy Studies Institute.

Normandale, S. (2001) 'A study of mothers' perceptions of the health visiting role.' *Community Practitioner 74*, 4, 146–150.

Oakley, A. (1980) *Women Confined: Towards a Sociology of Childbirth*. Oxford: Martin Robertson.

Oates, M. (2001) *Perinatal Mental Health Services. Recommendations for Provision of Services for Childbearing Women*, CR88. London: Royal College of Psychiatrists.

Oates, M.R. (2003) 'Perinatal psychiatric disorders: A leading cause of maternal morbidity and mortality.' *British Medical Bulletin 67*, 1, 219–229.

O'Hara, M.W. (1987) 'Postpartum "blues", depression and psychosis: A review.' *Journal of Psychosomatic Obstetrics and Gynaecology 7*, 205–227.

O'Hara, M.W. (1991) *The Use of the Edinburgh Postnatal Depression Scale with a U.S. Sample*. Paper presented at conference on *Prevention of Depression After Childbirth: Use and Misuse of the Edinburgh Postnatal Depression Scale*, University of Keele, UK.

O'Hara, M.W., Stuart, S., Gorman, L.L. and Wenzel, A. (2000) 'Efficacy of interpersonal psychotherapy for postpartum depression.' *Archives of General Psychiatry 57*, 1039–45.

O'Hara, M.W. and Swain, A.M. (1996) 'Rates and risks of postnatal depression – a meta analysis.' *International Review of Psychiatry 8*, 37–54.

O'Hara, M.W., Zekoski, E.M., Phillips, L.H., and Wright, E.J. (1990) 'Controlled prospective study of postpartum mood disorders: Comparison of childbearing and nonchildbearing women.' *Journal of Abnormal Psychology 99*, 1, 3–15.

Olds, D. and Kitzman, H. (1990) 'Can home visitation improve the health of women and children at risk?' *Pediatrics 86*, 108–116.

Olson, A.L., Kemper, K.J., Kelleher, K.J., Hammond, C.S., Zuckerman, B.S. and Dietrich, A.J. (2002) 'Primary care pediatricians' roles and perceived responsibilities in the identification and management of maternal depression.' *Pediatrics 110*, 6, 1169–76.

Onozawa, K., Glover, V., Adams, D., Modi, N. and Kumar, R.C. (2001) 'Infant massage improves mother–infant interaction for mothers with postnatal depression.' *Journal of Affective Disorders 63*, 201–207.

Onozawa, K., Kumar, R.C., Adams, D., Dore, C. and Glover, V. (2003) 'High EPDS scores in women from ethnic minorities in London.' *Archives of Women's Mental Health 6*, 2, 551–555.

Parker, G. and Barnett, B. (1988) 'Perceptions of parenting in childhood and social support in adulthood.' *American Journal of Psychiatry 145*, 479–482.

Patel, V., Rahman, A., Jacob, K.S. and Hughes, M. (2004) 'Effect of maternal mental health on infant growth in low income countries: New evidence from South Asia.' *British Medical Journal 328*, 820–823.

Patel, V., Rodrigues, M. and de Souza, N. (2002) 'Gender, poverty and post-natal depression: A cohort study from Goa, India.' *American Journal of Psychiatry 159*, 43–47.

Peckham, C. and Dezateux, C. (1998) 'Issues underlying the evaluation of screening programmes.' *British Medical Bulletin 54*, 4, 767–778.

Peindl, K.S., Wisner, K.L. and Hanusa, B.H. (2004) 'Identifying depression in the first postpartum year: Guidelines for office-based screening and referral.' *Journal of Affective Disorders 80*, 37–44.

Perry, B.D., Pollard, R., Blakley, T.L., Baker, W.L. and Vigilante, D. (1995) 'Childhood trauma, the neurobiology of adaptation, and "use-dependent" development of the brain: How "states" become "traits".' *Infant Mental Health Journal 16*, 271–291.

Philipps, L.H.C. and O'Hara, M.W. (1991) 'Prospective study of postpartum depression: 4 1/2-year follow-up of women and children.' *Journal of Abnormal Psychology 100*, 151–155.

Pignone, M.P., Gaynes, B.N., Rushton, J.L., Burchell, C.M., Orleans, C.T., Mulrow, C.D. and Lohr, K.N. (2002) 'Screening for depression in adults: A summary of the evidence for the U.S. Preventive Services Task Force.' *Annals of Internal Medicine 136*, 10, 765–776.

Pilgrim, D. (2005) 'Evidence, logic and power: What is a mental disorder?' *Clinical Psychology 4*, 9–12.

Pill, R., Prior, L. and Wood, F. (2001) 'Lay attitude to professional consultations for common mental disorder: A sociological perspective.' *British Medical Bulletin 57*, 207–219.

Pitt, B. (1968) '"Atypical" depression following childbirth.' *British Journal of Psychiatry 114*, 1325–35.

Pop, V.J., Komproe, I.H. and van Son, M.J. (1992) 'Characteristics of the Edinburgh Postnatal Depression scale in the Netherlands'. *Journal of Affective Disorders 26*, 105–110.

Priest, R.G., Vize, C., Roberts, A., Roberts, M. and Tylee, A. (1996) 'Lay people's attitudes to treatment of depression: Results of opinion poll for *Defeat Depression Campaign* just before its launch.' *British Medical Journal 313*, 858–859.

Rahman, A., Iqbal, Z. and Harrington, R. (2003) 'Life events, social support and depression in childbirth: Perspectives from a rural community in the developing world.' *Psychological Medicine 33*, 1161–67.

Reid, A.J., Biringer, A., Carroll, J.D., Midmer, D., Wilson, L.M., Chalmers, B. and Stewart, D.E. (1998) 'Using the ALPHA form in practice to assess antenatal psychosocial health.' *Canadian Medical Association Journal 159*, 677–681.

Roberts, H. (2000) 'What is Surestart?' *Archives of Diseases in Childhood 82*, 435–437.

Robinson, R. (1998) 'Effective screening in child health.' *British Medical Journal 316*, 1–2.

Robling, S.A., Paykel, E.S., Dunn, V.J., Abbott, R. and Katona, C. (2000) 'Long-term outcome of severe puerperal psychiatric illness: A 23 year follow-up study.' *Psychological Medicine 30*, 1263–71.

Rodrigues, M., Patel, V., Jaswal, S. and de Souza, N. (2003) 'Listening to mothers: Qualitative studies on motherhood and depression from Goa, India.' *Social Science and Medicine 57*, 1797–1806.

Rose, G. (1985) 'Sick individuals and sick populations.' *International Journal of Epidemiology 14*, 32–38.

Ross, L.E., Gilbert Evans, S.E., Sellers, E.M. and Romach, M.K. (2003) 'Measurement issues in postpartum depression. Part 1: Anxiety as a feature of postpartum depression.' *Archives of Women's Health 6*, 51–57.

Roy, A., Gang, P., Cole, K., Rutsky, M., Reese, L. and Weisbord, J. (1993) 'Use of Edinburgh Postnatal Depression Scale in a North American population.' *Progress in Neuro-psychopharmacology and Biological Psychiatry 17*, 501–504.

Royal College of Psychiatrists (2000) *Perinatal Mental Health Services. Council Report 88*. London: Royal College of Psychiatrists.

Sanderson, C. (1995) *Notes for Sheffield Health Visitors about Screening for Postnatal Depression.* Department of Community Paediatrics, Sheffield Children's Hospital.

Schaper, A.M., Rooney, B.L., Kay, N.R. and Silva, P.D. (1994) 'Use of the Edinburgh Postnatal Depression Scale to identify postpartum depression in a clinical setting.' *Journal of Reproductive Medicine 39*, 620–624.

Schore, A.N. (1994) *Affect Regulation and the Origin of the Self.* Hillsdale, NJ: Erlbaum.

Scottish Intercollegiate Guidelines Network (2002) *Postnatal Depression and Puerperal Psychosis: A National Clinical Guideline.* Edinburgh: Royal College of Physicians.

Sechrest, L. (1963) 'Incremental validity: A recommendation.' *Educational and Psychological Measurement 23*, 153–158.

Seeley, S. (2001) 'Strengths and limitations of the postnatal depression screening scale.' In *Postnatal Depression and Maternal Mental Health: A Public Health Priority: Conference Proceedings.* London: Community Practitioners' and Health Visitors' Association.

Seeley, S., Murray, L. and Cooper, P. (1996) 'The outcome for mothers and babies of health visitor intervention.' *Health Visitor 69*, 133–138.

Shakespeare, J. (2001) 'An evaluation of screening for postnatal depression against the NSC handbook criteria.' www.nelh.nhs.uk/screening/adult_pps/shakespeare_final_paper.pdf

Shakespeare, J. (2002) 'Health visitor screening for postnatal depression using the EPDS: A process study.' *Community Practitioner 75*, 381–384.

Shakespeare, J., Blake, F. and Garcia, J. (2003) 'A qualitative study of the acceptability of routine screening of postnatal women using the Edinburgh Postnatal Depression Scale.' *British Journal of General Practice 53*, 614–619.

Sharp, D. (1994) *The Effect of Depression on the Development of the Child. Postnatal Depression Symposium.* London: Royal Postgraduate Medical School.

Sharp, D., Hay, D., Pawlby, S., Schmuker, G., Allen, H. and Kumar, R. (1995) 'The impact of postnatal depression on boys' intellectual development.' *Journal of Child Psychology and Psychiatry 36*, 8, 1315–36.

Shaw, C.M., Creed, F., Tomenson, B., Riste, L. and Cruickshank, K.L. (1999) 'Prevalence of anxiety and depressive illness and help seeking behaviour in African Caribbeans and white Europeans: Two phase general population survey.' *British Medical Journal 318*, 302–306.

Shinfuku, N. (1998) 'Mental health services in Asia: International perspective and challenge for the coming years.' *Psychiatry and Clinical Neuroscience 52*, 269–274.

Sinclair, D. and Murray, L. (1998) 'Effects of postnatal depression on children's adjustment to school: Teacher's report.' *British Journal of Psychiatry 172*, 58–63.

Small, R., Brown, S., Lumley, J. and Astbury, J. (1994) 'Missing voices: What women say and do about depression after childbirth.' *Journal of Reproductive and Infant Psychology 12*, 89–103.

Smith, G.D., Chaturvedi, N., Harding, S., Nazroo, J. and Williams, R. (2000) 'Ethnic inequalities in health: A review of UK epidemilogical evidence.' *Critical Public Health, 10*, 4, 375–408.

Snaith, R., Constantopoulos, P., Jardine, M. and McGuffin, P. (1978) 'A clinical scale for the self assessment of irritability.' *British Journal of Psychiatry 132*, 163–171.

Sobowale, A. (2002) 'Postnatal depression in South Asian Women: A search for a culturally appropriate and accurate detection tool.' Final Report to the Health Action Zone (HAZ), Department of Health, London.

Spielberger, C.D., Gorsuch, R.L. and Lushene, R.E. (1970) *The State-Trait Anxiety Inventory*. Palo Alto, CA: Consulting Psychologists Press.

Stamp, G.E., Williams, A.S. and Crowther, C.A. (1995) 'Evaluation of antenatal and postnatal support to overcome postnatal depression: A randomized control trial.' *Birth 22*, 138–143.

Stewart-Brown, S. and Farmer, A. (1997) 'Screening could seriously damage your health.' *British Medical Journal 314*, 533–534.

Strauss, A. and Corbin, J. (1990) *Basics of Qualitative Research: Grounded Theory Procedures and Techniques*. London: Sage.

Tabachnick, B.G. and Fidell, L.S. (1996) *Using Multivariate Statistics*. New York: HarperCollins.

Tam, L.W., Newton, R.P., Dern, M. and Parry, B.L. (2002) 'Screening women for postpartum depression at well baby visits: Resistance encountered and recommendations.' *Archives of Women's Mental Health 5*, 79–82.

Templeton, L., Velleman, R., Persaud, A. and Milner, P. (2003) 'The experiences of postnatal depression in women from black and minority ethnic communities in Wiltshire, UK.' *Ethnicity and Health 8*, 3, 207–221.

Thomson, R., Lavender, M. and Madhok, R. (1995) 'How to ensure that guidelines are effective.' *British Medical Journal 311*, 237–242.

Tucker, L. and Lewis, C. (1973) 'A reliability coefficient for maximum likelihood factor analysis.' *Psychometrika 38*, 1–10.

Tully, L., Garcia, J., Davidson, L. and Marchant, S. (2002) 'Role of midwives in depression screening.' *British Journal of Midwifery 10*, 374–378.

Twinn, S. (2000) 'Professional artistry: The contribution to the search for health needs.' In J.V. Appleton and S. Cowley (eds) *The Search for Health Needs*. Basingstoke: MacMillan.

US Preventive Services Task Force (2002). 'Screening for depression: Recommendations and rationale.' *Annals of Internal Medicine 136*, 10, 760–764.

Verkerk, G.J.M., Pop, V.J.M., van Son, M.J.M. and van Heck, G.L. (2003) 'Prediction of depression in the postpartum period: A longitudinal follow-up study in high-risk and low-risk women.' *Journal of Affective Disorders 77*, 159–166.

Walker, A., Maher, J., Coulthard, M., Goddard, E. and Thomas, M. (2001) *Living in Britain: Results from the 2000 General Household Survey*. London: Stationery Office.

Weel-Baumgarten, E.M., van den Bosch, W.J., van den Hoogen, H.J. and Zitman, F.G. (2000) 'The validity of the diagnosis of depression in general practice: Is using criteria for diagnosis as a routine the answer?' *British Journal of General Practice 50*, 284–287.

Welburn, V. (1980) *Postnatal Depression*. London: Fontana.

Wells, K.B., Sherbourne, C., Schoenbaum, M., Duan, N., Meredith, L., Unützer, J., Miranda, J., Carney, M.F. and Rubenstein, L.V. (2000) 'Impact of disseminating quality improvement programs for depression in managed primary care: A randomized controlled trial.' *Journal of the American Medical Association 283*, 2, 212–220.

Wheatley, S. (2001) *Nine Women, Nine Months, Nine Lives*. Leicestershire: Potent.

Whitton, A., Warner, R. and Appleby, L. (1996) 'The pathway to care in post-natal depression: Women's attitudes to post-natal depression and its treatment.' *British Journal of General Practice 46*, 427–428.

Whooley, M.A., Avins, A.L., Miranda, J. and Browner, W.S. (1997) 'Case finding instruments for depression: Two questions as good as many.' *Journal of General Internal Medicine 12*, 439–445.

Wickberg, B. and Hwang, C.P. (1996) 'Counselling of postnatal depression: A controlled study on a population based Swedish sample.' *Journal of Affective Disorders 39*, 209–216.

Wickberg, B. and Hwang, C.P. (1997) 'Screening for postnatal depression in a population-based Swedish sample.' *Acta Psychiatrica Scandinavica 95*, 62–66.

Wieck, A., Kumar, R., Hirst, A.D., Marks, M.N., Campbell, I.C. and Checkley, S.A. (1991) 'Increased sensitivity of dopamine receptors and recurrence of affective psychosis after childbirth.' *British Medical Journal 303*, 613–616.

Williams Jr, J.W., Mulrow, C.D., Kroenke, K., Dhanda, R., Badgett, R.G., Omori, D. and Lee, S. (1999) 'Case-finding for depression in primary care: A randomized trial.' *American Journal of Medicine 106*, 36–43.

Wilson, J.M.G. and Jungner, G. (1968) *Principles and Practice of Screening for Disease.* Public Health Paper 34. Geneva: World Health Organisation.

Wisner, K.L., Perel, J.M., Peindl, K.S., Hanusa, B.H., Findling, R.L. and Rapport, D. (2001) 'Prevention of recurrent postpartum depression: A randomized clinical trial.' *Journal of Clinical Psychiatry 62*, 82–86.

World Health Organization (2000) *Women's Mental Health: An Evidence Based Review.* Geneva: WHO.

World Health Organization (2001) *The World Health Report 2001: Mental Health: New Understanding, New Hope.* Geneva: WHO.

Worth, A. and Hogg, R. (2000) 'A qualitative evaluation of the effectiveness of health visiting practice.' *British Journal of Community Nursing 5*, 5, 221–228.

Wrate, R., Zajicek, E. and Ghodsian, M. (1980) 'Continuities in maternal depression.' *International Journal of Family Psychiatry 1*, 167–182.

Yonkers, K.A. and Chantilis, S.J. (1995) 'Recognition of depression in obstetric/gynecology practices.' *American Journal of Obstetrics and Gynecology 173*, 632–638.

Yonkers, K.A., Ramin, S.M., Rush, A.J., Navarrete, C.A., Carmody, T., March, D., Heartwell, S.F. and Leveno, K.J. (2001) 'Onset and persistence of postpartum depression in an inner-city maternal health clinic system.' *American Journal of Psychiatry 158*, 1856–63.

Zeanah, C.H. and Zeanah, P.D. (1989) 'Intergenerational transmission of maltreatment: Insights from attachment theory and research.' *Psychiatry 52*, 177–196.

Zigmond, A.S. and Snaith, R.P. (1983) 'The Hospital Anxiety and Depression Scale.' *Acta Psychiatrica Scandinavia 67*, 361–370.

Zigmond, A.S. and Snaith, R.P. (1994) 'The Hospital Anxiety and Depression Scale with the Irritability-Depression-Anxiety Scale and the Leeds Situational Anxiety Scale.' Windsor: NFER Nelson.

Zlotnick, C., Johnson, S.L., Miller, I.W., Pearlstein, T. and Howard, M. (2001) 'Postpartum depression in women receiving public assistance: Pilot study of an interpersonal therapy oriented group intervention.' *American Journal of Psychiatry 158*, 638–640.

The Editors

Carol Henshaw is a Consultant Psychiatrist with Cheshire and Wirral Partnership NHS Trust and a Senior Lecturer at Keele University. Her interest in perinatal mental health began during a research project investigating the relationship between postpartum blues and depression which eventually led to her MD. During higher clinical training she became a member of the Marcé Society, a scientific society devoted to mental illness related to childbearing and, in September 2004, became President. She is on the Executive Committee of the Royal College of Psychiatrists' Perinatal Section and chairs the KEPEU Steering Committee, which in addition to the training trainers programme, oversees and runs a variety of courses and conferences several of which have focused on the detection of perinatal mental disorder.

Sandra Elliott is a Consultant Clinical Psychologist in the MAPPIM perinatal mental health service in the maternity unit at St Thomas' Hospital, London, UK. Her interest in identifying the unmet emotional needs of childbearing women began in 1977 with a longitudinal study from early pregnancy to one year postnatal. The observations in this study led to an attempt to predict postnatal depression with an antenatal questionnaire (Leverton Questionnaire) and to prevent it in more vulnerable women. The antenatal approach was combined in an educational package with the postnatal detection and intervention approach of Holden, Sagovsky and Cox (1989) to provide training for health visitors. Sandra Elliott currently runs the Keele Perinatal Mental Health Education Unit (KEPEU) trainer training programme for multidisciplinary mental health and primary care teams who train midwives and health visitors. The advantages, disadvantages and prerequisites of systems to increase detection of perinatal mental health problems are a central part of the programme.

The Contributors

Cheryll Adams is the Professional Officer for Research and Practice Development with the Community Practitioners' and Health Visitors' Association in the UK. She leads the Association's Postnatal Depression and Maternal Mental Health Network.

Walter Barker is Director of the Early Childhood Development Centre, Bristol, UK.

Bryanne Barnett is Conjoint Professor, School of Psychiatry, University of New South Wales and Director, Infant, Child and Adolescent Mental Health, South Western Sydney Area Health Service, New South Wales, Australia.

Cheryl Tatano Beck is a Professor, School of Nursing, University of Connecticut, USA.

Caroline Bell was a research assistant in the Discipline of Psychological Medicine, Westmead Hospital, University of Sydney, Australia.

Philip Boyce is Professor of Psychiatry and Head of the Discipline of Psychological Medicine, University of Sydney, Australia.

Tony K.H. Chung is Chair and Professor of Obstetrics and Gynaecology at the Chinese University of Hong Kong.

Jan Cubison is Service Co-ordinator, Sheffield Maternal Mental Health Service, UK.

Mary Ross-Davie was midwife coordinator, MAPPIM project at St Thomas' Hospital, London and is now Surestart midwife, Borders NHS Trust, Scotland, UK. She is a member of the Scottish National Perinatal mental health network group.

Dawn Edge is Lecturer, School of Health Care Professions, University of Salford, UK.

Robert K. Gable is Emeritus Professor, Neag School of Education, University of Connecticut, USA.

Ann Girling has a clinical background in health visiting and now works as an independent healthcare consultant.

Patricia Glossop is Perinatal and Early Infancy Programs Co-ordinator, Infant, Child and Adolescent Mental Health Service, South Western Sydney Area Health Service, New South Wales, Australia.

Josephine M. Green is Professor of Psychosocial Reproductive Health and Deputy Director of the Mother and Infant Research Unit at the University of York, UK. The research drawn on for her chapter was carried out while she was at the Centre for Family Research at the University of Cambridge, UK.

Lucinda Green is Consultant Perinatal Psychiatrist, MAPPIM team, St Thomas' Hospital, London, UK.

Dominic T.S. Lee is Professor of Psychiatry at the Chinese University of Hong Kong, and Lecturer of Social Medicine, Harvard Medical School, USA.

Tessa Leverton is a Locum Consultant Child and Adolescent Psychiatrist at St Mary's Hospital, London and Honorary Clinical Senior Lecturer in Imperial College, UK. She works with Westminster Surestart.

Stephen Matthey is Research Director, Infant, Child and Adolescent Mental Health Service, South Western Sydney Area Health Service, New South Wales, Australia.

Jane Munro is Research and Development Midwife at Sheffield Teaching Hopsitals NHS Foundation Trust, UK.

Margaret Oates is Senior Lecturer in Psychiatry, University of Nottingham, UK and Consultant Perinatal Psyhiatrist. She is Chair of the Perinatal Section of the Royal College of Psychiatrists and Central Psychiatric Assessor for the Confidential Enquiries into Maternal and Child Health Care (CEMACH).

Michael W. O'Hara is Professor of Psychology, University of Iowa, USA.

Kathleen S. Peindl is Research Assistant Professor at Duke University Clinical Trials Division, Department of Pschiatry, Durham, North Carolina, USA.

Sheelah Seeley was previously a researcher at Reading University, UK and is now a consultant in Perinatal Training in Primary Care.

Lisa S. Segre is Associate Research Scientist of Psychiatry and Adjunct Assistant Professor, Department of Psychology, University of Iowa, USA.

Judy Shakespeare is a GP in Oxford, UK. She is a Senior Research Fellow in the Department of Primary Care, University of Oxford and Research Associate attached to the National Perinatal Epidemiology Unit in Oxford.

Abi Sobowale is a health visitor, Sheffield South West Primary Care Trust, UK.

Helen Stewart is Director of Nursing, Women's and Child Health, Liverpool Health Service, South Western Sydney Area Health Service, New South Wales, Australia.

Subject Index

Author Index